Kurt Tucholsky.
The Short Fat Berliner Who Tried to Stop
a Catastrophe With a Typewriter

By Harold L. Poor

KURT TUCHOLSKY

The Short Fat Berliner
Who Tried to Stop a Catastrophe
With a Typewriter

By Harold L. Poor

New Edition
New York and Berlin, 2019

Kurt Tucholsky.
The Short Fat Berliner Who Tried to Stop a Catastrophe With A Typewriter.
By Harold L. Poor

Reprint of:
Kurt Tucholsky and the Ordeal of Germany 1914–1935
Proofreader: Kemery Dunn

© 2019 by Berlinica Publishing LLC
165 West 83rd St., Suite 51
New York, NY, 10024, USA

ISBN: 978-3-96026-098-1
ISBN ebook: 978-1-935902-84-3
ISBN Germany: 978-3-96026-015-8
LCCN: 2019938459

Cover: Eva C. Schweitzer
Cover picture: Kurt Tucholsky Stiftung

Photo credits:
Kurt Tucholsky Stiftung (p. 16a, p. 20a, p. 148)
Landesarchiv Berlin (p. 16b, p. 36b, p. 176)
Kurt-Tucholsky-Museum Rheinsberg (p. 20b)
National Library of Scotland (p. 36a)
Bundesarchiv (p. 36a, p. 52a. p. 108, p. 164a)
Public Domain (p. 52b, p. 70a, p. 70h, p. 134a, p. 134b, p. 164b)
Eva C. Schweitzer (p. 206a, p. 206b)

Printed in the United States
All rights reserved under International and Pan-American Copyright Law. No part of this book may be used or reproduced in any manner whatsoever without written permission except in the case of brief quotations embodied in critical articles and reviews.

https://berlinica.com/

For Matile

Author's Acknowledgments

At last with a concrete product I may attempt to thank Tucholsky's widow, Mary Tucholsky, for her great kindness in receiving my wife and me into her home for a period of several months. The Kurt Tucholsky Archive, which she maintains, is a model of completeness and organization. Not only did Frau Mary open her collections to me without limitation, but she also provided me with every comfort and convenience including a private study. Best of all, the friendship begun there has continued by means of a rich correspondence in which I have been kept abreast of all developments in Tucholsky scholarship. Such kindness can never be adequately repaid. Also I must mention the attentions and culinary arts of Frau Mary's sister-in-law, Irene Gerold. She makes the banks of the Tegernsee a joy for gourmets as well as for scholars.

It is a distinct pleasure to acknowledge my gratitude for the help and encouragement received from my teacher, Fritz Stern of Columbia University. His gentle confidence and incisive criticism were invaluable. Istvan Deak, also of Columbia University, gave me additional encouragement and confidence. He has long been a brave and true friend.

Beate Ruhm von Oppen gave generously of her time in order to read and comment upon the manuscript. The long conversations in which she made available her critical judgment and unfailing good sense will be remembered as one of the most pleasant associations during the writing of this book.

I wish also to thank Klemens von Klemperer and Allan Mitchell, both of Smith College, whose thoughts and insights were of great aid. In addition, there are other members of the Smith College and Rutgers University faculties, too numerous to mention individually, whose aid and comfort were of inestimable value. In particular I would like to mention the kind attentions and infinite patience of the Smith College librarians.

I wish also to thank my friends and faithful critics, Lawrence Bonaguidi and Philip Greven, for their confidence and enthusiasm. Thanks are also in order to my former colleagues, Eileen Z. Cohen and Minna F. Weinstein, for their interest and encouragement during the early days of writing. To Thomas Davis, History Editor at Scribner's, and his assistant, Nina Di Pierre, go my gratitude for their unfailing patience and good judgment. Needless to say, the responsibility for all opinions and errors rests solely upon me.

To Louise Zahareas, who typed the manuscript, goes a debt of gratitude whose size can be appreciated only by writers as poor as I at the typewriter. She was the personification of speed, accuracy and efficiency.

Wives are always mentioned last in these acknowledgments. That is as it should be, for their contribution should be longest remembered. I therefore thank my wife, Matile Rothschild Poor, for her patience in listening to endless repetition of Tucholsky stories, for her unfailingly good scholarly judgment and for her sustaining love.

H. L.P. Highland Park, New Jersey August 10, 1967

 HAROLD L. POOR was one of the most gifted and charismatic teachers in the Rutgers History Department, focussing on cultural, political and intellectual aspects of 19th and 20th century German and European history. He also pioneered in the teaching of gay history. Born in 1935 in Missouri. he grew up in Birmingham, Alabama, attended Harvard College and Columbia University, and taught at City College New York, Temple University, and Smith College. In 1968, he published his dissertation on Kurt Tucholsky; he was was the co-author of the musical revue *Tickles by Tucholsky*, which premiered 1976 on Off-Broadway. From 1981 through 1983, he served as the national Chairperson for the Committee on Lesbian and Gay History. He died of AIDS on January 24, 1992.

NOTES

In citing articles by Tucholsky, the name of the article is listed first, then its place in the *Gesammelte Werke*, followed by an abbreviation of the particular pseudonym with which Tucholsky signed it, and then the particular publication in which it first appeared.

Abbreviations used in Notes:
G.W. Gesammelte Werke
I.W. Ignaz Wrobel
K.H. Kaspar Hauser
K.T. Kurt Tucholsky
P.P. Peter Panter
Th.T. Theobald Tiger

Contents

Acknowledgments

	Kurt Tucholsky and the Traps of Today	11
	My Father, Tucholsky, and Frau Mary	13
	Prologue by Harold L. Poor	17
I.	"An Entirely Consistent Person…"	21
II.	The Slaughter	37
III.	Berlin in Defeat and Revolution	53
IV.	The Voice of the 'Homeless Left'	71
V.	Battles of the Weimar Republic	109
VI.	The Rise and Fall of the Communists	135
VII.	The Paris Years	149
VIII.	Games of War	165
IX.	"Prelude to Silence"	177
X.	A Man Who Was Always Hunted	207
	Publisher's Afterword	230
	Tucholsky's Books in English	232
	Important Dates in Tucholsky's Life	237
	Sources	238
	Index	247

KURT TUCHOLSKY AND THE TRAPS OF TODAY

BY BELINDA DAVIS

DESPITE ALL HIS truly bitter words against his contemporaries and his skewering of those in power, Kurt Tucholsky's humanity is among the most palpable features in his writing. When political and economic instability bring deep social division—and greater concern for authority than for democracy—as in much of the Weimar period, a Tucholsky is necessary, indeed, many Tucholskys. It is such a person who refuses to play cynical games of dissemblage, and at the same time one who forces others to stop and see the humanity of political "enemies." It is little wonder that Tucholsky's words—written, spoken, and sung—caused the Nazis no small concern in their first years in power, even from abroad. The culture wars of the present call for a recognition of Tucholsky's successes up to a century ago. They call no less for acknowledgment of the alarm bell that rung out to mark the limits of contemporaries to ward off "catastrophe"—and concerted efforts to prevent our falling into the same traps.

Still, for English speakers at least, writing about satirist, cabarettist, librettist, and journalist Kurt Tucholsky seems to have gone out of style. There are arguably too few Anglophone works on Tucholsky altogether, still fewer historical works. This makes the republication of Harold Poor's 1967 book a welcome occasion, all the more alongside Berlinica Publishing's publication of five Tucholsky translations, among them Harry Zohn's *Germany? Germany! Satirical Writings: The Kurt Tucholsky Reader*. Tucholsky is forgotten at our peril; in his essential form, he is as relevant today as he ever was. Erich Kästner described Tucholsky (a bit uncharitably) as a "short, fat Berliner" who "tried to stop a catastrophe with a typewriter"—the "catastrophe" being the downfall of the Weimar Republic, from within as well as without. Tucholsky was alarmed not only for the rise of Nazi strength: after all, the Nazi party drew meaningful electoral support only well after Tucholsky had left Germany for Paris in 1924. He cast widely his concerns, expressing them with withering sarcasm along with a soaring wit.

These concerns included Social Democrats who, finally in power, cooperated all too eagerly with Conservative authorities of the former authoritarian German Second Empire in violently putting down protestors. He excoriated the German "bourgeoisie," members of which, in their concern to preserve their "most holy right: exploitation," expressed only "hate" and "disgust" toward German workers, signaling a particular "lack of imagination" concerning Germany's future. He ridiculed the flights of fancy among some fellow nationals in entertaining the virtues of renewed war—and of military control.

Yet far less turbulent times also call for a Tucholsky, and for the memory of Tucholsky himself. At moments of public complacency, it is the effect of a Tucholsky to shake people out of self-absorbed political apathy. The time at which Harold Poor, an acclaimed professor at the Rutger's History Department, first published his book in the late 1960s was itself a moment in West Germany that revealed Tucholsky's legacy, notwithstanding his death already three decades earlier. The effects of Tucholsky, and of Karl Valentin in Munich, are manifest, along with contemporary cabarettists Wolfgang Neuss in West Berlin, Matthias Beltz in Frankfurt, Dietrich Kittner in Hannover, the Gründgens siblings in northern Germany, and others, along with and as part of the contemporary Situationism, and "provo" politics. This was the critical challenge to political complacency in the postwar era, deploying biting humor to question just how completely the new Federal Republic and the Cold War West represented the forces of democracy and light.

It was a politics in the 1960s and 1970s that moreover, like those of the 1920s and early 1930s, refused to back down in the name of playing nice. Indeed, in Germany, at least, Tucholsky has remained well-remembered for his political temerity as for his talent—and at the highest levels of government, as well as among oppositional activists. So for example in the mid-1990s, both the parliament and Federal Constitutional Court were brought to weigh in on the legality of contemporary pacifist charges that cited Tucholsky's blunt assertion that "soldiers are murderers"; the phrase rose to high-level debate once again in 2010.

It is difficult to think of a time when a Tucholsky—and this Tucholsky—wouldn't matter. And so we are fortunate to again have Harold Poor's thoughtful and affecting historical biography to offer insight into Tucholsky's life, thought, effect—and inspiration.

Belinda Davis is Professor of History at Rutgers University and Director of the Rutgers Center for European Studies. Davis writes on popular politics and social change. Her most recent book is The Inner Life of Politics: Extraparliamentary Opposition in West Germany, 1962-83 *(Cambridge, forthcoming).*

MY FATHER, TUCHOLSKY, AND FRAU MARY

BY CHRIS POOR

My father, Harold Poor, first encountered the writings of Kurt Tucholsky when he was a young exchange student, living in Germany in the early 1950s. Despite the bombed out ruins, the loss of human life and two major war defeats in less than fifty years, my father's host family would pull a Nazi flag out of a hiding place and read *Mein Kampf* by candle light. This fascinated my father. Why would somebody still be attached to something that seemed to have been an utter failure on every count? He found many of his answers in the writings of Kurt Tucholsky. Tucholsky's writings, my father recognized, incised deeply into the German character. He seemed to feel a dissonance between their willingness to embrace the new Weimar Democracy and their attachment to the militaristic tradition of the Kaiser's Empire. Tucholsky captured this disconnect very well and this made it clearer to my father what had happened in Germany.

My father had been drawn to Tucholsky originally because the Nazis had burned his work, since he was always attracted to dissident and outsider voices. It was in his essays that my father found a kindred spirit. It was only years later, reading Tucholsky in English in the translation of Harry Zohn, a refugee from Vienna who became a professor at Brandeis that I could see how my father's sarcastic and cynical sense of humor was certainly heavily influenced by the man and his work.

My father set about writing his book on Tucholsky in the early 1960s. In March 1961, he traveled to Germany with my mother, and they stayed well into 1962. They visited Mary Tucholsky, the wife of the late, famous author, who lived in Rottach-Egern, at the Tegernsee, a beautiful lake in Bavaria. They had lunch with Mary every day, and Mary's sister Irena cooked for them. My mother was working on her dissertation on the French philosopher Denis Diderot. She learned German, tutored by a friend of Mary. A lot of Tucholsky fans visited the house, and my parents got to meet them.

In 1968, my parents did another trip to Germany, and this time, my sister and I went with them. I was around three and my sister was four, and we were all moving to Munich for a year. My father was doing research on the 1960s students movement. He told us that we were to meet someone very important who was to be called "Frau Mary". We even were prepared to follow old German manners: bowing and curtsying and some German phrases to introduce ourselves. I was wearing lederhosen and my sister a dirndl, and dressed like this, we went to Frau Mary's chalet at Tegernsee. We were to visit four or five times over the next few years. Frau Mary was like a grandmother to us; she sent us checks for Christmas until we were adults.

Kurt Tucholsky and the Ordeal of Germany was published amid little fanfare. In the United States, Tucholsky was obscure and unheard of. My father said later that he had the most profound moment of professional heartache he ever felt when he went to a large New York City bookstore and saw his book in the discount bin, less than a year after release. He told me he decided then and there that "publishing and perishing felt like the same thing." He never wrote another book on history. Instead, he dedicated his time to educating his students at Rutgers on the rise of fascism and its terrible impacts on humanity. However, Tucholsky was not done with him yet.

In 1973, my father was approached by Louis Golden. Golden was a New York stage author and a huge Tucholsky fan and he wanted help creating a musical based on Tucholsky's work. My father and he worked on this, with dad also working day and night to raise money for the show. Meanwhile, I was eight or nine years old, and I remember being kept up at night as the two of them banged on the floor and sang in English and German as they adapted music and lyrics. Brandeis University got involved, enthusiasm for the musical bubbled up, and the producers even found a famous director, Moni Yakim. Yakim had directed a musical on Jacques Brel, which had revived a lot of interest in the famous singer and songwriter from Belgium. Now Yakim hoped to achieve the same with Tucholsky. Well-known players were recruited for "Tickles," among them Helen Gallagher; Al Hirschfeld did a drawing of her. For us kids, it was a great time. We were hanging out with "show folks", going to rehearsals, watching sets being built, and costumes sewn. I was thrilled with parties and getting to meet famous people. And it was all due to and for Kurt Tucholsky. Finally, on April 26, 1976, the show premiered, at the Theater Four on West 55th Street, an Off-Broadway theatre.

But the musical received poor reviews. One critic wondered why everyone seemed so sad in the show. Perhaps because it was about the rise of Nazism and the Holocaust? Another one thought it "unstructured". I thought it was very imaginative, since it pulled on imagery from the Berlin Dada art movement. This included some grotesque scenery. At one point, an actor was dressed in a huge yellow cowboy/clown suit (I think he meant to be Goering) and he ranted and raved nationalistic and anti-Semitic slogans while in the background, wind-up monkeys were banging cymbals together. The sets meant to capture the feeling of being in a cabaret in the Weimar Republic while the songs ranged from wistful ballads to intense and graphic anti-war songs. But sadly, "Tickles by Tucholsky" closed in less than one month.

My father, after a book that no one read and a show no one wanted to see, was done with Tucholsky. But he stayed in touch with Frau Mary. I saw her one last time in 1985. She was eighty-seven years old and would die two years later. This was the time I had just started college. My parents had divorced in the late seventies, and my mother went back to school and became a social worker. My sister was studying to be a nurse.

Later, a few years after my father had died in 1992, I was in a bar in Eugene, Oregon, talking to a student from Germany. I mentioned my dad was a professor for German history. The student found this fairly novel, as he had not met any Americans who knew anything about his country. I mentioned Tucholsky, and this young man began to gush so much admiration around his work. He said everyone he knew thought Tucholsky was a groundbreaking writer, whose pacifist and anti-fascist stance was still highly relevant and important. Suddenly I knew why my father had seized upon such a seemingly obscure person and attempted to bring him to a wider audience, during a time a political turmoil and war. Hopefully, reading my father's work on Tucholsky will help the reader capture the humor and pathos that drew him to devote so much time and energy to this important German writer.

Chris Poor is the son of Harold L. Poor. He lives in Portland, Oregon, where he works as an employment specialist. He helps people with severe and persistent mental illness to find rewarding work.

Above: Kurt Tucholsky in the early 1930s.

Below: The Nazi book burning in Berlin, March 1933. Tucholsky's books were among the first to be burned.

PROLOGUE

BY HAROLD L. POOR

NIGHT, MAY 10, 1933. The flickering torches carried by thousands of uniformed youths made their way down Berlin's via triumphalis, Unter den Linden. The euphoria of spring reinforced the sense of righteous invincibility of the young men as they marched to the ceremonial climax. Finally they reached and lined the square in front of Friedrich Wilhelms University. Torches dipped and soon there was a large bonfire. The infamous book burning had begun, that twentieth century autodafe which marked the end of Weimar culture and signified the attempt to imprison the German intellect. Thirty-four German writers were honored that night by being burned in effigy of their works. One by one their names were called, their books cast into the fire—Sigmund Freud, Bertolt Brecht, Heinrich Mann, Ernst Toller... Some names, little known outside Germany, were suddenly given international fame and significance as representatives of decency and civilization. The loudspeakers blared out across the square: "Because of insolence and arrogance! With honor and respect for the immortal German folk spirit! Consume also, flames, the writings of Tucholsky...

I heard these words on a tape recording of the ceremony, in the Kurt Tucholsky Archive, Rottach-Egern, Germany, where I was a guest or Mary Gerold, Tucholsky's wife. Kurt Tucholsky, German satirist, chansonnier and cultural critic, was one of the most feared of the intellectuals hated by the Nazis. His liberal political convictions coupled with his satiric wit and immense public popularity frightened the Nazis and caused them to direct the huge force of their propaganda machine against him. Tucholsky's fortunes rose and fell with those of the Weimar Republic. Its life delimited his brilliant career. Tucholsky's struggle was the Republic's struggle; his defeat, its defeat.

Tucholsky began his professional writing career in a time of hope and chaos. The German revolution of 1918 held forth the promise of a new society based upon democracy and equality of opportunity. Simultaneously, the confusion and despair wrought by the war and the defeat rendered difficult the fulfillment of the revolutionary expectations. Like others of the non-Communist left, Tucholsky was at first heartened by the establishment of the Republic and he lent his considerable talents to its support. Before the conflict, liberal intellectuals had fought the materialism and authoritarian repressiveness of the imperial regime. In their eyes, the war and the defeat proved the bankruptcy and corruption of the Empire. At last Germany had a chance for a clean break with the past. But Tucholsky and his colleagues were not satisfied with the changes that occurred. In dismay, they watched the continuing power and the influence of the old forces—the generals, the judiciary, and the bureaucracy of the Empire. They were horrified by the betrayal of the revolutionary ideal when the Social Democratic leaders cooperated with Prussian generals and ordered soldiers to put down proletarian demonstrations. The leftist intellectuals came to believe that the Republic was nothing but the Empire in semantic disguise. And they continued to attack the new political structure much as their predecessors had attacked the imperial order, except that now they were more bitter and more intense.

The left-wing intellectuals found themselves in the curious position of advocating democracy while simultaneously denouncing the regime, which claimed to be democratic. They have been severely criticized for not strengthening the weak republican plant to help it ward off the blight of its right-wing enemies. But to the liberal intellectuals, there never was a republic; the influence of the conservative right wing was still paramount. As Carl von Ossietzky, who would soon become the editor of *Die Weltbühne,* wrote in 1924, "One hears people say that this republic is without republicans. Unluckily, the situation is just the opposite: the republicans are without a republic."

Because many of the reactionary forces remained alive in the Republic, it appeared that by their support of the republican regime the left intellectuals would contribute to the continuation of the power of reaction. Tucholsky and his friends opposed the *Scheindemokratie*—the mock democracy, which tolerated the reactionary Prime Minister Gustav von Kahr in Bavaria, but ousted legally elected Communist cabinet members in Saxony and Thuringia. They could not bring themselves to approve of a government whose judges sentenced Socialists to death while letting fascists go free for identical crimes. To change this intolerable state of affairs, the intellectual left styled itself as "negativist," entering into opposition in order to make way for new beginnings. They eventually recognized that their era's particular conjunction of social, economic and political crises made their cause all but hopeless. Nevertheless they continued to struggle for human decency and equality in Germany until they were finally swept away by barbarism.

Of all the left-wing intellectuals—Ernst Toller, Kurt Hiller, Siegfried Jacobsohn, Carl von Ossietzky, to name only a few—the most outstanding in terms of energy, insight and satiric brilliance was Kurt Tucholsky. Tucholsky with his democratic idealism, his humanitarian sympathies and his hatred of the Republic's hypocrisy, represents the epitome of the quandary of the democratic intellectual in Weimar.

The chaos of Weimar presented a disheartening challenge to an intellectual of Tucholsky's nature. Tucholsky could and had to sympathize with a society which having first undergone the shock of a hideous war, was further burdened by a punitive peace. Yet he also recognized that outside forces such as the Versailles Treaty were too often used as excuses for inordinate self-pity. Tucholsky found himself in the curious position of hating the sham republic and advocating its destruction while simultaneously defending it against the nihilism of the extremists. He lived in a tragic and curious era in which all order appeared to be reversed. It was Alice's dream transformed into a nightmare. All sophisticated societies are characterized by complexity, but seldom have irony and paradox been as blatant and confusing as in Weimar Germany. Brown shirts fought red shirts in the streets and voted together in the Reichstag. While army maneuvers were conducted in Russia, *All Quiet on the Western Front* was read at home, the famous pacifist novel of Erich Maria Remarque. The strains of the *Internationale* and the *Horst Wessel Song* fused with the rhythms of the Charleston.

Communists were imprisoned, fascists allowed to go free under a constitution that guaranteed equal justice. Albert Einstein made his revelations to the world while some of his countrymen revived the myth of the *Protocols of the Wise Men of Zion*. At one time an American could spend a week at the Adlon Hotel for five dollars while a German had to spend the savings of a lifetime in order to ride a streetcar to work. Matthias Erzberger and Walter Rathenau, liberal politicians, were murdered; Adolf Hitler and a militarist like Erich Ludendorff treated with awe. Old patterns reestablished themselves in the midst of frightening innovations. Dissatisfaction, pessimism and foreboding beside complacency, optimism and prosperity. Creativity and chaos, brilliance and stupidity, mania and calm, paradox and contrast—such was Weimar. Such was the world in which Kurt Tucholsky lived.

Above: Kurt in 1898 with his sister Ellen, his mother Doris holding his brother Fritz, his father Alex, and his grandmother Rosalie.

Below: Tucholsky's desk in the Tucholsky-Museum in Rheinsberg.

I.

"AN ENTIRELY CONSISTENT PERSON"

Tucholsky was a member of an era that guarded its privacy. He felt no compulsion to confess to the public the details of his personal life, though it was more colorful than most and even at times traumatic. When he did refer to himself in his writings, he was either satirical or sarcastic. Even in his private letters, the self-references were usually oblique. Furthermore, through the use of different writing styles and pseudonyms, Tucholsky refused to present a single, unified personality to the public world. Indeed, his use of pseudonyms did not stop with himself, for he invented fictitious names for most of his friends as well. It was the habit of a playful and ironic temperament. Tucholsky was in no way a poseur, but the self behind the writings must be viewed through a scrim of hints, names, styles and illusions more hazy and more nearly opaque than the usual.

The oldest of three children, Tucholsky was born in Berlin on January 9, 1890. His father, Alex Tucholsky, was a successful Jewish businessman and banker, able to provide his family with material comfort and bourgeois luxury. Tucholsky's father possessed a sensitive, almost melancholy nature and provided the warmth and love, which the mother, Doris Tucholsky, was unable to give. Tucholsky often fondly remembered his father's extraordinary ability at the piano. Although a brother, Fritz, was born in 1896 and a sister, Ellen, in 1897 Tucholsky continued to be the favorite of his father who hardly ever failed while on his many business trips to send his son an affectionate postcard. Alex Tucholsky's untimely death in 1905 threw the young Kurt into a mild crisis and he left home for good at the age of fifteen. Thereafter, Tucholsky's contact with his family became tenuous and in later years was restricted to his brother and sister.

Doris Tucholsky, the mother, in contrast to her warm and gentle husband, was literal and rigid. Cold and aloof to her children, she was the kind of woman who observed all of the proprieties of motherhood, who saw that her children were well-fed, well-dressed and well-washed, but who did not understand how to love them. Tucholsky himself left behind one of the most bitter descriptions of his mother. In 1914 he wrote a review of Rosa Bertens' performance in Strindberg's *Funeral Pyres*. He praised Bertens and wrote that her portrayal presented the paradigm of mothers. As described by Tucholsky, Bertens presented a willful, tyrannical woman who would use any means to maintain her authority over her household. Tucholsky later admitted that his critique of Rosa Bertens was really a description of his own mother.[1] Excerpts from the 1914 review leave little doubt that Doris Tucholsky's eldest son was profoundly alienated from her:

> And then her unforgettable voice: "Shut the door, please!" What was that? She was afraid, she shuddered with horror. She sat on her upholstered chair and held tightly to its arms. Was she still the ruler? For fifteen or twenty years, perhaps longer, she had ruled. And they had been bitter years. But the whole time she had had her eyes open, she, the uncrowned queen of a live room apartment. There was not a stick of wood, not a lump of sugar or a slice of sausage which had not passed through her hands… She trembled with a lust for power and with the fear that she would be overthrown… She crouched over her special fire log, which she had pulled out of the fireplace while gasping with the desire for power. She stuffed it under the sofa and sat there growling like a dog over its bones. It was not a question of the wood; she had her will, her cursed will… . This was her kingdom… Here she ruled, ruled with every means, with force, with blows, with lies…[2]

Given this vision of his mother, it is understandable why Tucholsky placed little value upon his childhood family life. When he was three years old, the family moved to Stettin. This area near the Baltic coast provided Tucholsky's most vivid childhood impressions of nature and he always referred to the "eastern" landscape as being of greater beauty when others praised the sun of the Italian south. It was also in Stettin that he attended his first school in 1896. Little evidence remains of Tucholsky's early school years, but there is one small story— a poem written around 1897 which gives some indication of the patriotic teachings of his grammar school. The piece is entitled *The True German*. It portrays a German who lives near the scene of the Battle of Sedan during the Franco-Prussian War and who is forced to flee from his village. Yet he is curious to see the battle and hides himself behind a bush only fifty yards from the fray. While there, he sings a song of patriotic devotion. The man swears to remain true to the sentiment of the song "until his last breath."

> Suddenly he stopped, for he was hit by a bullet. Wounded unto death, he continued to sing the last verses, with an ever diminishing force.

Farewell, O — O World—I am leaving already—Oh, God, into your ha-hands-I-place-my-spirit-you were gracious unto me as long as I lived. Farewell, farewell, farewell. Then he died.
This is the true German, who swears an oath before God and keeps and remembers it until he softly passes away.[3]

This quite normal excursion of the seven-year-old schoolboy into patriotic sentiment resembled the later parodies of *Teutschtum*,[4] which the mature Tucholsky would write.

When Tucholsky's father became director of a bank, the Berlin *Handelsgesellschaft*, in 1899, the family moved back to Berlin and Tucholsky was enrolled in the famous French Gymnasium. The school was and remains one of the great centers of secondary education in Germany. Founded in 1689, by the immigrant French Huguenots to whom Friedrich, the Great Elector had opened the boundaries of his state, the French Gymnasium early became noted for the high quality of its teachers and for its classical and humanistic education.[5] It was natural for Alex Tucholsky to send his son there, since the school was the socially appropriate place for prominent Jews to send their children. The student body was made up of old and new aristocracy, old and new wealth and of the children of the many members of the diplomatic corps and the foreign colony in Berlin. With its French tradition and the diverse background of its students, the school provided a cosmopolitan and liberal atmosphere rare in most German secondary educational institutions of the time.

Tucholsky, however, was not impressed by these advantages. He later described his school days as "the lost years." He hated what he called the dryness of the subject matter, the uninteresting presentation and the stern discipline. Above all, he chided the school for not preparing him for practical life in the external world.

Nothing. Not once did they teach us correct thinking, not once correct insight, correct ways, correct work—nothing, nothing, nothing. We were made neither into good humanists nor into good practical men—nothing…[6]

Certainly this exaggerated attack upon the French Gymnasium says more about Tucholsky than it does about the school. Like many creative men, Tucholsky had an independent mind, which found formal education restrictive. He worked best in solitude. Tucholsky's view of his education was probably colored by the great personal problems which he experienced during his adolescent years. In 1905, after his father's sudden death,

Tucholsky's performance in school became poorer and poorer. Finally he left home, and the following year, quit school. He continued to study and write on his own until 1909 when he decided to take the examination for the "school leaving certificate" (the *Abitur*) as an "external student." (The so-called "one-year examination," successfully completed, reduced the required military service of the person from three years to one.) It was a traumatic experience for him and his tutor advised him to take the army exemption examination a second time to gain practice in test writing again. Tucholsky did so and was one of the two men out of twelve taking it who passed. This gave Tucholsky the necessary confidence and he managed to gain his *Abitur* on September 21, 1909.

In the meantime, Tucholsky began to create another career which would rival that of the student and scholar. Upon leaving home, Tucholsky styled himself as a writer and published his first work in 1907 when he was seventeen years old. Appearing in *Ulk*, the humor supplement of the *Berliner Tageblatt*, the piece was entitled "Fairytale" ("*Märchen*") and was an early indication of Tucholsky's future satirical abilities. It was a satire upon the characters of both Kaiser William II and his Empire. By having the fictional emperor of the tale sneeze upon his beautiful snuff box, Tucholsky depicted the crass disregard of the Empire and its leader for some of its most original and creative artistic talents:

> There once was an emperor who ruled over an immeasurably large, rich and beautiful country. And, like any other emperor, he also had a treasure room, which in addition to all the sparkling jewels also contained a snuffbox. What remarkable things were depicted on its lid! There was a landscape, small but full of life: a Thoma landscape with Böcklin clouds and Leistikow lakes, Reznicek like ladies turned up their noses at Zille figures, and a peasant maid a la Meunier carried an armful of Orlik flowers—in short, the whole artistic *avant-garde* was on this snuffbox. And what do you suppose the emperor did with it? He sneezed at it.[7]

It would appear that there was an almost unbroken evolutionary line extending from this first published work to Tucholsky's later fame as journalist and satirist. In his early years of maturity, however, Tucholsky was uncertain of his literary talents and in 1909 he decided to continue his education. In the autumn of that year, he became a student at the University of Berlin. Slowly his interests turned to law and he studied during the summer semester of 1910 in Geneva, after which he went back to Berlin. He had loved Geneva, but upon returning he found it as difficult as ever to achieve the single-minded concentration needed for formal study. His interests were too divergent; his curiosity too great. He vacillated between writing and the law; between a Bohemian life and scholarly studies. He was unsure of himself and of his future. Tucholsky was always to be a restless person, never satisfied with any one pursuit or any one subject of interest. It was journalism, which was ideally suited to his multiplicity of talents and interests. However, in 1911, Tucholsky determined to continue his study of law, a fact mentioned in the diary of Franz Kafka.

Tucholsky and his friend Kurt Szafranski (who would later illustrate his first novel, *Rheinsberg*) went on a "walking trip" to Prague and visited the writer Max Brod, who in turn introduced them to Kafka. Tucholsky was impressed by Kafka and would be the first literary critic to recognize his genius. Kafka was also sufficiently impressed by that single meeting with Tucholsky to describe it in his diary. Tucholsky did not give the impression of restlessness or of being at odds with himself, for Kafka described him as "an entirely consistent person" (*"ein ganz einheitlicher Mensch"*). In fact Tucholsky made some fun of his own talents and uncertainties according to Kafka:

> Tucholsky and Szafranski. The aspirated Berlin dialect in which the voice makes use of intervals consisting of "nich". The former, an entirely consistent person of twenty-one. From the controlled and powerful swing that gives a youthful lift to his shoulders to the deliberate delight in and contempt for his own literary works. Wants to be a defense lawyer, sees only a few obstacles and at the same time how they may be overcome: his clear voice that after the manly sound of the first half hour of talk pretends to become revealingly girlish—doubt of his own capacity to pose, which, however, he hopes to get with more experience of the world—fear finally of changing into a melancholic, as he has seen happen in older Berlin Jews of his type, in any event for the time being he sees no sign of this. He will marry soon.[8]

When Kafka met him, Tucholsky was on the threshold of maturity—in his own eyes as well as Kafka's. He was an "unserious" writer, soon to become a lawyer and be was in love. Tucholsky was engaged to Kitty Frankfurter, but he also ran around a lot with Else Weil, a medical student. In his prewar letters to Dr. Owlglass (Hans Erich Blaich), the writer for *Simplicissimus*, Tucholsky often mentioned "Claire," his nickname for Else. The war interrupted both of these romances, but Tucholsky's early simultaneous involvement established a pattern which be would always follow. He liked women, but be was unable to establish a lasting relationship with any single woman. It may have been his disastrous and unhappy relationship with his mother which caused Tucholsky to fear a binding attachment, it may have been his almost fanatic devotion to his career which made family bonds irksome. Whatever the reasons, Tucholsky exhibited an erratic and sometimes irresponsible behavior toward the women in his life.

Tucholsky grew into a man who was difficult to live with. The self-doubt noted by Kafka multiplied into a myriad number of anxieties and depressions. He drove himself often to the limits of nervous exhaustion. Throughout his life he searched for a geographic spot whose inhabitants possessed generous spirits and exhibited sensible, dignified behavior. A strange quest, but Tucholsky was shaken by the meanness, which he detected in the German public spirit after the war. A warm, tolerant, and compassionate person, Tucholsky was sometimes disagreeable because of his many simultaneous deadlines and obligations. In his personal relationships he was impulsive and he had peeves, which were difficult for less sensitive persons to understand. He hated barking dogs, finding it impossible to work to the accompaniment of growls, whines or yelps.

Because of the dog problem alone, he shifted his place of residence many times. During his period in Paris, he left his beautiful house in the suburbs of Le Vesinet, and moved in 1927 to Fontainebleau where he occupied the sixteen-room former residence of a cardinal. Dogs continued to plague Tucholsky for the remainder of his life, amounting to a minor preoccupation. He often jokingly referred to the presence or absence of dogs in his letters. While convalescing in Sweden in 1928, he wrote to Mary, his second wife, "I am recovering when I am not playing at being depressed.... Sometimes a dog screeches. I have retained something from Vesinet. What can one do?"[9]

The inordinate concern with barking dogs was but a simple part of the restlessness, the searching desire that permeated Tucholsky's spirit. Just as he found it impossible to live with one woman, so he found it difficult to live in one place. He was a wanderer in body and mind. Tucholsky himself once wrote:

> Longing—longing for fulfillment!... somewhere there lies a purpose, never to be reached!
> Much, almost everything can be satisfied in this world, almost any yearning can be met—only this one cannot be... What is it which drives us on, further, higher, forward?... To be happy, but never satisfied... There is no deeper longing than the longing for fulfillment. It can never be stilled.[100]

This is a passage from the short novel *Rheinsberg*, which Tucholsky published in 1912. After returning from Prague and the meeting with Franz Kafka, Tucholsky and his friend Kurt Szafranski decided to cooperate with each other in a literary and a business venture. The former was *Rheinsberg*, written by Tucholsky and illustrated by Szafranski. Like his final novel, *Gripsholm Castle*, *Rheinsberg* was a romantic tale for lovers, which was lyrical in its depiction of youthful love, but wistful in its knowledge that youth passes quickly. Tender and delicate, the novel was saved from sentimentality by a sharp, risque wit. Because it was the story of a summer vacation taken by a young, unmarried female medical student and her lover, *Rheinsberg* caused something of a sensation.[111] It was a critical success and in a brief time sold fifty thousand copies. Tucholsky was so inexperienced in drawing up contracts that he sold all rights to the book for only 125 marks.

As indicated earlier, Tucholsky and Szafranski did not end their cooperation with *Rheinsberg*, they also went into business together. In order to promote the sale of their book and to have fun, the two young men had the idea of opening a "book bar" in Berlin, a bookstore in which alcoholic beverages were served while the customers browsed. Tucholsky and his friend soon found themselves pouring drinks and making money.

But Tucholsky was not certain that he wanted to lead the often precarious existence of a writer or depend upon a succession of shaky enterprises such as the book bar for a living. Therefore, as Kafka noted, Tucholsky was determined to obtain a law degree. In 1913, he requested that the University of Jena waive the junior barrister examination and admit him as a candidate for a doctorate. He was accepted and in 1914, he submitted his dissertation. It was rejected, but Tucholsky quickly rewrote it and passed his oral examination in November 1914. The title of his dissertation might well have been one of Tucholsky's later satirical inventions: "Die Vormerkung aus 1179 BGB und ihre Wirkungen" ("The Memorandum from Paragraph 1179 of the German Civil Code and its Effects"). On February 12, 1915, Tucholsky was granted the degree, Doctor of Jurisprudence.

Tucholsky's dissertation was probably rejected because he had been too occupied with other writing. The law degree was respectability and insurance, but his heart lay in his journalism. In 1912, Tucholsky published three articles in *Vorwärts*, the organ of the Social Democratic Party. With the success of *Rheinsberg* that same year, it is understandable that Tucholsky came to the attention of Siegfried Jacobsohn, the editor and publisher of the *Schaubühne*. Founded in 1905, this was a journal of theater criticism and drama review, which gained Jacobsohn, along with Alfred Kerr, a high reputation as a critic. In addition, Jacobsohn had the most coveted editor's gift in abundance, the ability to recognize true writing talent. On January 9, 1913, Tucholsky's first article appeared in the *Schaubühne* and thus began the deepest friendship of his life.

Siegfried Jacobsohn was nine years older than Tucholsky and became a kind of mentor for his younger colleague. In later life, Tucholsky often referred to him as "my teacher" and during their long association, Tucholsky trusted Jacobsohn's judgment implicitly. With his blue pencil, Jacobsohn helped Tucholsky perfect his stylistic gift. There has seldom been a closer author-editor relationship, for Tucholsky wrote literally hundreds of letters every year to "S.J.", as he called Jacobsohn. (Most of the letters were confiscated by the Gestapo in 1933 and have disappeared.) Tucholsky numbered his letters to Jacobsohn, beginning with the numeral "1" each January. The letter of December 2, 1926, which Jacobsohn never received because of his death the following day, bears the number "244."[122]

Jacobsohn thus provided Tucholsky with a critical school in which his talent could develop and gave him a forum for the dissemination of his ideas. Tucholsky started as a drama critic, but with urging from Jacobsohn he began to write satiric poems and critical essays on subjects other than drama. Tucholsky's contributions were indeed prodigious. He wrote a total of 113 pieces for the *Schaubühne* between January 1913 and June 1914. After the war, Tucholsky returned to become the major and best-known contributor to the magazine, which by then had changed its name to *Die Weltbühne*. Between 1919 and 1932, Tucholsky wrote an average of one hundred to one hundred fifty articles and poems yearly for Jacobsohn's journal alone.

Tucholsky's contributions were divided among the areas of social satire, political commentary, cultural criticism and chanson poetry. Tucholsky was unable to restrict himself to any one of these talents, but developed them all and became famous for them all. To give himself a maximum amount of freedom to express these varied interests, Tucholsky assumed four pseudonyms. With rare exception, he signed all of his writings with one of the four pen names and each became associated with a particular style or type of article. The pseudonyms were invented partly as a joke, but Tucholsky feared that if he became known in one particular area, no one would take the other seriously. For example, known as a satiric humorist, the effectiveness of his political analysis would suffer. And thus the four names became expressions of different aspects of Tucholsky's personality. He himself described it as a "gay schizophrenia":

> The pseudonyms were brought out of darkness, thought up for fun and invented as a joke—that was at the time when my works first appeared in the *Weltbühne*. A small weekly must not have the same author appear four times in the same issue—thus as a joke these homunculi were born. They saw themselves printed and then turned confused somersaults; but they soon sat upright, became more certain, very certain, then bold. They soon were leading their own existence. Pseudonyms are like little

men. It is dangerous to invent names, to pretend to be someone else, to invent names—a name lives. What began as a joke ended as a gay schizophrenia. It was also useful to be able to appear five times, for who in Germany believes that a political writer can be humorous, a satirist, serious? Who credits a playful man with knowledge of the penal code or a describer of cities with being able to compose light verse? Humor discredits.[133]

It was, to be sure, fashionable during this period for writers to assume pseudonyms, but Tucholsky was genuinely fascinated by names with their power to characterize a personality and to effect humor. He always played around with fictitious names. He never had a close friend or acquaintance to whom he did not give a nickname which denoted both affection and good joking. His sister, Ellen, was "Hippel"; his brother, Fritz, was "Kohn." The two close friends, Erich Danehl and Hans Pritsche, were "Karlchen" and "Jakopp." The playwright, Walter Hasenclever, was known as "Max" and his second wife, Mary Gerold, was called "Meli" and "Mala." The process began when Tucholsky was very young. In his early letters, he often signed his name "Ignaz." The letters to Hasenclever were usually signed "Edgar," those to Mary Gerold with "Nungo."

Although the names were playful and served a practical purpose, there may have been deeper reasons for Tucholsky's fascination with pseudonyms. It may have been a part of the restless searching for peace (*Ruhe*) to which he often referred. By using a false name, Tucholsky could prevent a part of himself from being consumed by his intense involvement in the public world. The pseudonyms could act as a shield whereby he could divorce himself from public reality, whereby he could create and protect a private life. This would seem to be confirmed by Tucholsky's letters, for his private correspondence almost never reflected his public concerns. No matter how angry, indignant or despairing his writings in the *Weltbühne* may have been at any particular time, his private letters of the same period seldom contain a hint of that anger, indignation or despair. It was only after 1932 when he ceased to write for publication, that his letters began to be concerned with public events. Thereafter he was unable to separate his political despair from his personal life and he fell into an ever deepening and dangerous depression.

Questions of an individual's self-regard and sense of identity are always difficult, but the pseudonyms may have been indicative of Tucholsky's inability to focus on any one single purpose. They may have denoted a form of "identity crisis," the inability of Tucholsky to identify himself with any single cause, theme, interest or party. Given Tucholsky's Jewish background and the assimilation into a bourgeois society which respected Jewish wealth but rejected Jewish birth, it would have been difficult to establish identity in normal times. But the additional chaos of the postwar era when there were a myriad number of political problems, social causes and public needs made an intellectual of Tucholsky's talent run the danger of an atomization of his creative powers.[144]

Kafka wrote that Tucholsky feared "changing into a melancholic, as he had seen happen in older Berlin Jews of his type" ("*Verwandlung ins Weltschmerzliche*"). His Jewish origin was a subdued theme in Tucholsky's life, an undercurrent of which the observer is only half-aware, but which was nevertheless present. Tucholsky formally left Judaism early and for reasons of expediency became a Protestant in 1917. But his enemies never let him forget his Jewish origin. He wrote later, "In 1911 I 'seceded' from Jewry. I know one can't do anything of the sort, but that was the legal formula."[155] Thus he was and was not a Jew. There was an involvement-noninvolvement, a commitment and indifference, which forced Tucholsky to combine the qualities of prophet, critic, poet, enemy and lover of Germany in his one person. The fact that society simultaneously rejected and accepted him because he had been a Jew enabled Tucholsky to regard that society with an eye more detached (but not indifferent) than was possible for a more "integrated" person. Yet Tucholsky's Jewish background was not dominant, it was rather a kind of nuance, a distant awareness of exclusion, which prevented total involvement in the society. Although Tucholsky at the end of his life returned to a serious consideration of the problems of Judaism, it was not Kafka's "Jewish melancholy" which finally overcame him. It was rather the intellectual despair, which anyone who has loved and lost may suffer.

Tucholsky would probably laugh at these deep and serious speculations about his identity problems and use of pseudonyms. But even he admitted that it was dangerous to invent names. Many intellectuals possess a kind of double consciousness, an acting self and an observing self. They become so introspective that they project a consciousness outside themselves and observe themselves "performing" like characters in a play or novel. With a third eye, they observe themselves in conversation, making love, writing books. At its worst, this introspection leads to neurosis and immobility. At its best, it allows for a more objective self-view, a healthy self-irony which prevents one from taking one's self too seriously. Tucholsky's use of pseudonyms heightened this process of self-observation. In 1919, he published an article entitled "Interview with Myself" ("*Interview mit sich selbst*") in which his ironic self-view and his own amusement at his multiple personality traits were amply expressed. In the piece, Tucholsky interviews one of his pseudonyms, Peter Panter:

"Herr Panter will see you now!" said the butler. I stepped closer. The great door to the master's study opened, the butler swept back the portier, I stepped inside, the door closed behind me.
There sat the master, massive at his desk, an almost fat man. He exhibited a well-cared—for Caesar profile-only the double chins added a somewhat disturbing note. His bristly hair projected into the air. In his bright eyes lay a rich, satisfied contentment.[166]

Herr Panter asks Tucholsky to take a seat in order to discuss the questions in his "remarkable letter." Fascinated, Tucholsky sits down and watches as Herr Panter lays down his fat hands so that the observer cannot escape noticing his highly polished nails. "You ask what counsel I have for your future and add that you are consumed by the struggle for a high ideal. You are offended by a life that appears sharp edged—those were your words—and you want advice from me. Now, young man, you shall have it!" Panter enquires what Tucholsky's profession is and receives the shamefaced answer, "Nothing." "Hm—then why do you need my advice? In any event—I am at your disposal." Tucholsky asks how to achieve success, the success that Panter enjoys. He motions toward the beautifully appointed room with its leather-bound books, the gilded pages, the rich bronze lamp, the generous ashtray of black marble. "How did you obtain all of this?"

> The master smiled strangely.
> "Success? You want to know how I have achieved success, young man? Young, young hothead! Well—I humbled myself. I have made compromises."
> "Never would I do that. Never!" I said emphatically.
> "You must do it," he said. "You will do it... ."

The rich, comfortable Panter advises his young alter ego to make concessions. It is the only way to get ahead. Tucholsky answers melodramatically that he is concerned with ideals, with truth. "I am a storm and stresser and I shall remain so!" He will call murder, murder even if a flag flies over it. It is mankind that he wants to help.

Panter replies that he must see reality. There will be a wife, children, a house. And then he will bow before necessity—just a simple nod of the head, a slight bending, a little loss of principle. He must learn when to say yes and when to be quiet. Panter contends that silence costs nothing; it is the pearl in the crown of human art. Panter advises him to kneel before money, before power and before women—and the reward will be great. Panter tells how he welcomes into his own house priests, physicians, officers and artists. He gives them wine, asks no questions and they buy his books. Panter further advises his young friend to marry the daughter of a rich man. "There is room in the smallest villa—but it must be a villa."

> "Listen to me. I am standing high on the ladder that you are only beginning to climb. Success is everything. You may achieve it in several ways: through compromise, through silence, through listening and through flattering the old people. If you can understand this, then you will be made. And it is so pleasant to be made."

Tucholsky then departs, hearing the master at his magnificent desk ring for tea. As he opens the wrought iron gate in front of the house, Tucholsky mutters, "What a disgusting fellow!"

Tucholsky was, of course, poking fun at the values of capitalist society and at the clichés that its critics used when denouncing it. He was also laughing at himself, for it was at this very time that he was also writing some of his most strident articles denouncing the old regime and calling for a moral revolution. He was writing the most uncompromising manifestoes demanding the establishment of equality before the law and the abolition of the military. Yet the interview with himself shows that at the same time he was ironically observing his youthful passion for justice and was even half-amused by it. That did not make his belief in his values any less certain, but it did make Tucholsky more human. And it was precisely this close knowledge of himself which made Tucholsky so appealing, his awareness of how he sounded, of the humor as well as the seriousness of his own situation. His readers always knew that if one of the pseudonyms made an ass of himself, another of the pseudonyms was bound to comment upon it. This was also dangerous, for it was the kind of humorous self-view—the recognition of the place of ideals within the context of one's whole personality—which could cause the melancholy Tucholsky feared.

Tucholsky was also making fun of his own refined tastes and tendency toward opulence. He never really lusted after the "success" described in the interview, but he did love good food, magnificent surroundings and beautiful women. At the same time he had a respect for simplicity and held the obsessions of the acquisitive society in contempt. He was an idealist, a crusader for justice, and social reform, causes which usually denote Spartan grimness. Tucholsky was that rarest of all characters—a jovial missionary, a self-indulgent reformer, a lover of mankind who also loved women.

Peter Panter was not the only mirror through which Tucholsky could view himself. In addition, there were Theobald Tiger, Ignaz Wrobel and Kaspar Hauser. Tucholsky once described his view of each of the characters. Panter, as would be guessed from the interview, looked more like Tucholsky than the others, for he was a rotund, rather short man who often made references to his weight. Panter was responsible for literary criticism, theater reviews, light satire and cultural vignettes. When not sleeping, Theobald Tiger was writing verses. It was under his name that almost all of Tucholsky's famous chansons for the Berlin cabaret appeared. Kaspar Hauser was a bewildered man who opened his eyes after the war and beheld a world he did not understand. Hauser engaged in much the same activity as Panter. Ignaz Wrobel was an acid, bespectacled man, slightly hunchbacked and redheaded. Tucholsky considered the name to be particularly grating to the ears and thus used the Wrobel pseudonym for most of his political commentary and the more biting social and cultural criticism.[17]

Although the pseudonyms represented different aspects of his personality, Tucholsky regarded them all as having one and the same purpose. "We all stem from one father and this common origin is not obscured by what we write. United we love—united we hate—we march separately, but we all attack the same enemy.... . We are five fingers on one hand."[18]

The enemy. The central fact of Tucholsky's life was struggle—struggle against irrationality and injustice. Tucholsky saw his, "their," most important purpose as being to destroy all vestiges of the old monarchical, "Prussian" spirit in German public life and to instill a democratic sensibility in his countrymen.

In 1919, Tucholsky asked, "What can satire do?" and he replied, "Everything."[19] And indeed the most potent weapon in Tucholsky's intellectual arsenal was satire. He satirized everything from minor human failings to the moral and political systems of modern society. Because of its pungent and flamboyant quality, satire easily attracts attention and it follows naturally that Tucholsky's fame rests mainly upon his satiric abilities. With such pieces as " 'n Augenblick mal—!" ("One Moment Please!"),[20] a satire on the telephone, or "Wo kommen die Löcher im Käse her?" ("Where Do the Holes in the Cheese Come From?"),[21] a satire on what happens to friendship when an attempt is made to answer a child's innocent question—with pieces such as these, Tucholsky soon became famous as a humorist. But his satire was at the same time deadly serious. His Herr Wendriner, a caricature of the middle-class Jewish businessman, became the German Babbitt—George F. Babbitt was the main character of a popular Sinclair Lewis' novel of the same name. The sketch of 1930, "Herr Wendriner steht unter der Diktatur" ("Herr Wendriner under the Dictatorship"),[22] is horrifying in its accurate vision of life and behavior under National Socialism. It was, of course, Tucholsky's political satire, which caused the strong German reaction to his works. It was his ironic exaggeration of the difference between ideal and practice, which caused his enemies to hate and his friends to applaud.

Satire, however, can be as destructive to the critic as to the criticized. Satire is written because of a dual motive of love and hate and that was precisely Tucholsky's attitude toward his own country—a *Hassliebe* motivated by the gulf between the real and the ideal Germany. At even his most humorous moments, there was a serious and tragic undercurrent reminiscent of the title of one of his books *Lerne Lachen ohne zu Weinen*, (*Learn to Laugh Without Crying*).[233] His mental pacing back and forth between ebullience and despair, love and hatred was a kind of sickness which gnawed at the spirit and in the end cost Tucholsky his life.

In his attempt to abolish his hatred for Germany in order that love might triumph, Tucholsky struggled indefatigably against all the forces in the society which he hated. He possessed unflagging energy that enabled him to meet as many as seven publishing deadlines a week, carry on a formidable correspondence and lead a complex personal life. He was the type of courageous man whom the Berliners would describe as having *Herz und Schnauze*. He foresaw all too clearly the future of nihilistic barbarism and the whole of his career was an attempt to divert Germany from that path. He implored the people to cast off their indifference and become aware of the dangers threatening them. He fought the nationalists and anti-republicans, jeered at the Jews who compromised with Hitler and presented amazingly accurate predictions of life to come under the dictatorship. His contemporary, the author Erich Kästner, says that he tried to "stop a catastrophe with a typewriter."[244]

All five Tucholskys died in the attempt to do just that. Tucholsky was not only the most significant representative of the defeat of an intellectual political orientation, but he was also an individual who suffered a deep personal tragedy. He devoted his life to an ideal and to a country that in the end offered him nothing but a vial of poison. In 1923, long before his death, Tucholsky knowingly wrote his own epitaph; it is, nonetheless, a good summation of his fortitude and character:

Here lies a golden heart and a brassy mouth!
—Good night!

NOTES

1 Letter to Mary Gerold Tucholsky dated September 4, 1918. "... Concerning Rosa Bertens. That is not simply Strindberg's character or Bertens' portrayal; it is also my mother." KT, Ausgewählte Briefe, 1913-1935 (Hamburg, 1962), p. 399.

2 KT, "Rosa Bertens," G.W. (Hamburg, 1960), I, 190f; K.T., *Die Schaubühne*, X/19 (May 7, 1914), 520.

3 KT, "Der echte Deutsche," quoted by Klaus-Peter Schutz, *Kurt Tucholsky in Selbstzeugnissen und Bilddokumenten* (Hamburg, 1959), p. 12.

4 A play on *Deutschtum*. The word Teutsch is an archaic form of Deutsch. Tucholsky caricatured the superpatriotic Germans by calling them *Teutschen*, thus indicating their reactionary nature and lending to them a comic Colonel Blimp quality.

5 See letter by Henry H. H. Remak, "Brief aus USA" in "Der Collegianer," *Notre Parole* (Berlin, April, 1964), pp. ff..

6 KT, "Ein Kind aus meiner Klasse," G.W., II, 53-55; P.P., *Die Weltbühne*, XXI/9 (March 3, 1925), 315

7 Harry Zohn (ed. and trans.), *The World Is a Comedy, A Tucholsky Anthology* (Cambridge, Mass., 1957), p. 226. Also in: *Germany? Germany?* (Berlinica, New York, 2017).

8 Max Brod (ed.), *The Diaries of Franz Kafka* 1910-1913 (New York, 1948), p. 71 (entry of September 30, 1911).

9 KT, *Ausgewählte Briefe*, p. 485.

10 KT, *Rheinsberg, Ein Bilderbuch für Verliebte* (Zürich, n.d.), pp. 54f; and G.W., I, 40f. English translation by Cindy Opitz; *Rheinsberg. A Storybook for Lovers*, (Berlinica, New York, 2014).

11 The medical student was modeled after Else Weil, who became Tucholsky's first wife. In the novel, her name is "Claire" and in life Tucholsky referred to her as "Claire Pimbusch."

12 See KT, *Ausgewählte Briefe*, p. 512.

13 KT, "Start," G.W., II, 1004; K.T., *Die Weltbühne*, XXIII/52 (Nov. 27, 1927), 964.

14 See the discussion of the literary critic, Hans Sahl, "The Man with the Five Pseudonyms," *Politics*, V/3 (New York, Summer, 1948), 171.

15 KT, Ausgewählte Briefe, p. 333. The translation is by Ralph Mannheim from *Politics*, VI/3, 173.

16 KT, "Interview mit sich selbst," G.W., I, 471; P.P., *Berliner Tageblatt* (September 3, 1919), p. 414. In English translation by Cindy Opitz in *Berlin! Berlin! Dispatches From the Weimar Republic* (Berlinica, New York, 2013), pp. 38–40

17 KT, "Start," G.W., II, 1004.

18 KT, "Wir alle Fünf," G.W., I, 1041-43; K.T., *Die Weltbühne*, XVIII/34 (Aug. 24, 1922), 204.

19 KT, "Was darf die Satire?" G.W., I, 364; I:W., *Berliner Tageblatt* (Berlin, Jan. 27, 1919).

20 KT, 'n Augenblick mal—!", G.W., I, 1097; P.P., *Acht Uhr Abendblatt* (Berlin, May 26, 1923).

21 KT, "Wo kommen die Löcher im Käse her?" G.W., II, 1212; P.P., *Vossische Zeitung* (Berlin, Aug. 29, 1928).

22 KT, "Herr Wendriner steht unter der Diktatur," G.W., III, 547; K.H., *Die Weltbühne*, XXVI/41 (October 7, 1930), 559. All three stories are translated by Cindy Opitz in *Berlin! Berlin! Dispatches From the Weimar Republic* (Berlinica, New York, 2013)

23 KT, *Lerne lachen ohne zu weinen* (Berlin, 1931).

24 Erich Kästner, "Begegnung mit Tucho," *Gruss nach Vorn* (Hamburg, 1948), p. 291.

Above: A dead German solidier in the trenches in World War I. Germany lost two million soldiers; 4,5 million were wounded.

Below: Scheidemann proclaims the Republic from the Reichstag in 1919.

II.

THE SLAUGHTER

TUCHOLSKY WAS a member of the "war generation," the group of young men whose lives were ripped apart by the event, which closed the nineteenth century and opened the twentieth. Like many others, Tucholsky spent much of the rest of his life trying to put the pieces back together again. On the other hand, Tucholsky was twenty-four years old when the war began; he had reached maturity and had a promising career as a writer before him. The war thus was not the formative experience that it was for younger men. The lives of the men of Tucholsky's generation were interrupted, perhaps even shattered, by the war, but they did not receive their primary education in the trenches. They could not escape their nineteenth century mold. Yet after the slaughter, life could never be the same again and for this reason they felt themselves to be forever separated from life and therefore lost.

Much has been written about this generation born in the late eighties and early nineties, the generation in which the sons were more conservative than the fathers—conservative in that they turned away from the ideals of democratic liberalism and moved toward ideas of national renewal which bordered on the mystical.[1] In France the fathers "had done battle for the innocence of Dreyfus and fought the power of the 'reactionaries' and the clergy. Their children were as likely as not to embrace the counter-revolutionary, monarchist politician Charles Maurras and his *Action Francaise*, or the milder version of conservative nationalism preached by the novelist Maurice Barres."[2]

In Germany, there was the Youth Movement, composed of those bands of middle-class adolescents who wandered through forests and over mountains in an attempt to discover through nature the individual life. Girded with Nietzschean ideas, they longed to establish an order beyond the state with its constitutions and superficial institutions. Beyond the ugliness of industrial modernity and commercial uniformity lay "inner freedom" and the individual's independent responsibility to shape his own life.[3] Thus would they create the ideal man who would compose a "new mentality" above the degradation of the modern world. They were slightly anarchic and they were anti-authoritarian, but they were also in search of authority and new allegiances.[4] These young idealists provided most of the volunteers in 1914. It was the war that became the experience of their lives through which "meaning" became even more anarchic and irrational.

Tucholsky was also opposed to the culture of Wilhelmine Germany, but he placed no faith in the Youth Movement. Writing in April 1914, he maintained that in actuality the movement had become a "conservative, chauvinistic program." It was no longer a contending political faction, but on the contrary had been swallowed by the government. He believed that the youth, because of their vagueness, had unwittingly passed into the service of the monarchical state. Their "rebellion" served only to buttress the state that they seemingly opposed. "We are not well. We have a hundred dogmas of reflection, but barely one of action. We resemble the millipede that was immobilized because he couldn't decide which leg to move first. He was lost in self-contemplation. Power and intellect (*Macht und Geist*) are two factors further apart than ever."[5]

Through their willed indifference to the crass external world, through their talk of "inner freedom," the youth insured the triumph of the forces they opposed. Tucholsky was dissatisfied also, but he believed that moral and spiritual transformation could come only if the practical world of political and social relationships were changed first. To ignore politics was to court disaster, for while the idealists were enjoying inner freedom, the politicians would be imprisoning and executing the people. Tucholsky wrote in 1917 that small details were as much the stuff of life as the ideals of the philosophers.[6] No matter what the visionary pronouncements of the Youth Movement might be, no matter how lofty the goals proclaimed by William II for the German people, what really mattered was the quality of the everyday life of individuals and their treatment at the hands of power.

The way to the fulfillment of the individual that the Youth Movement sought lay not in a form of nationalist religion or in vague cultural idealism. In his pre-republican writings, Tucholsky sought political freedom, democratic politics, social justice—the liberal ideals expressed in the rhetoric of the (failed) German revolution of 1848. "We have lost the ideals of the pre-March period [of 1848], but have retained the reaction. Politics has degenerated into squabbling; opposition into un-influential rowdiness. God give us a pair of good fellows who can bring us out of this lazy pre-March and into a genuine Spring."[7]

The new springtime of democratic liberalism which Tucholsky wanted did not come. Instead there was World War I, the event that gave meaning to being for those who dreamed of a "life of action." In horror, Tucholsky watched the youths marching joyfully to the front. For him, their joy proved the self-deception and bankruptcy of their ideals. It demonstrated conclusively the decadence of Wilhelmine culture.

Searching for an ideal and a faith, the young men of 1914 greeted the slaughter with songs and garlands. The limbo of waiting for something to happen was over; the active life had begun. Seldom has a war been entered with greater idealism on the part of all combatants. In Paris, London, Berlin, cheering crowds greeted the declarations of war. The letter of a young German soldier written in 1914 is typical of the general ecstasy with which Europe hailed the war and of the particular hopes that a part of the German youth played in it:

> Leipzig (unfortunately still here)
> August 3, 1914
> Hurrah! At last I've received my orders. It was this morning in a noisy tavern. Hour after hour, I had waited for them. This morning I saw a young female acquaintance and I was almost ashamed for her to see me still in civilian clothes. You, my good parents, will also be proud of me. I no longer belong to peaceful Leipzig.
> Dear Mother, please remember what I said to you in the confusion of parting: in these times when we think of those who belong to us we become small and weak. But when we think of our people, of the Fatherland, of God, of the all-embracing universe, then we become courageous and strong.[8]

For many Germans in the light of their history of disunity and particularism, the war appeared to offer a unifying ideal, which would obscure the differences of the past. The majority of the personal memoirs of the period referred to 1914 as the year of sudden and unexpected national unity.[9] The liberal author Rudolf Binding wrote: "On the streets and in the squares, people looked each other in the eye and rejoiced in the community of feeling."[10] The philosopher Max Scheler spoke in almost mystical tones of the abolition of the sense of loneliness by the common effort in war: "No more were we what we had been for so long. Alone! The broken contact between individual, people, nation, world and God was suddenly reestablished…"[11]

Perhaps the most lyrical description of that ecstatic August is found in Stefan Zweig's autobiography, *The World of Yesterday*. Again the emphasis is upon solidarity, unity and good feeling. Even a man as humane and sensitive as Zweig admits the excitement, which filled his own breast in 1914:

> And to be truthful, I must acknowledge that there was a majestic, rapturous, and even seductive something in this first outbreak of the people

from which one could escape only with difficulty. And in spite of all my hatred and aversion for war, I should not like to have missed the memory of those first days. As never before, thousands and hundreds of thousands felt what they should have felt in peacetime, that they belonged together. A city [Vienna] of two million, a country of nearly fifty million, in that hour felt that they were participating in world history, in a moment which would never recur, and that each one was called upon to cast his infinitesimal self into the glowing mass, there to be purified of all selfishness. All differences of class, rank, and language were flooded over at that moment by the rushing feeling of fraternity. Strangers spoke to one another in the streets, people who had avoided each other for years shook hands; everywhere one saw excited faces. Each individual experienced an exaltation of his ego, he was no longer the isolated person of former times, he had been incorporated into the mass, be was part of the people and his person, his hitherto unnoticed person had been given meaning...[12]

A few months after August, the writers who had hailed the outbreak of war regretted their initial enthusiasm.[13] But Tucholsky had not succumbed to the madness which overwhelmed the others, a fact which testifies to his practical sense and clarity of judgment. He was not in the slightest way seduced by the rationalizations of the "ideas of 1914," that pathetic attempt to create a special concept of German freedom to oppose the "decadent" liberalism of the West. Authors and politicians like Thomas Mann, Ernst Troeltsch, Friedrich Meinecke, Johann Plenge, Walther Rathenau and others of equal fame and intelligence tried to give the war meaning through the definition of a national purpose—the ideas of 1914 over the ideas of 1789.[14]

Tucholsky, on the other hand, never confused the war with Geist.

He saw it as a stupidity and a horror; it had nothing to do with ideals or personal purpose. Kafka's judgment that Tucholsky was an entirely consistent person showed remarkable insight, for Tucholsky never wavered from his past evaluation of the Empire. In all of the excitement that tragic August, Tucholsky never lost sight of the reality behind the rhetoric.

Tucholsky was thus not one of the millions who rushed to the colors in 1914. He continued to pursue his law studies and received his doctorate in Jurisprudence early in 1915. However, in April 1915 he was duly inducted into the army, but he had the extreme good fortune to be sent to the east rather than to the deadly western front.

In 1915 Tucholsky wrote nothing for publication, his time being spent completing his legal studies or taken up by induction into the army. During the remaining years of the war, he published little because he did not wish to conform to the censorship. He found time and inclination to write only some literary criticism and allegorical satire. He composed the "bourgeois fables" such as *The Enchanted Princess* and *Walpurgisnacht* which portrayed substantial bourgeois types in the forms of witches, devils and other fairy-tale characters.[15]

In 1918, Theobald Tiger wrote a poem admonishing Peter Panter for being so silent about the war. He accused him of being "frivolous," of dealing with nonessentials instead of politics and "reality."[16] The following week, July 18, 1918, Peter Panter replied in prose to Theobald Tiger's verses and justified his silence about the war. In the article, Panter thanks Tiger for his "friendly song" and points out that both of them are privileged to be pseudonyms. Even so it is easier to be a poet who makes rhymes than to be a writer who composes "simple German." On the question of politics and the war, Panter maintains that he has absolutely no propensity for martyrdom. Others might climb on their soapboxes, but he was unsuited for such a role. Fat bellies cannot arouse the necessary pathos. In the end, Panter contends, it is a question of either falling into the nationalist line or maintaining the opposition of silence. What he began as a kind of quip, Tucholsky ended on a deadly serious note:

> And you must understand that for an honorable man, in these matters there is a single either—or: he either goes into opposition (which can be effected by silence) or he cooperates. He who was never before concerned with the state falls into line with a rhythmic or epic clatter, rhymes the blood of others with his own welfare—and that makes a very pretty sound—and justifies the necessity of this war cosmogenetically. And meanwhile the blood flows and flows.
> The first war year I was totally silent. I believe today that it is possible—but always with this silent reservation—to speak of secondary things. But about the main thing I can say nothing because it does not seem logical to me to leave the front to attend a premier of the drama of human nature. Either Christ or the sergeant, but not this mean proportional. You will realize, dear Herr Tiger, that it was not estrangement from the world or snobbery, which caused me to prattle on about everything but not about the one thing.
>
> I am yours sincerely,
Peter Panter[17]

Tucholsky often maintained that to know when and how to remain silent was half the battle. And when circumstances such as the censorship robbed him of a voice that would not serve his opponents, then his silence was deafening. During the war, his voice of protest was conspicuous by its absence, just as it was to be again after the Nazis came to power.

When he chose to report the "secondary matters" he did so exceedingly well. The single, direct account of his war experience was made in 1917 in an article for the *Schaubühne* entitled "Unterwegs 1915" ("Underway in 1915"). It was a wistful and humorous portrayal of Tucholsky's journey with the troops to the east. Trains to be loaded and unloaded, gear to be packed and unpacked, orders to be deciphered by the light of torches and waiting, waiting, waiting. "Arrival at the train station. We remain there for hours... the wind blows, but it is not wind; the lovely clouds are not clouds, the rain is not rain." On their way to the Latvian province of Courland, they finally arrive in the city of Tilset where they must transfer to barges. After the confusion of loading is over, Tucholsky and his friend, the "melonhead," go below to the galley and are astounded:

> On the sofa in the tiny room sits a magnificent youth. He is so beautiful that I must continually look over at him. He is a combination of child and English choirgirl. He has delicate movements, long eyebrows and can smile—! But when he opens his mouth, it is all almost lost—a repulsive, drawn out east Prussian accent (*Platt*). But then he ceases speaking and sleeps—heavenly! But where did he come from? The mother, in a manner of speaking, is a hideous, bony hag who is supposed to cook for us. Also we want to sleep there—even both in one bed if necessary. In the next room? No, she cannot recommend the next room to us. We look in: a dark, low place. Suddenly there appear a huge white goose and a goat. Not for us....

They return to the table in the kitchen. Tucholsky finds a Bible and begins to leaf through it absentmindedly. The old woman sermonizes about her religious experiences "when I was a seamstress in Berlin." "Aha," thinks Tucholsky, and is drawn to stare at the boy who opens his eyes and with a dreamlike expression sighs and begins to pick his nose. As the mother shouts at the boy, Tucholsky finds a letter stuck in the Bible, marking the Ninetieth Psalm. Secretly he reads it: "In the case of Bechereit versus Schmalmofsky, I wish to inform you that you have met with success. It was ruled that your brother-in-law must pay 286 marks plus 6 per cent interest to begin the 12th of August this year. Attorney at law, Martin." Tucholsky sighs, "Ah, the pious."[18]

Such was the way in which Tucholsky described his personal war experience—the attention to detail, the description of longings for home, uncanny coincidences, the elucidation of the foibles of little people met along the way.

But hardly a hint of the only important matter—the slaughter. Tucholsky was waiting until his views could be expressed with some effect.

It was much the same with his private letters in these years. He never complained openly about his privations. He concentrated instead on humor and criticism of the books he was reading. He had some time to read because he was not a participant in actual combat. Having no previous military training, he was placed in an equipment supply unit which "fought the Russians and the flies," as he wrote his sister, Ellen, in August 1915.[19]

His correspondence with his younger sister was touching, but could hardly be as serious as that with Dr. Owlglass. "Owlglass" (a play on Eulenspiegel) was the pseudonym for Hans Erich Blaich, a well-known contributor to the satirical magazine *Simplicissimus*. In 1912, Tucholsky and Szafranski, while on their way to Prague, had visited Dr. Blaich at his home in Feldbruck near Munich. A rich correspondence ensued until a misunderstanding in 1920 caused Dr. Blaich to break it off, much to Tucholsky's regret.[20]

It was in his letters to Blaich that Tucholsky first betrayed some of his impressions of the war and his hopes for the future. The letters reveal a man intensely concerned with literature and determined to hold on to the remnants of a "civilized" life. On December 18, 1916, Tucholsky wrote that army life in the east reminded him of an ox that repeatedly ran its head against a thick wall. His performance was magnificent, but he failed to ask if it had a purpose. "Time crumbles in our fingers; I have a heavy heart concerning the rebirth post festum. Short and sweet: the world goes wrong again and one's own house is the best.... Don't hold the old soldier-writer's pessimism against him—he can't help it."[21]

As the slaughter continued, Tucholsky began to despair that a new age of humanity would be possible. He feared the advent of a materialistic age of social indifference. He found himself withdrawing from a world, which was too cruel and stupid. In 1917, his personal experiences in the war began to shake him:

> If the great humorists have all been serious men, then I must be a Gulliver. I have a belly full of the bitterest gall... Day before yesterday, they shot a couple of Russians-spies—I assisted. Naturally only with the court action, not with the carbines. It was a wretched business. Humanity hacks its way through flesh and blood—the path of "the Idea" through living men. Those lofty phrases sound pretty later in the primers — just so one didn't have to be there.

It was all too wearying, the killing, the inhumanity, the irrationality. And the army—the cold and unearthly way in which the officers looked at the enlisted men, holding in contempt those who had fewer buttons than they. "Yes, you may say softly, it's not as bad as all that," wrote Tucholsky to Blaich on March 8, 1918, "but I believe it is very bad and I no longer want anything to do with it."

Throughout 1917 and 1918 Tucholsky became increasingly convinced that in comparison to the barbaric future, the prewar era would seem a paradise of graciousness and tranquility. Whatever might come in the future, the "old time" was past forever. On April 17, 1917, he wrote, "Claire writes correctly that we at least had a gleam of the past. Our grandchildren will not be able to say that." And a few months later in June came the lament to Blaich, "But our, my time is past. You at least ladled off a little more *crème*—for us they put the lids on after the soup... "

By January 1918 he was writing that he felt like an old man who constantly shuffles along looking for his past—unable to keep up with the times.

Tucholsky felt himself withdrawing from the world like others of his generation who made a separate peace or bade a "farewell to arms." He began to have dreams of emigrating from Germany to some quiet, unbelligerent country. In 1917, he wrote cryptically, "I have never been a deserter and have no desire to be one—but these boots don't really fit me. The best would be to pull them off. For two years Sweden has been in my head. What do you think of that?" Tucholsky did finally settle in Sweden, but he never withdrew before the advent of the Nazis into an exclusive, private concern. He abandoned any allegiance to governments or ideologies, but he remained intensely involved in society and culture. And try as he might, he was never able to shake off his German boots.

The one saving grace about Tucholsky's military experience was that it forced him to go to Courland, where he found the woman he was to love the rest of his life. On May 21, 1918, he wrote to Dr. Blaich, "In Courland I have become acquainted with a young lady (her name is Mary Gerold) who loves poems such as you are able to write."

Tucholsky's education and talent enabled him to obtain a transfer to the flying school in Courland where he became a noncommissioned officer and director of the military library. He also edited a soldiers' newspaper, *Der Flieger* (*The Pilot*). Mary Gerold worked in Autz, a small town near Riga. She was a shy but urbane girl in whom Tucholsky found a good match for his own wit and intelligence. In late 1917 Tucholsky first made Mary's acquaintance. Almost immediately he began writing letters to her, even though she might be only a few blocks away. He would see her during the day and write in the evening, telling her of his feelings of affection, chiding her for her shyness or attempting to clear up a misunderstanding. The letters to her in 1917 and 1918 were tender and playful love letters, at once sophisticated and intimate, in which Tucholsky revealed much about his background and ideas of himself. Above all, he expressed his hopes and fears for the future. This was but the beginning of a correspondence that was to continue for the rest of Tucholsky's life. There is no better record of the charm and earnestness of Tucholsky's personality than in these letters to Mary. They span his life, from the prankish enthusiasm of his youth to the utter desolation of his final days.

Tucholsky's first meeting with Mary was a disaster; he had been presumptuous and forward. He had offended her and he wrote her a note of apology in a stilted, mock-formal style:

November 13, 1917
My very honored, gracious Fräulein,
I do not believe that it was the occasion for such a punishing glare.
I know very well that the little note was unthinkable in orderly relationships—that it does not do to wave to a lady as the grand sultan tosses the silken handkerchief to his favorite, which means nothing less than "come!" But you must also please consider that Autz is not a salon and local conditions cannot be compared to those in a large city in time of peace. The note was a bit direct, but it was the only thinkable way out in that moment.
You say that there is no reason for such things to happen. I don't know. (You don't either.) You say that I do not know you. That is an error, which may easily be corrected. And allow me to say that it is no deprecation to a young lady if someone says that he would like to become acquainted with her. And herewith I shall solemnly and a little ruefully (with a consciously prankish face) withdraw completely the invitation. Up to the point of the "happy eyes"—I cannot take that way, for it is written and must remain so.
And so I thus beg of you to allow me this evening to ask if for only twenty minutes you will be unfaithful to that firm, but bad resolution made this evening to be completely pure. We shall smoke the long peace pipe and I believe that a small stroll along the eastern battlefield will repair what was written in an unthinking but joyous moment.
With a formal bow which would find approval in the eyes of even the strictest great aunt—
The acquainted unacquainted

Mary did indeed forgive Tucholsky his first impetuous behavior and accepted his invitation for an afternoon walk. In the evening, Tucholsky returned home and wrote another letter. Mary was somewhat taken aback by what she termed a correspondence from "house to house." But Tucholsky insisted that he wanted to give her his fresh impressions, to share his thoughts by means of his most comfortable mode of expression, the written word.

After their first encounter Tucholsky was in no way halting about expressing his feelings.

> As far as it was possible in the darkness, I recognized in you: temperament—no blood in the veins, but champagne, thank God; tingling nerves, a feeling for rhythm—you dance well. In toto, someone who does not deserve the usual admirer who says graciously after the first night, "Well now, my little one… " (You would brush him off at once.) Result? Result: not "I love you"—those are not the right words. But: "I would like to learn to love you." ("But you have no idea—" You want to say.)

Tucholsky continued that he knew that they would never quarrel because she was a "good comrade," a partner who understood nuances, who heard the half and quarter tones. Even her distaste for hand-holding would never cause them to quarrel. In short, they understood one another. Whether their relationship would become "serious" or not was another matter. "If it's all right with you, we'll toss the beach ball back and forth for a while longer—we shall wait." Tucholsky added mischievously that a room would be much nicer to wait in than a dirty street. He confessed that it would be a steep and difficult way, but certainly the end would be worth it—"Allons! I shall take that path. Surely you will allow me to."

Mary, however, remained suspicious of Tucholsky's intentions. He seemed so hasty, so overwhelming in his conviction that they were perfect for one another. After all they had only been acquainted for a few months, and he was a soldier away from the restraints and responsibilities of home. She remained cautious, shrinking from the slightest physical contact. "Please do not think me too hurried," he wrote on November 17, 1917, "I only want—don't laugh—to save time. I don't want to fritter away this beautiful, precious time. What kind of an opera would it be if the overture lasted two hours?"

Tucholsky continued the metaphor by saying that the best moment in the theater occurs when the lights begin to dim, the curtain rustles and one settles back comfortably in one's seat and lets come what may. He carefully explained to Mary that his reason for wanting to stroke her hand was not out of a "boring need for physical tenderness." It was rather like the husband in Turgeniev who can only stare at his beloved wife, and in spite of himself he cannot take his eyes away from her. "This evening, carefully and shyly, I looked at you from the side until I thought: now she notices, you must stop. It was so difficult for me to sit quietly in my chair and not go to you and say, 'God, you are a wise and fabulous girl—come!' "

These tender explanations did not convince Mary that the friendship should go beyond a pleasant conversation. A letter to her on November 21 described a traffic signal with two arms, one of which said "yes," the other "no." Tucholsky pleaded that it might be yes—yes to a winter filled with quiet days before the fire while snow fell outside. They would laugh, smoke cigarettes and read. To no avail. Mary remained friendly, gay and aloofly correct.

There are no letters for December. On January 12, 1918, Tucholsky proposed an "armistice." On the sixteenth he explained that forms were necessary, but people who are dear to one another cannot continually approach one another in top hats. Juliet's telling Romeo not to go, that it was the nightingale and not the lark, was not socially refined, but it was the truth.

On the following day, January 17, Tucholsky wrote a letter entitled "Longing." "Whoever says, 'I think of you day and night, my love,' is lying. There is no such thing, but there is the unconscious sense. In the unconscious there rests something; it doesn't sleep, it rests…. And in quiet hours, it gets up, lifts its head and says, 'I am still there.' It is still there. It is always there and will and must see the light of day. Help it to—."

The letter of the seventeenth was the last time that Tucholsky used the formal form of address, Sie, to Mary. On January 18, 1918, he wrote a love poem in which he used the familiar du. Touched by Tucholsky's perseverance and convinced of his honorable intentions, Mary relented. On January 25, 1918, Tucholsky wrote:

My dear blonde one,
You are here: Your hand lies on my shoulder, I see your hand tremble in the light. I stroke your hand. And clearly I sense your being—so close, so close. I feel the warmth of your body—and I only want one thing—that you will always be here.

For the next three months, there was an outpouring of poems and tender sentiments. But the idyll soon ended. In April Tucholsky received orders, which transferred him to the German occupation in Romania. He was to be attached to the police commissar's office in Turn-Severin. He and Mary would not see each other again until her arrival in Berlin in 1920.

Tucholsky received a few days furlough in Berlin while on his way to Romania. At the end of April, he wrote Mary from his Berlin flat. He tried to reassure her that he was not "deserting" her, that he would never forget her:

April 27, 1918

And now the first word to you from Berlin, which is bright and full of spring. The trip was not fun, nor would it have been if the people had not been sitting on top of one another like sardines.
And how are you? Have you been washing behind your ears like a good girl? And your feet? (No, one doesn't need to wash the feet.)... I thank you for what was in the little envelope. If it were not in your dear hand, I would strike out one phrase—"Left behind?" No. That means never again. When you feel abandoned, write "left alone." That means only for a span of time. And it is only, only, only a span of time, little Mely!

Tucholsky's intense longing for Mary grew. He fell deeply, hopelessly in love. In his few letters during the brief stopover in Berlin, he began to speak openly of their future marriage: "Dear little Mely, lovers who swear eternal fidelity are slightly ridiculous. Time has greater power than they imagine. But if everything does not change, can we not be together, belong together?... It would not be bad if it could become a reality. 'It'? Always to be with each other."

Through the next two years, Tucholsky wrote to Mary an average of twice a week—long, thoughtful letters in which he expressed not only his admiration and love for her, but also his ideas about literature, politics and the war. Because of his enforced separation from Mary, it is not surprising that he disliked Romania. He much preferred the Baltic landscape and northern weather. He loved wind and rain: "It's raining outside. Every person has a weather, which is just right for him, which makes him feel best. Sunshine for some, storms for others. I have several weathers—those connected with a falling barometer. But—forgive me—weather without girls is never right."

Tucholsky often spoke of his reading and recommended books to Mary. He urged her to read *Buddenbrooks*, saying that Thomas Mann's character, Hanno, would become a life-long friend. He read copiously in French and often sent to Mary translations of chapters or sections of books that he particularly liked. He constantly spoke of his desire to share his experiences with her, to speak with her of his impressions of the people and the country in Romania:"... I always think, 'What would she say about that?' And, 'You must show her that someday.' And, 'She should be with me....' Nothing is really any fun unless you are sharing it with me."

Mary wrote Tucholsky about the misery of some prisoners-of-war she had seen. Tucholsky was moved to respond, "You do not do it, I know, but one must never say, 'The poor Russians!' One must say, 'The poor men!'" He marveled at how quickly men could be reduced to the status of animals. He related scenes of wounded Russians and Germans lying on straw with glazed eyes, silent and filthy. No one bothered to give them a drink. The worst, however, was to see two hungry Russians begging for food and groveling on the floor when it was brought to them.

"I had to leave," wrote Tucholsky, "I can see people suffer, but this was a terrible humiliation. I had to ask myself—how would I behave under such conditions?" He speculated that some people were reduced to animality sooner than others. As far as nationalities were concerned, the Russian probably succumbed the fastest, the German soon thereafter with the Englishman holding out to the last. Tucholsky expressed the opinion that men became brutal because they lost sight of the individual and his suffering. idealists were always saying that the individual did not count, that it was useless to remember that "he also has a mother who loves him and for whom he is the hub of her small world." But it was only the individual who counted. "The people [*Volk*] and the whole are imagined things which we have made up ourselves."

Tucholsky always maintained this conviction that one must never look beyond the individual man. Ideologies, religions, causes and struggles served only to mask individual suffering, served to conceal the horror and justify murder. Tucholsky became a confirmed and dedicated pacifist as a result of his war experience. He began to pronounce what would become a constant theme of the pacifists in the twenties, namely that a man who killed another man was a murderer even if he were a soldier in uniform on a battlefield. Tucholsky maintained that most morality was based upon practicality. Thievery was harmful to property as was murder. But murder could sometimes be justified—in war—because of its usefulness to property. "After six thousand years," Tucholsky lamented, "it has not yet gotten through man's head that blood is blood and that there is no such thing as a holy murder."

Such ignorance would continue until the madness of states ceased. It was the anarchy of the nations and the religious devotion of men to the state, which perpetuated the killing. Tucholsky expressed the hope that just as the state had established its authority over the feuding families, tribes and cities, so would an international authority end warfare among the states. Men were, after all, not herds of animals, even if the shouts of the warmongers were enough to make one believe that men were only dumb brutes. "What a mongrel man is: not an animal, not a god, but something of both. But there are those who see only the earth, who shout 'War!' They call cowardly traitors those of us who believe that there is perhaps something more worthwhile than shooting men in their faces."

Thus did Tucholsky in his war letters to Mary begin to work out the principles and convictions for which he would fight after he returned to Germany.

But in the last year of the war, he also dealt in specifics as well as generalities. By the summer of 1918, it was clear that the German spring offensive in the west had failed. Tucholsky's letters then became more concerned about the immediate future of Germany and Europe. From July through October he constantly reiterated the phrase *"Ich sehe schwarz"* (The future looks dark). He feared that something like the cultural desolation of the period following the Thirty Years' War would occur again. As the fall of Austria neared (Austria sued for a separate peace on October 27, 1918), Tucholsky wrote that soon not only would it be the end of Germany's war effort, but of the old Europe as well. He foresaw a Europe full of petty, squabbling states:

> Outwardly everything is quiet, the worst is yet to come. All of that which has been so carefully glued together, that which we hoped to see grow together—will now fall apart. And an evil patchwork of petty states begins which will cast Europe centuries into the past. "I am independent!" "No one can tell me what to do!" "I have my own flag." "We also want our own king, our own courts and officialdom and police and tariffs—" In such manner, it all comes crashing down. That which we held dear has been beaten into pieces—intellectual life cannot bloom in this arid mixture…

In the long run, Tucholsky was remarkably correct in his predictions in 1918. Europe did enter a political and intellectual balkanization from which she is only beginning to emerge after fifty years. It was a melancholy prospect to think of returning to so-called normal life not only in a war-torn continent, but also in a defeated country.

The war stopped with the conclusion of the armistice on November 11, 1918. Tucholsky was ordered to return to Berlin; Mary was trapped in Courland where invasion and civil war appeared to be imminent. The pundits proclaimed that a new period in European history was beginning, but Tucholsky found little consolation in that. As he wrote in his last letter from Romania to Mary, "It is little fun to have to live through *two* eras—*one* would have been plenty for me."

NOTES

1   See Klemens von Klemperer, *Germany's New Conservatism, Its History and Dilemma in the Twentieth Century* (Princeton, 1957).
2   H. Stuart Hughes, *Consciousness and Society, the Reconstruction of European Social Thought 1890-1930* (New York, 1958), p. 341.
3   See the declaration of the Free German Youth made at a gathering on the Hohen Meissner Hill in the vicinity of Kassel in 1913, quoted in Howard Hecker, *German Youth: Bond or Free* (London, 1946), p. 100.
4   Klemens von Klemperer, *Germany's New Conservatism*, p. 44.
5   Kurt Tucholsky, "Vormärz," G.W. (Hamburg, 1960), I, 169; K.T., *Die Schaubühne*, X/14 (April 2, 1914), 381.
6   Kurt Tucholsky, "Meinen Freunden den Idealisten," G.W., I, 238-39; I.W., *Die Schaubühne*, XIII/3 (February 1, 1917), 107.
7   Kurt Tucholsky, "Vormärz," G.W., I, 170.
8   Philipp Witkop (ed.), *Kriegsbriefe gefallener Soldaten* (Munich, 1928), p. 7.
9   Hanna Hafkesbrink, *Unknown Germany. An Inner Chronicle of the First World War Based on Letters and Diaries* (New Haven, 1948), p. 34.
10   Quoted by Hafkesbrink, p. 35, from Rudolf Binding, *Erlebtes Leben* (Frankfurt/M., 1928), p. 237.
11   Quoted by Hafkesbrink, p. 37, from Max Scheler, *Der Genius des Krieges und der deutsche Krieg* (Leipzig, 1917), pp. 1-2.
12   Stefan Zweig, *The World of Yesterday* (New York, 1943), p. 223.
13   See Hafkesbrink, pp. 51-75 and *passim*; also William K. Pfeiler, *War and the German Mind* (New York, 1941).
14   See Ernst Troeltsch, "Die Ideen von 1914," written in 1916 and published in *Deutscher Geist und Westeuropa* (Hans Baron, ed., Tübingen, 1925); Thomas Mann, *Betrachtungen eines Unpolitischen* (Berlin, 1918); Johann Plenge, *1789 und 1914. Die symbolischen Jahre in der Geschichte des deutschen Geistes* (Berlin, 1916); Otto Hintze, Friedrich Meinecke, Hermann Oncken, Hermann Schumacher, eds., *Deutschland und der Weltkrieg* (Leipzig, 1915); Friedrich Meinecke, *Die deutsche Erhebung* (Stuttgart-Berlin, 1914). For a discussion of the "ideas of 1914," see Klemens von Klemperer, *Germany's New Conservatism*, pp. 47-66.
15   Tucholsky published a collection of these fables in 1920 under the title, *Träumereien an preussischen Kaminen* (Reveries by Prussian Firesides) (Berlin, 1920)
16   Kurt Tucholsky, "An Peter Panter," G.W., I, 285-286; Th.T., *Die Weltbühne*, XIV/28 (July 11, 1918), 42.
17   Kurt Tucholsky, "An Theobald Tiger," G.W., I, 286-287; P.P., *Die Weltbühne*, XIV/29 (July 18, 1918), 62.
18   Kurt Tucholsky, "Unterwegs 1915," G.W., I, 248; I.W., *Die Schaubühne*, XIII/35 (August 30, 1917), 35.
19   Kurt Tucholsky, *Ausgewählte Briefe*, 1913-1935 (Hamburg, 1962), p. 83.
20   Dr. Blaich wrote Tucholsky on March 10, 1920, that he had accidentally read his critique of Ludwig Thoma's *Erinnerungen in the Weltbühne* (see G.W., I, 604). Because of the criticism of *Simplicissimus* contained in the article, Blaich felt himself constrained to end the correspondence.
21   This and all the following quotes are from: Kurt Tucholsky, *Ausgewählte Briefe*, p. 39, 47, 56, 48, 50, 55, 49, 57, 341, 342-343, 343-344, 347, 348, 349, 356-357, 360-361, p. 373, 372-373, 372, 395, 411, 413.

Above: After the Kapp Putsch in 1920s Berlin, a failed right-wing coup, soldiers and Freicorps men are controlling the streets.

Below: Marlene Dietrich in The Blue Angel, *the famous 1930 movie.*

III.

BERLIN IN DEFEAT AND REVOLUTION

AFTER THE armistice that ended World War I, Tucholsky made his way back to Berlin, a city in misery. In defeat, the great capital looked like a provincial town, or, as Tucholsky described it, "a fourth class waiting room full of misfortune."[1] Nothing was certain. It was unknown whether or not the armistice would endure. Two million German soldiers and more than half a million German civilians had died in the war. Many more were crippled. Famine was a likely possibility. The form of government was difficult to determine. In the confusion, Tucholsky did not find time to write Mary until December 19, over a month after the Republic had been proclaimed.

> What's going to happen here no one knows. For some time now I have daily expected the Entente to march in. And it would be no wonder given the unreasonable behavior of our Berliners. They no longer work, instead they hold meetings and run around.[2]

Tucholsky was as surprised by the so-called revolution as anyone else. Indeed he found it difficult to discern anything more than a few workers' demonstrations, speeches on street corners and much talk about the formation of "councils." To be sure the monarchy had fallen, but so far there had been little change in the actual structure of government. Tucholsky was waiting to see what would happen, for he knew no more than anyone else.

In contradiction to the contentions of right-wing critics, Tucholsky and the other men of the intellectual left had nothing actively to do with the destruction of the monarchy and the establishment of a republic. There were no plots; they were as surprised as anyone else by the turn of events. Just as the left intellectuals never formed any kind of party or organization, so were they during the war only in the loosest communication with one another. They planned nothing. How could they? They were in the field fighting, for the most part. Their speculations showed them to be passive or at least to have no special access to information.

On September 17, 1918, Tucholsky wrote to Mary:

> There is nothing new. Everything seems to be holding its breath. According to my information, everything at home looks so bad that I cannot write about the details. The country is shaken to its very foundations-not outwardly. There will be no revolution, no lanterns will be shattered, no people murdered—but morally and inwardly everything is teetering. The opposite poles have become so sharp and pointed that there is much to fear.[3]

Tucholsky foresaw a moral and philosophical crisis, which would certainly have political overtones, but he did not see an immediate political revolution. He believed that the spiritual emptiness and political ineptitude of imperial policy was now being paid for by a nation in defeat. He believed that there would have to be changes in the very fabric of the nation if it were to survive, but as far as a practical political revolution was concerned, he was as much in the dark as anyone else. On October 23, 1918, he wrote to Mary:

> ... One may say that the fate of Germany for the next two hundred years hinges upon the next few weeks. It looks dark—so dark that your ink in comparison is white as an angel. And we must wait. It is a small stupid satisfaction to realize that everything we wrote for years long before the war is now true and clear and admitted by everyone. At that time they almost spat upon us for it... the realizations that are in everyone's mouth today (I have never before written to you so openly) have been bought and paid for at a very high price.[4]

Those few weeks which Tucholsky spoke of were filled with violence and seeming revolution. Beginning with the mutiny of the sailors at the city of Kiel on October 28, 1918, the revolt spread to other seaports and finally to the cities of the interior of Germany. On November 8, a radical left Bavarian republic was proclaimed. In many cities, workers and soldiers formed revolutionary councils, following the model of the Russian soviets.

In Berlin there was a last, abortive attempt to save the monarchy when on the morning of November 9, Max von Baden, Chancellor since October, took matters into his own hands and announced the Emperor's abdication. (William had not been able to bring himself to take that drastic, but necessary step.) Later in the day, Prince Max appointed Friedrich Ebert, a Social Democrat, as Chancellor, after extracting from him a promise that a nationally elected constituent assembly would decide the future form of government for Germany. Both Ebert and his colleague, Philipp Scheidemann, had given their cooperation to Prince Max in the days before and they now agreed that the monarchy should be preserved if at all possible. That very afternoon, however, Scheidemann shouted, "Long live the German Republic" from the Reichstag window because he had been informed that the radical Karl Liebknecht was about to proclaim a "Soviet Republic" from a balcony of the royal palace. Germany became a republic through an accidental, impulsive decision inspired by a desire to thwart the radical left.

Scheidemann's action settled little of the confusion. It ended neither the menace of leftist extremism nor the possibility of a resurgence of the old conservative forces. The proclamation of the Republic was but the beginning of the struggle for political control. The councils were still holding their meetings; the Spartacist League (the base of what later became the Communist Party) was grouping to make a bid for power.[5] The armies were returning, bringing with them the possibility of a white terror, like in Russia. In Berlin during November and December 1918, thousands of people occasionally wandered the streets ready to be fused into mobs. More often the streets were empty. There was a sinister quality of expectancy. Would the victorious Entente invade? Would the Spartacists gain control of the workers' and soldiers' councils? Would there be a revolution on the order of the October Revolution in Russia? Would the blockade continue and cause mass starvation? "The universal unhappiness is horrible," Tucholsky wrote on December 19, 1918. "It is greater than even we bitterest pessimists are able to paint it... ."[6]

A few days later, on December 23, 1918, almost a month of chaos and violence began in Berlin, which ended in the triumph of the army as a force independent of the civilian government. In order to prevent further revolution, Friedrich Ebert (in the famous telephone agreement with General Wilhelm Groener) obtained the support of the army for his provisional government by agreeing to cooperate in the preservation of the Officers' Corps.[7] The officers thus enthusiastically cooperated in putting down demonstrations by the radical left. In their fear of Karl Liebknecht's Spartacists, the Majority Socialists relied upon the old army organization and made it all but impossible to create a loyal, republican armed force.

In the ranks of the political left the struggle for political control was ruthless. There were three factions. The Spartacists wanted a government by councils resembling the Russian soviet system. The Independent Socialists (who had split with the majority of the Socialist Party during the war) desired a combination of councils and parliament, while the Majority Socialists opted for simple parliamentary democracy.[8] By its cooperation with the generals, the Social Democratic Party (SPD) alienated not only the Spartacists, but also the Independents. The Independents had cooperated with the majority party in the provisional government, but they became restive when Ebert refused to countenance their demands for immediate socialization of industry. After December 16, when the Congress of Workers' and Soldiers' Councils repudiated extremism and refused to seat the Spartacist leaders, Karl Liebknecht and Rosa Luxemburg, the leaders of the more leftwing, Independent Socialists (USPD) threatened to withdraw from the Ebert regime.

The break came when violence erupted on December 23, 1918. The sailors of the People's Naval Division rioted for their overdue salaries. The men surrounded the Chancellery and threatened to make Ebert their prisoner. Although the main telephones were cut off, Ebert used his secret line to army headquarters at Kassel and appealed for help. While the army was on its way, Ebert came to an understanding with the sailors and tried to rescind the appeal, but the army attacked anyway. The result was a brief victory for the Independents and the Spartacists who had made the sailors' cause their own in a test of Ebert's power. The eight-hundred-man army managed to subdue the sailors after two hours, but the army was in turn attacked by a hostile civilian crowd of men and women. The troops panicked and ran away. The Independents resigned from the Ebert government, thus giving it effective control over organized authority.

The "victory" of the Spartacists was, of course, deceptive. Real power was in other hands. Despairing of the use of war-weary soldiers against the extremists, General Groener decided to recruit volunteers for a free corps, the soon-dreaded *Freicorps*. Soon the various generals began to form and train the volunteer groups which were to become the shock troops of political reaction.[9]

Thus was prepared the ground for the showdown between the two extremes of socialism: the Spartacists and revolutionary shop stewards on the left who wanted a sovietized *Reich*; and the Majority Socialists on the right who wanted a parliamentary republic created by an elected national assembly. It was ironic and an ominous portent that the conflict between Ebert and Liebknecht was settled by the reactionary military organization.[10]

Although ideology was the real issue, violence again broke out when the SPD dismissed Emil Eichhorn, an Independent Socialist, from his position as head of the Berlin security police. The Spartacists and the Independents called out some 200,000 men and formed armed columns in the Tiergarten. They were able to occupy the building of the *Vorwärts*—the party paper of the SPD—and the Wolff Telegraphic Bureau. Ebert, determined to rid himself of the Spartacist headache, called in the army and the Free Corps, which after initial delays attacked on January 10, 1919. The tactics were merciless. Using flame throwers and heavy artillery, the generals forced the workers to capitulate. By January 15, the threat of a Bolshevist revolution in Germany was ended.[11]

Tucholsky was horrified by the actions against the Spartacists. He was not a follower of Liebknecht, but he questioned whether the Republic had been placed in less danger after the defeat of the extreme left. On January 15, 1919, Liebknecht and his political compagnon Rosa Luxemburg were murdered in cold blood by right-wing officers of the Guard Cavalry Division. Tucholsky wrote a poem dedicated to their memory, but he repudiated their methods:

> Martyrs—? No,
> But victims of the mob.
> They dared. How rare that is today.
> They stepped forward, became activists.
> They wanted to be more than theorists.
> He: a muddle-head of middle measure.
> In the streets he sought human treasure,
> Poor guy, that's not where it is,
> There are many ideals; he was true to his,
> He wanted to raise the oppressed.
> With a human life they should be blessed,
> They betrayed the idealists,
> The sea god drowned by his own waves.
> They broke the cash box, the riot raged—
> Poor guy, is that what you wanted?
>
> She: the real man of the two.
> A life of suffering in prison.
> Ridicule and scorn and black-white chicanery
> And nevertheless faithful to the flag, the Fahne!
> And again and again—arrest and prison
> Interrogation and oppression
> And again and again—prison and arrest—
> She had the stronger male power.
>
> ... God knows that we aren't Spartacists,
> But honor to two fighters!
> May they rest in peace !![12]

For Tucholsky, the extraordinarily light sentence given to the murderer of Rosa Luxemburg was an indication of the future of the revolution in the hands of a triumphant right wing. Tucholsky could not support the Spartacists, but he also could not sanction the means used against them. He never forgave the Socialists for their pact with the army leaders and contended that if Liebknecht did not hold the solution, then neither did Ebert, for militarism was as dangerous as Communism. On May 8, 1919, Tucholsky sarcastically wrote, "We have not had a revolution in Germany, but we've had a counterrevolution."[13]

It was during these terrifying and violent events that Tucholsky decisively entered his career as a writer and a journalist. Almost at once, his earlier uncertainty disappeared. Perhaps his anger at the past and the treatment meted out to the workers grew to the point that he was overwhelmed by his zeal to transform German society. After his return to Berlin, Tucholsky began furious literary activity, publishing some 150 essays and poems in the fourteen months from November 1918 through December 1919. In these writings he sought to expose the true horror of war, to discredit Prussian authoritarianism and, as he put it, to make a true revolution in German life.

Part of the certainty about his career came, no doubt, from his success. Almost immediately after his return to civilian life, Tucholsky became involved in the Berlin cabaret. The name "Theobald Tiger" became one of the best known and popular in the whole of that bright field. Through his chansons for the cabarets of Berlin, Tucholsky early achieved fame in the Weimar Republic, a fame that led many to seek out his other writings.

After the strict censorship of the war years the audacity of the cafe theater was heady and breathtaking. Young people flocked to the cabarets to hear the generals and the Emperor denounced, to hear the admonitions that they must create a better world, or perhaps simply to be entertained by witty songs about life and love in the modern world. It was in the cabaret theater that one had the sense of being a part of the modern, of riding the crest of the avant-garde wave. It was there that the idealism and cynicism of youth found expression. In the darkness of the cafe, young persons in despair before the political madness around them, could find communion with like-minded friends and see their frustrations acted out on the stage. While listening to the songs of cynicism and hope, of longing for liberty and justice, of hatred of war and love of peace—the lyrics of humanity and equality—they could convince themselves that the very rationality and righteousness of their cause had to insure that they would yet prevail.

It is difficult for Americans to comprehend the importance of the theater in German intellectual life, much less the German political cabaret. The drama is the most important expression of German cultural life. The general heading of "theater" includes the cabaret, a form which has reached its greatest popularity and perfection only in Central and Eastern Europe. Perhaps the reason is that the strict censorship in those areas made the cabaret form necessary. In Germany and the Austrian Empire the censorship continued through the First World War necessitating the veiled criticisms of satiric innuendo and ironic symbol—forms, which find their most effective expression in a live performance on stage. Writers and poets were able to "get away with" dissenting commentary and biting opposition impossible in books and journals. The satiric cabaret came thus to be one of the most important and trenchant sources of political and cultural dissent, to which the greatest performing and acting talents were attracted. It was no coincidence that a man of Tucholsky's ability and seriousness invested his time and energy in the cabaret.

Tucholsky wrote for the famous Nelson Theater, the Kurfürstendamm home of Rudolf Nelson's reviews. Nelson was a talented composer and performer who before the war had operated the popular cabaret *"chat noir."* Tucholsky's works were performed in other well-known cabarets such as *"Schall und Rauch"* ("Noise and Smoke") and the *"Wilde Bühne"* ("Wild Stage"). In these establishments the most famous singers of the day interpreted Tucholsky's chansons. Among the women were Gussy Holl and Claire Waldoff, the stirring, deep-voiced Trude Hesterberg, the tragic, somber Rosa Valetti and the brilliant Kate Kühl, for whom Tucholsky wrote the greatest number of songs. The most famous male performers were Paul Graetz and Ernst Busch, the latter noted for his performance of revolutionary songs and working-class ballads. Tucholsky composed the music for some of the chansons himself, but well-known artists such as Werner Richard Heymann, Friedrich Holländer and Rudolf Nelson more often set the lyrics to music.

Tucholsky composed many songs of light whimsy and humor and a few expressing tender sentiment. Among the most interesting and evocative are those dealing with politics and society. The highly topical songs might describe a particular social condition or political event with a light-hearted, tripping beat. Then the tone would suddenly become harsh or mocking and the lyrics would make a deadly accusation by the unexpected use of a hackneyed party slogan or other political cliché in a new context. Tucholsky constantly made references to prominent political figures such as Gustav Noske, the Socialist Minister of Defense, who cooperated with the army leadership in quelling the Spartacists. There were songs encouraging the working class to demand its rights; there were others inciting the people to revolution—militant, intense and stirring. But of all the political songs, the most moving are those concerned with the war and the suffering it caused:

They lay four years in the trenches,
It was the great time!
They froze, crawled with lice and had
At home a wife and two small boys—
Far, far—!

And no one dared tell the truth,
No one dared protest,
Month after month, year after year—

… And the hordes of hack journalists shouted:
"War! War!
Victory!
Victory in Albania and victory in Flanders!"
And who died? The others, the others, the others
… Who is that enthroned above,
Covered with medals from head to toe
And who commands only, "Murder! Murder!—"

… Brothers, brothers, close the ranks! Brothers!
It must not happen again!
War against war!
And on earth, peace!'[14]

The music for the above, *"Krieg dem Kriege"* ("War against War"), begins in a low hushed tone rising to a shout of indignation and ending with a militant marching tempo suggesting the invincibility of the determination of the pacifists to create peace. The song "Red Melody" was written in a similar vein in 1922, three years later. Dedicated to Erich Ludendorff, the former WWI-general, the song was the lament of a woman for her dead son. In a low weeping voice, she describes the pain of the war years. Then in the chorus her voice rises to a shout of fury as she screams at the general not to dare try it again. In each chorus she warns that the "reds" are coming to get him and indeed in the closing lines of the song, she imagines that the millions of dead have pushed up out of their graves and have come to take Erich Ludendorff and all of militarism away. Rosa Valetti made the song famous:

A woman sings:

I am alone
All is gone
My son fought the Russians,
A cattle horde,
Away they roared,
To the front—in Omnibuses.
And there—the guard was not back in time—
Haho! He lay in slime.

The years, the years
Were long and numb formed,
The tears, the tears
Taste of the Baltic Sea—
General! General! Don't dare it again!
The dead are shouting! Think of the reds!
Hear the clanging, muffled chorus!
We are coming closer—
Cannon man! Out of the grave—push up!

I saw the world
In fire enfurled—
The women bent with sorrows, The reaper cut
And they were struck
With a hundred thousand horrors.
And for what did they scream and die?
Haho! For a filthy lie!
The corpses—the corpses—
They lie in the earth,
We women—we women—
Now what are we worth?

General! General! Don't dare it again!
The dead are shouting! Think of the reds!
Look out! Look out!
Hear the clanging, muffled chorus!
We are coming closer—Cannon man!
From the grave—push out!

In darkest night, Not a light—
They climb out of the depths
The fusilier
The musketeer,
Those who have no rest.
The dead battalions arrive—
Haho! To him who is alive.
Summoning, summoning,
Hear it in the wind's tone,
They're coming! They're coming!
Around his house they moan!
General! General!

> Don't dare it again!
> The dead are shouting!
> Think of the reds!
> Look out! Look out!
> Hear the subterranean chorus!
> We are coming closer—cannibal man!
> In step!
> Come with us—![15]

Tucholsky's prose pieces dealing with the same theme naturally lend themselves better to translation. During the war years, the War Academy building in Berlin was a place of daily sorrow. On its walls were posted the lists of those killed in action. After his return, Tucholsky often passed the academy and he noticed how the lists of dead, pasted on the walls, were slowly washing away. Some had become mere white spots. The memory of the days when the lists were new moved Tucholsky to write a brief essay entitled "The Spots."

> People say to me that I do not know how the German man is able to die. I well know. I also know how the German woman is able to weep. And I know that in her weeping today she is slowly beginning to recognize for what he died. For what—
> I grind salt into the wounds, but I would like to cauterize those wounds with the fire of heaven and cry out to the mourners: he died for nothing, for madness, for nothing, for nothing, for nothing.
> In the course of the years, the spots will gradually disappear, washed away by the rain. But there are others, which cannot be eradicated. In our hearts are scratched lines which will not go away. And each time that I pass the War Academy with its brown marble and white spots, I say quietly to myself: promise yourself. Make a solemn vow. Work. Try. Tell the people. Free them of the madness of nationalism, you with your small powers. You owe it to the dead. The spots are crying out. Do you hear them?
> They cry: *Nie wieder Krieg*—!
> Never again war—![16]

Tucholsky was approaching the height of his new-found success and popularity as a writer for the cabaret when Mary suddenly arrived in Berlin. Because of the political uncertainty, Mary had decided to flee from Latvia, but she was in a quandary as to where to go. Tucholsky had not really invited her to Berlin; he had not really made a formal proposal of marriage. In fact, he had indicated in the past that much would depend upon his financial condition, upon whether he could support her properly. He had implied that it was best for her to remain in Courland until both the political situation in Germany was clear and he had established himself upon some firm financial foundation. When Tucholsky heard that Mary had to flee, he of course urged her to come to him in Berlin. She was naturally reticent lest it appear that she was trying to force herself upon him. She also did not know what Tucholsky would expect of her once she came to Berlin. Above all she did not want him to make any financial sacrifice for her sake. He wrote her at length trying to calm her fears:

> No one is giving up anything; it is only a question of duty. Matz, who would believe you are coming to Berlin in order to—baby! Twenty-year-old. Little, terribly stupppppppid Meli. I shall say it this time. Cut and dried, this is the way things are: I ask you to come here and then we shall see how we shall live with one another. You are not a child and I know that you will not perish without me. But first I want to do everything for you that I can—even a Mimosa opens up sometimes.[17]

Things were not to go smoothly for them. Two months after her arrival in early January, they broke their relationship. Tucholsky later wrote that she arrived four months too early. He had had no money and was really unable to help her financially. Ironically, later in the year he made a lot of money, but they had already broken up. Almost immediately after Mary's arrival, Tucholsky knew that something was wrong. He wrote on January 20, 1920, "… something isn't right between us. It doesn't do to speak of these things, but I've had this feeling the whole time you've been in Berlin. You are so withdrawn, you do not give of yourself as earlier."

Tucholsky wracked his brain for reasons. It was not just a question of adjustment to the city, it was as though something had died. There was no communication. He speculated that perhaps Mary needed simple officer types, not literary men around her. She needed blond not "dark" men. On January 30, he wrote another questioning letter—"I shall try to write as though this letter were going to Courland and not Friedenau—which isn't easy." Tucholsky admitted that they were estranged because of many external circumstances beyond their control. The question was whether it was merely external.

Nothing improved; the estrangement continued. On February 16, 1920, Tucholsky wrote the breaking letter:

> I don't know what it is. For two years, I loved you as only one human being can love another. And now what is happening? It is as though a glass wall stands between us and I can't break it.

> I spoke with you freely and openly on those evenings last winter when I sat at the typewriter—when you were not present. And I also speak to you in the same way today—but I don't know what it is that weighs upon my breast. Something is wrong.
> I don't know what it is. I confront a riddle and I see no way out.
> I neither can nor want to forget. I have no hopes either. I must let it and you go.
> I ask nothing of you—if you ever need anything, call on me.
> Not small and withdrawn, but as one who turns naturally to her friend.
> I want to remain at least that, if not more.

Tucholsky was hurt and angered by Mary's aloofness from him. Mary was deeply wounded by his precipitate decision to break off contact with her. It appeared that he was adding insult to injury when a few months later on May 3, 1920, Tucholsky married Else Weil ("Claire Pimbusch"), his medical student friend from before the war, now a full-fledged Berlin physician.

Tragic as it was, it was perhaps inevitable that the break between Tucholsky and Mary occurred. They had known each other but for a brief time and under unusual circumstances. Tucholsky later wrote that in all of their years of knowing one another, they had only been really together a total of four days. When they saw one another it was in a theater or a cafe or in her room where there was no real privacy. When he first met Mary in Courland, Tucholsky was too impulsive and impatient. Mary quickly fell in love with him, but she was extremely shy. She was inexperienced in love and unsophisticated. She needed patience on the part of a lover. Absence and loneliness often force a projection of past intimacy between friends and lovers, which may never have existed. In his loneliness in Romania, after leaving Mary, Tucholsky poured out his heart and dreamed of a perfect and fulfilling love, which Mary felt but which she could not give.

With the vulgarity and crudity of army life, Tucholsky had an almost desperate need for companionship, for civilized conversation and feminine gentleness. These qualities he found in Mary and he fell hopelessly in love with her. She, on the other hand, saw Tucholsky as a young man who had suddenly intruded upon her life, proclaimed his devotion to her, and overwhelmed her with his sophistication and intense longings for affection. Just as she was beginning to become accustomed to him, he was snatched away to Romania. She naturally felt deserted and her reaction was defensive and withdrawing. While Tucholsky in his particular need asserted that the relationship could grow and mature in spite of ink and distance, Mary fell back into her old life and remained skeptical about the future with Tucholsky even though she was in love with him. When she became a fugitive, she was forced to go to Tucholsky still uncertain about her feelings for him and his for her.

When she arrived in Berlin, not only was Tucholsky virtually penniless, but began to act too quickly, to make assumptions about the intimacy of their relationship which she could not yet tolerate. She was a young girl in a strange and alien city, forced to flee from a home to which she would never return. And she had her pride. She was both frightened and exhilarated by the novelty of her experiences and she needed time for adjustment. As Tucholsky later wrote:

> Now I realize everything. How you arrived at an inopportune moment when I had no money, or at least little money. How I was ashamed to confess that I found everything so strange, uncomfortable—strange, strange and strange again. How I loved you and how you at the same time annoyed me—annoyed me without wanting to. How I was much, much too impatient, too fast, too quick—too quick in the erotic as in the human. How I made mistake after mistake and knew that I was making them—how I felt everything disappearing through my fingers…

On the other hand, Tucholsky was a sensitive man and he probably would not have pushed so hard if Mary had been able to be more open with him. She was so quiet, so enigmatic that he was driven almost mad by the pain, which her aloofness caused. Tucholsky later complained that there had been whole chambers of her heart upon whose doors was inscribed "entrance forbidden." He could not and would not have broken them down, but it had been so unbearably painful for him to realize that the past, the two years in Courland, the intimacy seemed to have counted for nothing. "I knew half of you. Had I known the other half, I would probably have been more relaxed. But I knew nothing and you said nothing –and you remained silent. And I was silent also."

Not once had she told him that she loved him and for that he had suffered greatly. When finally she did give him an indication of her affection, he confessed that it was too late.

Tucholsky's impulsive marriage to Else Weil was not a success and he fell into despair about the absurdity and confusion of his life. Once in a while he would see Mary on the street or on a train platform and he would be shaken by a renewed desire for her and sickened by his emotional misery. In August, only three months after his wedding, Tucholsky began to keep a secret diary in which he recorded his glimpses of Mary and began to analyze why he had not been successful with her. What was most painful was that he realized that he still loved her. Slowly, the diary became a description of his continuing love for her and a kind of record of his progress in renewing their relationship. Finally he began to reestablish direct contact with her. In October 1920 he sent her a birthday greeting, but, not being able to remember the exact date because she was born under the old Russian calendar, he wrote, "One can forget the date—not the woman." At the same time in his diary, he expressed his anguish and self-recrimination, "For two years I wished and longed for you and then you came and I had no patience. I have to close my eyes when I think of it… if only you were here. But you are not here. And I long for you just as much as I ever did. And you will not come again. Never—?"

The following year on May 17, 1921, Tucholsky dared to send Mary a brief greeting as he departed for a vacation trip. He asked her please to call on him if she needed anything. Tucholsky was almost beside himself with longing; he was almost mad with self-hatred and lovesick despair. A few days later on May 22, he confided to his diary after receiving a pleasant letter from Mary:

> I am going away and have almost driven myself crazy. Probably forever. I am going away and am taking that and you with me. For I have not ceased to desire you, to love you and to want you with me always. I am hot and cold—and I cannot describe that. I cannot do that. Farewell.

Tucholsky's deep personal depression continued throughout the following year, but he became more open in his communications with Mary. By April he was writing to her some of his ideas concerning why things had originally gone wrong for them. He asserted that he knew he had no right to say anything to her and that if she was in love with someone else, then so be it. However he now realized how he had made the two worst mistakes of his life, his breaking off of their relationship and his hasty marriage thereafter: "I know only that I have never forgotten you. You are the only woman from whom I can conceive being given a child."

He asked only for the privilege of sending her flowers now and then.

Mary did not discourage him and by June he was writing, "I never believed that there was such a word as 'always.' " Whereupon he signed the letter "Always." That same month in his diary he wrote a long analysis of their relationship, expressing in detail what he believed both his guilt and hers to be. It was a catharsis necessary before their new relationship could begin in earnest. He knew then that he would someday show Mary the diary and he wrote so that everything would be in the open between them. In November 1922 he invited her to a performance at the Nelson cabaret and she accepted.

In the course of the following months, they saw more and more of each other until on March 2, 1923, Tucholsky asked her to marry him. He sent her the secret diary and said, "… Give me your hand. You are everything to me. I want to be the same to you. Friend, companion, comrade, beloved and your husband."

Mary accepted Tucholsky's proposal, but it was impossible for them to be married immediately. Tucholsky was already married and would have first to obtain a divorce. That was relatively simple. But there was another factor: the great inflation of 1923. In the very month that Tucholsky asked Mary to be his wife, the mark began a downward spiral until August when it reached the ludicrous value of four trillion marks to the dollar. It was obvious that all thought of marriage would have to be postponed for a time. The delay was frightening to both Tucholsky and Mary. She worried that he might abandon her again. He feared that she had not really given herself to him and that he could not make her happy. Perhaps he was too old for her; perhaps he and his life were too complicated:

> Sometimes I think: she would be a thousand times happier with a blond cavalry officer, because he would be less complicated and would perhaps better master life. He would know no difficulties and have no scruples. No, I am no victor in a dance tournament… .

Then Tucholsky added that no matter what might hypothetically be best for her, he could not live without her. He maintained that she did not seem to realize how much she meant to him. He knew, if they should part, even that would pass, but he would receive a wound from which he would never recover. And if there should be a separation, which he could not even conceive of, he would forever be haunted by the echo, "But you could nevertheless have made her happy and how good that would have been—!" A few years later these final doubts and reservations were to appear to have been a sad prophecy. But for the moment:

> Dear one, be happy—! It must work out. And don't be angry at Nungo—be angry at the country and the time. I need rest—and would like to come to Meli, lie still on her breast and have blond hair cover my eyes and say nothing. And belong to you. Completely and alone to you.

NOTES

1 Kurt Tucholsky, *Ausgewählte Briefe*, 1913-1935 (Hamburg, 1962), p. 415.
2 Ibid., p. 415.
3 Ibid., p. 410.
4 Ibid., p. 412.
5 In 1916, Rosa Luxemburg wrote a series of articles which were published as "Spartacus Letters." The radicals began to call themselves the *Spartakusgruppe*. On November 11, 1918, they officially adopted the name *Spartakusbund*. See: Ossip K. Flechtheim, *Die Kommunistische Partei Deutschlands in der Weimarer Republik* (Offenbach, 1948).
6 Kurt Tucholsky, *Ausgewählte Briefe*, p. 415.
7 See John W. Wheeler-Bennett, *The Nemesis of Power, The German Army in Politics*, 1918-1945 (New York, 1954). This study indicts the army for its malevolent influence upon the Republic. Wheeler-Bennett's interpretation of the Ebert-Groener telephone agreement on the evening of November 9, is an indication of the general position of his study: "Thus, in half a dozen sentences over a telephone line, a pact was concluded between a defeated army and a tottering semi-revolutionary regime, a pact destined to save both parties from the extreme elements of revolution but, as a result of which, the Weimar Republic was doomed at birth [p. 21]."

For the opposite point of view, see Harold J. Gordon, *The Reichswehr and the German Republic* (Princeton, 1957). Professor Gordon maintains that while the army's influence was not necessarily benign, it, nevertheless, was not destructive. A yet more recent book takes issue with Professor Gordon's thesis, F. L. Carsten in *The Reichswehr and Politics, 1918 to 1933* (New York, 1966), maintains that the army was a force for instability in the Republic and that it resisted even the most minimal respect for the Republic.

8 The standard history of the Independents is Eugen Prager, *Geschichte der U.S.P.D.: Entstehung und Entwicklung der Unabhängigen Sozialdemokratischen Partei Deutschlands* (Berlin, 1921).
9 See Robert G. L. Waite, *Vanguard of Nazism, The Free Corps Movement in Postwar Germany*, 1918-1923 (Cambridge, Mass., 1952).
10 The Ebert-Liebknecht struggle was but the final stage of the ideological conflict which had plagued the left wing from its beginnings in the mid-nineteenth century. The conflict may be given the general title of revisionism versus Marxist orthodoxy. The standard work on this subject is Peter Gay, *The Dilemma of Democratic Socialism*, Eduard Bernstein's Challenge to Marx (New York, 1952). Another good general history of the divisions within Germany's left wing is A. Joseph Berlau, *The German Social Democratic Party 1914-1921* (New York, 1949). Carl E. Schorske's competent study, *German Social Democracy, 1905-1917, The Development of the Great Schism* (Cambridge, Mass., 1955) also traces the events which led to the formation of the Independent Socialist Party and eventually the Spartacists. Schorske's view is that the split came about because of the "new revolutionism" rising after 1905 as well as because of the older "reformism."
11 Gordon A. Craig, *The Politics of the Prussian Army*, 1640-1945 (Oxford, 1955), p. 360. For a detailed study of Spartacus Week, see Brie Waldman, *The Spartacist Uprising of 1919 and the Crisis of the German Socialist Movement: A Study of the Relation of Political Theory and Party Practice* (Milwaukee, 1958).
12 Kurt Tucholsky, "Zwei Erschlagene," G.W., I, 361f.; K.H., *Die Weltbühne*, XV/4 (Jan. 23, 1919), 97. It is interesting to note that a recent scholar supports Tucholsky's judgment of Liebknecht and Luxemburg. Werner Angress (Angress, *Stillborn Revolution. The*

Communist Bid for Power in Germany, 1921-1923 (Princeton, N.J., 1963), pp. 31f.) maintains that although their joint martyrdom has indissolubly linked them in the Communist tradition, the two leaders were very different in character, aim and idea:

> Rosa Luxemburg was first and foremost a Marxist theorist, but Liebknecht was a man of action rather than a thinker. Although he was virtually born into the Marxist revolutionary movement, he never became well versed in Marxian theory. He shared with Luxemburg the dream of a future Socialist society but had no clear idea of how it should be realized. Lacking both Luxemburg's sensibility and sensitivity, his approach to revolution was impulsive, pragmatic, and at times downright rash. While his rousing oratory, his personal courage and the sincerity with which he stated his convictions made him one of the most effective radical agitators, his lack of critical judgment at times involved him in adventures without regard for the possible consequences.

13   Kurt Tucholsky, "Preussische Studenten," G.W. (Hamburg, 1960), I, 407; I.W., *Die Weltbühne*, XV/20 (May 18, 1919), 532.
14   Kurt Tucholsky, "Krieg dem Kriege," G.W., I, 432.
15   Kurt Tucholsky, "Rote Melodie," G.W., I, 1026.
16   Kurt Tucholsky, "Die Flecke," G.W., I, 547. "Die Flecke" ("Spots") and numerous of Tucholsky's anti-war poems appear in English in *Prayer After the Slaughter. Poems and Stories From World War I*, Berlinica, New York, 2015), translated by Peter Appelbaum and James Scott.
17   This and the following quotations are from: Kurt Tucholsky, *Ausgewählte Briefe*, pp. 404, 440-41, 444, 445-46, 457, 451, 455, 453, 447, 450, 460, 461.

Above: The author Walter Hasenclever, a close friend of Tucholsky, and the Weltbühne *editor Siegfried Jacobsohn, his mentor (right).*

Below: Editor Carl von Ossietzky, who was killed by the Nazis in 1938.

IV.

THE VOICE OF THE HOMELESS LEFT

THOUGH TUCHOLSKY quickly achieved fame for his cabaret songs after the war, his real career, which he proclaimed as his profession, was as a writer and critic. Tucholsky belonged to no political party, subscribed to no ideology, and joined few organizations, but he was a member of the group which has come to be loosely classified as the "left intellectuals." They were the writers of the non-Communist left who desired liberal, democratic, socialist reforms, but who could find no political party which they believed would accomplish their goals. Because of their alienation they came to be called Germany's "homeless left."[1] Yet even this phrase perhaps implies too much unity. Unlike Communist intellectuals, the writers of the democratic left hardly looked upon themselves as a group at all. About the only things they had in common were the journals in which they published. They met in the pages of their magazines, where they expressed their views and argued with one another. Their publications gave them unity and identity.

Of all of his colleagues, Tucholsky was the most brilliant and prolific. His work expressed their "program" and formed their manifestoes. He set the tone of their most important publication and thus gave direction to whatever "movement" may be said to have existed. Although he appeared in almost every kind of publication that could conceivably be called liberal, most of Tucholsky's work appeared in a few well-known journals. He wrote for *Freiheit* (organ of the Independent Socialists), *Vorwärts* (organ of the Social Democrats), and for the *Vossische Zeitung* of the great Ullstein publishing complex.[2] Tucholsky's most important association, however, was with the *Weltbühne*, for which he became the major writer and for a brief time its editor.

Because it was so wide-ranging, it is difficult to describe the small magazine which described itself as a "weekly for politics, art and economics." When confronted with the task, a former contributor and one of the most notable of Tucholsky's colleagues, Kurt Hiller, exclaimed, "It wasn't a magazine. It was an institution."[3] In short, the journal has become the most noted left-wing publication of the Weimar period and indeed has recently been termed by one writer as the 'organ of the 'intellectual left.'"[4] It included in its stable of writers almost all of the democratic intellectuals. Yet the phrase "organ of the left" is not meant to imply uniformity of opinion. It was precisely because the magazine contained works by the whole of the non-Communist left that it was unable to present little more of a political program than protest. Kurt Hiller has written a memoir of the great days of the magazine. He speaks of the diversity of its writers:

> The contributors even in the most brilliant period did not form a "philosophically" or politically homogeneous circle. Its diameter extended from Otto Flake to the social anarchist Erich Mühsam on the left. In between there were the liberals and democratic pacifists Hellmut von Gerlach, Rudolf Olden, Ludwig Quidde (also Ossietzky may be placed in the left wing of this group). There were Social Democrats such as the famous and enlightened sexologist, Magnus Hirschfeld, or such as Heinrich Ströbel, who was Prime Minister of Prussia for a brief time. There were leftist Socialists such as Axel Eggebrecht and Fritz Sternberg, who proved an exception by becoming an orthodox Stalinist. Most richly represented was the group of revolutionary pacifists: Tucholsky; the economist, Alfons Goldschmidt; Walter Mehring; Ernst Toller; and me [Hiller].[5]

While the magazine never stated a formal political position, its writers were obviously dedicated in general terms to a democratic socialist ideal. Through caricature, satire and political analysis, they portrayed and criticized the Republic and its leaders. They fought the militarists and their secret plans, denounced the malevolent influence of heavy industry, and chided the Socialists for their timorous attitude toward blatant social and political injustice. And they argued with each other. The pages of the *Weltbühne* may be said to present a kind of microcosm of the conflicts inherent in the left wing of the Republic. As Tucholsky wrote in 1929:

> The *Weltbühne* is a tribune in which the whole of the German left, in the broadest sense of the term, has a voice. From our coworkers, we demand clarity, personal cleanliness and good style. Whether or not this is a correct principle is another question.... The *Weltbühne* consciously renounces any kind of strict dogma; we are interested in discussion.[6]

Although there was broad disagreement among its writers, the *Weltbühne* came as close as any formal publication to presenting a coherent program of this politically "homeless" intellectual left. It was not a program whose points could be listed in a party platform, but the contents of the *Weltbühne* over the years, through the men and institutions attacked, and the proposals made at a particular time, revealed an outlook upon society and an expectation of reform which can be loosely termed a "program." The *Weltbühne* was not an official party publication, nor was it connected with any particular party line or dogma. These were precisely the reasons for its success. Official organs such as *Vorwärts* or *Die Rote Fahne* were too restricted by party dogma or, in the eyes of some writers, were "compromised" in some way. Independent magazines such as Maximilian Harden's *Zukunft* or Karl Kraus's *Die Fackel* were either "passe" and unread or they were associated with the eccentricities and opinions of a single man. As Kurt Hiller wrote in 1940, explaining why the *Weltbühne* became the tribune of the German left:

> ... Harden's *Zukunft* visibly declined, Naumann's and Gertrud Bäumer's *Hilfe* became increasingly Philistine. The Marxist revues, because of their party narrowness, were unable to enter the mainstream of intellectual life. (On the other band, Wilhelm Herzog's superior *Forum* was in the middle of the stream and remained without a radius of action.) Thus, the *Weltbühne* became the best and most influential magazine of the German left, or more exactly stated: it became the magazine in which members of the German left, in terms of quality and actual effectiveness, met each other in the most favorable, healthy and productive relationship.[7]

The magazine, however, was not begun as a journal of leftist opinion. The *Weltbühne* evolved out of a prewar weekly of theater criticism, *Die Schaubühne*, founded in 1905 by the respected drama critic, Siegfried Jacobsohn. As a literary magazine, the *Schaubühne* was far from being avant-garde and was looked upon as being an "opposition journal" by the literary leftists.[8] Indeed, they hardly paid it any attention, for the journals of the left were Herwarth Walden's *Sturm* and Wilhelm Herzog's *Pan*, both established in 1910. A third magazine was added in 1911 when Franz Pfemfert began to publish *Die Aktion*. None of these publications survived the war intact. *Pan* failed financially, *Sturm* became an ardent supporter of the war and *Aktion* moved so far left that it became irrational and was referred to as being "left of itself."[9] The gap was filled by the *Schaubühne*, metamorphosed into the *Weltbühne* in April 1918. During the war, the character of the magazine had begun to change as increasing space was given to political and economic events. Although Jacobsohn had been forced in the midst of the war by the authorities to print the patriotic verbiage of "Germanicus" (Robert Breuer), it was clear that the weekly journal was leaning to the political left. This tendency was confirmed and insured as Tucholsky's influence upon Jacobsohn continued to grow after 1918. With its new name and orientation, the reputation of the *Weltbühne* became ever more illustrious until in 1930, a person who expressed interest in politics was considered uninformed if he had not read the latest issue. The circulation of the magazine was rather small relative to its importance. In 1917, Jacobsohn published 1200 copies and in 1925, the number had grown to only 12,600.[10] It is unlikely that the number of issues ever exceeded 15,000, comparatively a very small circulation. There were mass magazines such as the *Berliner Illustrierte*, which by October 1929 had reached an edition of almost two million copies. The higher quality Ullstein magazines such as *Uhu*, which contained articles and fiction of general interest or the more technical *Koralle* had circulations of around sixty thousand. Of more significance for comparison to the *Weltbühne* was *Querschnitt*, the exclusive and snobbish Ullstein prestige magazine. At its height in 1931, *Querschnitt* had a circulation of 25,000.[11]

Yet the size of a magazine's circulation may sometimes be less important than who reads it. The *Weltbühne* was read by responsible members of the rightist intelligentsia as well as by the left.[12] The subscription list contained names from all of the countries of Europe and the magazine was available on most of the newsstands in the larger cities of the Continent. In 1931, the *Weltbühne* achieved German and perhaps even world fame when its editor, Carl von Ossietzky, was tried and imprisoned for allegedly revealing "military secrets" in a 1929 article which told of German secret and illegal aeronautical rearmament. Thereafter, the magazine was denounced by the right wing in terms that would make the *Weltbühne* seem to have been one of the most powerful publications in Germany.

The right wing, of course, magnified the *Weltbuhne's* actual importance. Their extraordinary dislike of the magazine may be explained by its purpose and style. The men of the right hated its cosmopolitan outlook and its lack of respect for "Germanic purity" as exemplified in its frequent use of unorthodox spellings and grammatical forms. This was in addition to the explicit mockery of upper-class speech forms, aristocratic social pretensions and rightwing political jargon. To the conservatives, the leftist writers appeared to be brash young men intent upon destroying all traditional values. The conservatives despised the left-wing writers precisely because they were not members of the official academic or bureaucratic establishment. As independent journalists, authors, artists and playwrights, they were automatically without status. The university professor was considered to be the true "intellectual." The public was suspicious of the free intellectual, the "writer," who had claim neither to rank nor to title.[13] In the university establishment and to some extent in the popular mind, the writer hardly deserved the title intellectual at all. Instead he was often contemptuously termed *Literat* and his writings were called *"Asphaltliteratur."* Only in a country such as Germany where "culture" was worshipped almost as a religion could the distinction be made between the official high priests of the universities and the self-appointed acolytes from "the streets."[14]

The final horror for the right was that many of the writers for the *Weltbühne* were Jewish. Being iconoclastic and Jewish, the magazine naturally fell heir to the charge that was always made against a free exchange of ideas: it was a "corrosive" and divisive influence when unity and resolution were needed in a time of national frustration and humiliation.

In 1927, Tucholsky wrote, "Since 1913, I have belonged to those who believe the German spirit to be almost unalterably poisoned..." The is difficult to define what Tucholsky meant by spirit or *Geist*, but in general it was the culture, the public mentality as represented in social institutions, the unconscious, everyday assumptions about politics and society. The "poison" was the lack of a sense of fair play, the greed, the snobbery, the cruelty and the militarism which Tucholsky believed permeated the body of German culture.

On March 3, 1919, Tucholsky published an article that was a kind of catalogue of those things that the left intellectuals hated. Titling the article, "We Negativists" ("Wir Negativen") and using his real name, Tucholsky gave the reasons why he and his colleagues could not take a more positive attitude toward Germany:

> The accusation is often made against us writers for the *Weltbühne* that we say no to everything, that we are not positive enough. We withdraw and merely criticize and thus dirty our own German nests. And what is worst of all—we fight hate with hate, force with force, fist with fist.... Are we dirtying our own nests? It is impossible to dirty an Augean Stable and it is insane to sit on the fallen roof of an old shed and sing national anthems.
>
> We should make positive proposals, but positive proposals are of no use if a basic honesty (*Redlichkeit*) does not permeate the country. The reforms that we want cannot be accomplished with simple formulas, nor with the new national agencies in which so many people place their hopes. We do not believe it is enough to set up offices with multiple personnel.... We believe that the essence of the world lies behind its things and that a mentality of decency is able to cope with and turn to good use even the worst of situations. But without it, nothing can be done.
>
> What we need is this sense of decency.

We are not yet able to say yes. We cannot strengthen a sensibility that forgets the humanity in man. We cannot strengthen a people that believes its greatest duty is to build scarecrows of honor before the workers and thus hinder any kind of real work. We cannot say yes to a people whose outlook is still such, that, had the fortunes of war been reversed, we would have had great cause to fear the worst. We cannot say yes to a land beset by collectivities and in which the corporation is more important than the individual. We cannot say yes to those whose accomplishments are held up as examples to the younger generation—those who form a decadent part of the society, infected by a childish hunger for power internally and by an indifference to the outside world. We cannot say yes to those for whom cash is more important than courage and who have contempt for all storm and stress which is not of the moment. They are without fire, without hate and without love. We are supposed to run, but our ankles are tied. We cannot say yes.

...The *Realpolitiker* fight us because we see no value in compromise, because we see no cure in insignia and new official documents. We know well that ideals cannot be made real, but we also know that nothing is created, is changed, is effected without the fire of an ideal. And that is what appears to be the danger to our opponents—and they are right—for we do not believe that the light of an ideal should only serve to decorate the heavens. It must burn here below in the cellars where the termites live and in the palaces of the rich; it must burn in the churches where the old miracles are rationalistically betrayed and burn beside the moneychangers who have made a temple out of their stalls.

...We stand before a Germany full of unheard—of corruption, full of profiteers and sneaks, full of three hundred thousand devils, each of whom uses the law in order that his black person may remain untouched by the revolution. We mean him and only him.

And if we have the opportunity to choose, shall we fight him with love, shall we fight him with hate? We want to fight with hate growing out of love...[15]

With words such as these, Tucholsky joined the line of brilliant cultural critics extending from Heinrich Heine to Friedrich Nietzsche. Although he was a critic on the left, it is striking how similar some of his language was to that used by the conservative intellectuals. It had long been their contention that Germany was infected by self-seeking party bosses, corrosive politicians, and greedy profiteers. In "We Negativists," Tucholsky made comparable accusations. While it is obvious that his goals were vastly different, it is confusing that he should share a terminology with some of his most bitter philosophical and political opponents. Certainly it is legitimate to ask what in fact distinguished the intellectual left from the intellectual right. Did Tucholsky unwittingly work to the favor of his enemies? To answer these questions, a careful examination must be made of the bases and assumptions behind Tucholsky's cultural view. Such an investigation is fundamental to an understanding of Tucholsky's career, for he made his greatest contribution to the German intellectual tradition while serving in his role as a cultural critic.

After the unification of Germany in 1871 and the capitulation of German liberalism to power, German cultural criticism traditionally came from the conservatives, or perhaps better stated, from the anti-liberals. The defeated liberals were too busy accommodating themselves to the new order to be able to offer criticism. The radical left, the Socialist intellectuals, of the Empire devoted their energies either to Marxist theology or to party organization. Being antinationalist and internationalist, the Socialists were "scientists" concerned with world culture, with mankind, with human society, but not with Germany as a separate or particular embodiment of any of those generalities. German cultural criticism was thus a rarity on the left. And when it did come, as with Tucholsky, it was natural that it should sound much like the right since both leftist and rightist dissidents opposed the same *status quo*.

One of the most potent anti-liberal pre-war cultural critics was Julius Langbehn. Hating the Bismarckian Reich, but devoted to "Germany," Langbehn was a "failure," a man dogged by unhappiness and insolvency. He published his immensely popular *Rembrandt als Erzieher* (*Rembrandt as Educator*) in 1890. A programmatic book, unstructured, uneven and vague, it was a wild swinging attack—at times almost drunken—upon modernity and the divisions and corruption of modern life. It was a "rhapsody of irrationalism" expressing a longing for a simpler cultural past of purity, a past in which creativity, morality and virtue had been possible. The Columbia professor Fritz Stern has written eloquently of Langbehn's "Germanic irrationalism":

> Rembrandt, celebrated as a German, was to be the teacher of a new and final German reformation. Art, not science or religion, was the highest good, the true source of knowledge and virtue. And the old German virtues, now lost, were: child-like simplicity, subjectivity, individuality. *Rembrandt als Erzieher* was a shrill cry against the hothouse intellectualism of modern Germany which threatened to stifle the creative life, a cry for the irrational energies of the folk, buried for so long under the layers of civilization.[16]

Langbehn was a part of the "Germanic Religion" which developed in the closing years of the nineteenth century, an expression of discontent with modern culture and politics. Langbehn's irrationalism appealed to the generation of the Youth Movement, those young men who rushed to the colors in 1914. This generation since Tangiers had lived in a Europe filled with tension. After 1905 crisis followed crisis; the expectation of war was almost universal. The whole intellectual mood of Europe had changed. "Where the writers of the 1890's had restricted themselves to a questioning of the potentialities of reason, the young men of 1905 became frank irrationalists or even anti-rationalists."[17]

The imperial conservative configuration was a jumble of establishment writers, respectable academics, irrationalist visionaries and alienated social misfits. The establishment historian, Heinrich von Treitschke, and the outcast critic, Paul de Lagarde, were united in their hatred of Jews and liberalism. They both placed their faith in "authority" and "unity," but, as is apparent in Langbehn, the irrationalist critics hated the imperial establishment also because of its spiritual hypocrisy and social division. They bequeathed their ideas of organic unity and of the mystery of the *Volk* to the Youth Movement and to the post-war nationalist visionaries.

As did Langbehn, Tucholsky denounced imperial culture, but there was a crucial distinction since he rejected the irrationalists as well. Tucholsky always remained firm in his faith in the powers of intellect and reason. He distrusted the Youth Movement because it was vague in its idealism and because it became the dupe of power. Tucholsky was disturbed by the hypocrisy and mediocrity of the Second Empire, but he had nothing but contempt for Langbehn's *"Rembrandt-Deutschen"*—the "Rembrandt Germans"—as he called them.[18] Their chauvinistic pieties, their theatrical mysticism, and their apocalyptic visions were for Tucholsky illustrations of the bankruptcy of German culture, not a symbol of its rebirth.

After the war there developed two forms of German conservatism—the reactionaries and the nationalist visionaries. The former merely longed to restore the old authoritarian Reich and in its name they opposed the Republic. The latter, the mystic nationalists, sought to implement the pre-war ideas of the Germanic critics. They longed for the unity of blood and soil—the "Third Reich" which would bridge the chasm between classes through the common identification with the race, the nation, the Volk. Their vision was in part what was finally vulgarized into the Nazi slogan, *ein Volk, ein Reich, ein Führer*—"one people, one Reich, one leader."[19]

The nationalist visionaries opposed the Republic not only because it was the despised, divided liberal state, but also because it contained so much which had existed in the Empire. First the Empire and then the Republic prevented the "national revolution" of which they dreamed. Tucholsky also denounced the Republic because he believed it was only the Empire in disguise. But he also rejected his so-called right-wing "partners." For Tucholsky, the nationalists of the republican era were also part of the leftover baggage of the Empire. They were a continuing illustration that nothing had changed after the revolution.

Before the war, conservatives had rejected the "West" as a lesser civilization. The war only served to deepen the idea that the western tradition was alien to Germany, that democracy spelled the death of culture. But Tucholsky wholeheartedly embraced the "alien," western ideas of liberalism and democracy. He was a rationalist firmly in the tradition of the eighteenth century Enlightenment with its belief in reform through education, practical planning for social happiness and faith in political progress. Tucholsky's ideal of "basic honesty," the sanctity of the individual, the "sense of decency," and the recognition of human rights were goals, which he believed could be reached through concrete political changes. It was by means of rational, practical action within society that reform would be achieved. For Tucholsky, those conservatives who hoped to unite everyone in a mystic "Third Reich" were lost in a hopeless abstraction. They were the prisoners of power because they refused to use their reason.

Tucholsky's political goal was the establishment of democratic government and equality. His were the liberal ideals expressed in the rhetoric of the—failed—revolution against the monarchy of 1848. He was an eighteenth century democrat with expanded ideas of social justice. In 1922 he stated his democratic convictions in an essay entitled "All Five of Us" ("Wir alle Fünf")—a reference to himself and his four pseudonyms:

> All five of us love democracy, where a man may say what he has to, freely and responsibly. Democracy where men are not "equal" (*gleich*) like the stamped out members of a Prussian company that incarnation of the prison state—but where between the bank president and his doorman there is no longer a caste distinction. The only difference is economic and occupational. Whether they drink tea with each other is something else, but there can be no question that they are both human. We want to destroy the old Germany down to the last shoestring. This new Germany we want to build—all five of us… We are five fingers on one hand.[20]

Tucholsky absolutely rejected the organic conception of the state in favor of a pluralistic society. He wanted the abolition of uniformity, the rejection of the conformist ethic of the Prussian regiment. He desired an open society in which free discussion was welcomed and dissent encouraged. He wanted reason, clarity of purpose, and a generous cosmopolitanism to triumph over the anti-rationalism, the vagueness, and the racism of the Rembrandt Germans.

Tucholsky wanted the introduction of a democratic spirit into Germany, but the legacy of the past made the establishment of democracy difficult. The bitterness and chaos in 1918 made it almost impossible. Not only had no love of liberalism been inculcated into the German masses during the long tenure of the authoritarian Reich of Otto von Bismarck, the "Iron Chancellor," but the ideas of the Germanic critics had also found wide popular sympathy. The Germans then spent four years fighting the democratic west. They had been barraged by four years of propaganda touting the differences between Germany and the west, the superiority of the unique German *Kultur* over the mere "civilization" of the decadent west. It was unlikely that the Germans would suddenly embrace the ways of their former enemies—especially after the Treaty of Versailles.

Versailles, of course, was the much-disputed treaty between Germany and the victorious Entente after World War I. The treaty had determined Germany (and her Austrian-Hungarian allies) as the sole culprit in starting the war. It forbade the unification of Germany and Austria, the rearmament and, to a certain degree, the industrialization of Germany. It had specified war reparations mostly to France; Germany was forced to give Lorraine and the German-speaking province Alsace to France. In addition, 25,000 square miles of German territory with seven million ethnic Germans had to be ceded to Poland, mainly Upper Silesia, Posen, Eastern Pomerania, and parts of East Prussia, with the City of Danzig cut off from the German mainland. Germany signed the treaty under the pressure of the British hunger blockade and the threat to be invaded; the U.S., in the end, did not ratify it.

Tucholsky believed the defeat should have demonstrated to the people the bankruptcy and decay of the Empire. The collapse should have made them turn decisively away from the past. But the ideas of the Germanic critics through the medium of wartime propaganda had taken a far stronger hold than Tucholsky realized. Or perhaps he realized it all too well.

Tucholsky's resemblance to the Germanic critics was thus superficial. They both opposed imperial society, but they also opposed each other. For Tucholsky, the Rembrandt Germans were themselves a despicable product of Imperial Germany. They were its smugness, its narrowness, its chauvinism writ large and taken to extreme. He thus opposed the whole of the German establishment—the nationalists, the bureaucrats, the militarists and the Germanic visionaries. He implied that if these persons and their institutions were abolished, then democracy and, with it, cultural reform could be accomplished.

> And we hate that Germany which dares to style itself as the only true, original Germany, but which in reality is the poor caricature of an outlived Prussianism. That Germany in which the old lazy officials flour-

ish, who conceal their cowardice behind their rank. That Germany where the smart-alecks thrive, who in the war were officers and officers' candidates and who with every power—and with what means—attempt to have their underlings again. Their deepest ambition is not to be of some good, but only to be better than the others. They feel well only when they are humiliating someone else.... All five of us hate that Germany where the bureaucratic apparatus has become a purpose in itself.[21]

In his rejection not only of the imperial establishment, but of "Germanity" as well, Tucholsky resembled the most brilliant cultural critic of all, Friedrich Nietzsche. When Bismarck's authoritarian Prussia engulfed the Germanies and bound them together, Nietzsche predicted the end of German cultural greatness. He believed that the "intellectuals" would capitulate to power; they would serve the state and its needs, not the spirit.

Among Germans today it is not enough to have spirit; one must arrogate it, one must have the arrogance to have spirit.... One pays heavily for coming to power: power *makes stupid*. The Germans—once they were called the people of thinkers: do they think at all today? The Germans are now bored with the spirit, the Germans now mistrust the spirit; politics swallows up all serious concern for really spiritual matters. *Deutschland, Deutschland über Alles*—I fear that was the end of German philosophy.[22]

Tucholsky did not share Nietzsche's contempt for the masses; he was not an elitist, but he did characterize Germany with a similar style and phraseology. Nietzsche hated the *Reichsdeutsche*—the Germans who saw Bismarck's Reich as the culmination of German culture, those who strutted about because they belonged to a "great power." It was one thing to be proud of being "German," but quite another to take pride in being a *subject* in a German empire. When the definition of "German" came to be the political entity the Empire, instead of a cultural tradition, then Nietzsche considered German culture to be dead.

Tucholsky also saw the substitution of imperial nationalism for the old cosmopolitanism as a disaster for German civilization. His vision of the crassness, the bombast, the hypocrisy, and the mediocrity of imperial culture was identical to Nietzsche's. For Tucholsky, Germany was weighed down by a "poverty of civilization" (*mangelnde Kultur*) caused by subservience to statism and a sycophantic adulation of authority. It was an *Unkultur*—a "noncivilization" whose members seemed to have a passion for marching around and organizing themselves into disciplined hierarchies.[23]

It seemed to Tucholsky that Germans had to have submission and domination (*Über- und Unterordnerei)*; they had to satisfy some native "herd instinct." Tucholsky believed that Germans were possessed by a "Lord to underling" (*Herr zum Kerl*) spirit which made justice impossible. "This country has Lords and underlings. It doesn't have men."²⁴ Germany was a vast "barracks-square" (*Kasernenhof*) in which someone was always looking down on someone else and ordering him around. It was the spirit of "lordliness," of arrogance, which Tucholsky hated above all else.

To illustrate these "poisons" in the society, Tucholsky composed portraits of the "typical German," the "typical officer," the "typical bourgeois." It is this use of generality, which is both the strength and weakness of the cultural critic. He attempts to describe the quality, the tone, the nuance of a society, but his characterizations are often imprecise and unfair to individuals. Yet they strike chords of understanding and provoke insights, which more "objective" methods fail to accomplish. It is because they are so outrageous and yet so correct that cultural critics excite heated discussion and consternation. When Nietzsche wrote the *Twilight of the Idols* in 1888, he said both everything and nothing about German culture.

> What the German spirit *might* be—who has not had his melancholy ideas about that! But this people has deliberately made itself stupid for nearly a millennium: nowhere have the two great European narcotics, alcohol and Christianity, been abused more dissolutely. Recently even a third has been added—one that alone would be sufficient to dispatch all fine and bold flexibility of the spirit-music, our constipated, constipating German music. How much disgruntled heaviness, lameness, dampness, dressing gown—how much *beer* there is in the German intelligence!²⁵

Tucholsky used a similar method when he portrayed his typical German. Tucholsky, however, drew out his portrait more carefully and in greater detail than did Nietzsche, who was far more allusive, flinging down bolts of flashing single phrases and then moving on to another subject. Tucholsky's descriptions were longer, wittier and more explicit. Much of Tucholsky's method depended on his use of language. He was almost uncanny in his ability to depict dialect and ordinary speech habits. Like any good propagandist, Tucholsky was able to take words that were used almost unconsciously by the society, which were an integral part of the fabric of its speech and employ them in a way which would startle. By placing them in a different context, he gave ordinary words and phrases new definitions, and maintained they revealed the true character of the society. The method was a variation of the attempt at summation of the German national character by the foreigner who says: "Germany is a country in which everything is *verboten*." In the same manner

Tucholsky used other common words and phrases such as *Untergebene* or *Kerl* to depict the authoritarian mentality. He used dialect in a similar fashion. A caricatured general in Tucholsky's writings always spoke with a Prussian pronunciation that sounded arrogant and ignorant with its use of contractions (for example: *habnse* for *Haben Sie*) and the substitution of J's for G's. Yet, in the mouths of the working-class characters portrayed in the chansons, the same accent as Berlin dialect sounded quaint and sympathetic.

Tucholsky's use of dialect is, of course, untranslatable, but he wrote many equally effective pieces in straight German. "Face of a German" is a prime example of Tucholsky's portrayal of a human product of the German *Unkultur*:

To George Grosz who taught us to see such faces.

A rather thick head; a none too high forehead; cold, small eyes; a nose that likes to sink itself into a drinking glass; a mouth, which gives cold orders; an unpleasant toothbrush-like moustache: that's how this face looks. A well-cut black coat, a large knotted cravat with a sort of pearl in it, an always clean collar: these also can be seen. The hair is cut short around the ears; the whole man is well-scrubbed, cleans his fingernails in the morning, shaves or has the barber do it.
As a young man he pressed his way through the doors of lecture rooms, none too interested. His mama said to him: "Hubert, when will you be home today?"—and he gave her a not very friendly answer. He crammed. Passed exams. Was called on: "Hubert So and So." And then be rose, a bit subservient, a bit anxious, not very excited—cold, actually. Entered government service, rapidly climbed upwards.
Long forenoons with difficult paper work, with empty breaks during which breakfast was taken out of his briefcase; in it there was also an angry letter and one that promised a little off-duty entertainment in the evening. For the rest: cold to his heart. Occasionally read a book that was not relevant to his work; tried Spengler once, crazy stuff; went to see Hardt's Tantris with the secretary. Very poetic. Intermission: "It's possible that I'll be shifted to another department one of these days. Well, thank God... "
Company commander during the war. Inexorable, cold. Cold toward the office boys who could not defend themselves, cold toward the young clerks—"Had to go through this myself once!"
Cold toward the world, cold toward God. Married. Has two children. Loves them in his way. Likes to laugh sometimes, in the evening, at some fat joke; still knows three verses about the innkeeper's wife, unfortunately has forgotten the others. Firm conviction of the justness of the

> state structure, the legal system, the church, and moral foundations in general. Also has not given these things much thought. Does not look at all bad sitting there at the writing desk, briefly clearing his throat once as he puts many papers in order... After all, he is somebody. Feels in complete harmony with country, majority and national community. Not overly fond of the Prussian aristocracy, finds it unpleasant. But he is impeccably correct and polite, definitely a small bourgeois toward his superiors. To his underlings, he is an aristocrat himself.
> Plays the part. Furthers his career. Will probably soon be some big-shot-ambassador, head of a ministry, secretary of state, for all I know.[26]

This was the civilian whom Tucholsky believed typified the public spirit of Germany—selfish, greedy, smug, authoritarian and despicable. He was the standard of "success" in the society. And if he wore a uniform, the adulation was all the greater. Even if he were only a streetcar conductor, the uniform commanded respect and embarrassed obsequiousness. The Germans were the "controlled."[27]

It was the "barracks mentality" which had destroyed German civilization, Tucholsky believed. It was impossible to speak, in fact, of a civilization as long as militarism represented the supreme value of the society. He was tired of apologies for Germany, of the division of the culture into good and bad elements. Tucholsky contended that a time comes when the whole of the society must be judged and that which is found wanting be changed:

> A German civilization cannot exist, as Thomas Mann believes, with the exception of this and in spite of that. It can only exist without this—without this military and without this barracks square. Everything else is fiction and whitewash.[28]

Tucholsky was, of course, referring to Thomas Mann's *Betrachtungen eines Unpolitischen* (*Reflections of an Unpolitical Man*), a tract written shortly after the outbreak of the war.[29] The *Betrachtungen* sought to provide a "mission" for Germany in the war, to define a superior German culture as opposed to the inferior western democracies. It was a work bordering on chauvinism, but Mann had difficulty justifying the place of Prussian authoritarianism and militarism in his scheme. Tucholsky perceived Mann's at times apologetic tone and insisted that there must be no exceptions, no "not-withstandings" if Germany were to be worthy of the name civilization.

It is in his criticism of Thomas Mann that Tucholsky's essential opposition to Nietzsche is apparent. Nietzsche and Tucholsky were similar in their estimation of the German character, but their solutions for the reform of culture were profoundly dissimilar. And Tucholsky's contribution to the tradition of German cultural criticism is most obvious in his divergence from Nietzsche.

For all of the discomfort, which he would suffer there, Nietzsche must finally be placed in the German political tradition with the "conservatives," indeed with the "nationalists." For when one speaks of the influences upon the nationalist visionaries of Weimar, one must include Nietzsche as well as Langbehn and the other Germanic critics. Nietzsche had a profound effect upon the Youth Movement, whose surviving members translated his ideas into the mystic nationalism of the Weimar era. The conservative youth in the years immediately before the war, rejecting bourgeois society, enthusiastically took up Nietzsche's ideas of a revitalization of culture through a rejection of politics and the affirmation of the life forces within the individual. The ideas of primordial instincts preserved through transformation into civilizing but vital creative forces, the ideas of life courageously and joyously lived on the edge of the abyss provided the rhetoric and faith of the Youth Movement, whose members might indeed be called "armed Nietzscheans."

Since for Nietzsche civilization was represented only in the highest examples of the species, his ideas implied an elitism, a rejection of the mass of men. It is not surprising that Nietzsche and his followers were anti-egalitarian, for the leveling which liberalism supposedly represented was destructive of the opportunity for the creation of the unique, the superior individual—the genius, the only person who gave a purpose for humanity's continuing to exist:

> Liberal institutions cease to be liberal as soon as they are attained: later on, there are no worse and no more thorough injurers of freedom than liberal institutions. Their effects are known well enough: they undermine the will to power; they level mountain and valley, and call that morality; they make men small, cowardly and hedonistic—every time it is the herd animal that triumphs with them. Liberalism: in other words, herd-animalization.[30]

It was Nietzsche's anti-liberalism that made his idea so easily translatable into the rhetoric of visionary nationalism. Like Tucholsky, Nietzsche rejected both the Empire and Germanity, but the mystic Germans took Nietzsche's phrases about a superior race of men, a will to power, an instinctual strength and combined them with the irrationalism of the Germanic critics and used the combination to serve the very forces which Nietzsche hated—Germanic religion, anti-Semitism and concepts of the superiority of the German *Volk*. Nietzsche's mistake and his tragedy was that he did not consider the possible political consequences of his ideas. He rejected politics just as he rejected racism and nationalism and he possibly deluded himself into believing that he had abolished those tiresome realities through the very process of rejection. Nietzsche therefore unwittingly served the power state that he despised.

In 1914, Thomas Mann illustrated this tragic process when he tried to reconcile the cultural idealism of Nietzsche with the political reality of the German state. Indeed he tried to make them one and the same. Mann's was the expression of the longing for cultural unity, the desire for the organic society in which petty wants have been replaced by a larger spiritual purpose. For Mann, the western democracies represented a cacophony of contending narrow interests, of self-seeking greed and purposeless "progress." The false liberty of western liberalism was to be rejected for the "freedom" of German cultural idealism.

Thomas Mann eventually repudiated the *Betrachtungen*; Tucholsky had never subscribed to their principles. As did Nietzsche, Tucholsky believed that imperial Germany was permeated by a "herd instinct," but unlike Nietzsche, he believed that liberalism would abolish that instinct not deepen it. Nietzsche's solution was elitist, individual and psychological.

Although Tucholsky was sympathetic to psychology (he always kept a photograph of Freud hanging in his study), he also recognized the reality of and necessity for *society*. Tucholsky's solutions were bound up with society and its institutions. Unlike Nietzsche, Tucholsky believed that man could achieve greatness precisely through the political institutions of liberalism. Nietzsche believed that humanity achieved a claim to superiority only because certain individuals rose above the rabble. They were the only ones who counted in creating a culture.

Tucholsky believed that human grandeur could be achieved only if everyone counted, only if *society* as a whole was able to rise above itself. Only in society could the individual be freed, not through withdrawal from it. Only if all were free could anyone be free—and that freedom had to be actual as well as "spiritual." For Tucholsky, the conservative dream of organic unity and elitist leadership only served to hide the reality of subjection and servitude. A culture was the sum of all its parts and each had to be confronted honestly, for some might belie the very meaning of civilization. In the early days of the Republic, Tucholsky believed that the new regime was doing nothing to eliminate the evil parts. In 1919 he exclaimed, "We don't live in a republic. We live in a fettered monarchy."[31]

Even though Tucholsky and the nationalist visionaries hated each other, their voices often joined in denouncing the Republic. And Tucholsky and his colleagues have been bitterly criticized for their supposed "destructive" effect upon German democracy between the wars. Because they saw nothing but the old spirit of the Empire within the Republic, Tucholsky and his friends withdrew their support from it. They began a merciless attack upon the Republic's leaders for cooperating with and fostering the old elements. Above all they jeered at the Social Democrats. And thus even though they claimed to be the keepers of Germany's democratic conscience, the left intellectuals are accused of helping to kill democracy. It is said that because of their "impossible" idealism, their "hopeless" concern for political purity, the left intellectuals withdrew from participation within the society and rendered themselves politically "homeless" and therefore impotent. Professor Golo Mann, the son of Thomas Mann, is typical of the present-day liberal critics of Tucholsky and his colleagues:

> ... Even though this detached left expressed only contempt for the Republic and had little to do with Social Democracy, it was, nevertheless, looked upon by the right as the typical expression of the "system": "Asphalt literature," "corrosive Jewish thinking," or whatever the current expressions were. This radical literature did not belong to the Republic, but to the republican period—the only time in which their magazines and plays were able to gain such a loud voice. They did double harm to the Republic. They have unmercifully uncovered its weaknesses, while they themselves were regarded as the most valid expression of the republican spirit.[32]

Golo Mann's criticism suspiciously resembles that which he quotes from Tucholsky's contemporaries, those men who constantly accused the left intellectuals of "fouling their own nest" or of exerting a "corrosive influence" (*zersetzend*). These two phrases became (and remain!) the standard cant of those who distrusted diversity and dissent. Golo Mann thus implies, unconsciously perhaps, that the right was correct in its judgment of the left intellectuals. He makes Tucholsky and his colleagues somehow responsible for the sins of the right against the Republic, thus lightening the burden of guilt that the right should bear.

In any event, with their tradition of envy and fear of the outside world, the Weimar conservatives regarded self-criticism only as a force for weakness. Tucholsky and the left intellectuals were regarded as giving the "enemy," whoever he might be, one more opening in which to place his wedge. No matter what the failings, the shortcomings or the corruption of the society, they must not be exposed or talked about lest the body politic, weakened from within, be unable to fend off the thrusts from without.

In a healthy and free society, however, it is the role of the social critic to be separate from and "outside" of the institutions, which he criticizes and satirizes. Tucholsky was profoundly alienated from his society, but he used his alienation to become what he termed the "bad conscience" of Germany. He stood apart in order to point out the discrepancy between ideal and reality. His very lack of participation helped to insure his constructive effect. Professor Daniel Bell in *The End of Ideology* raises a legitimate voice in defense of the "divisive" social critic. He is speaking of American dissent, but his words may with equal justice be used to defend the activity of the left intellectuals in Germany:

> Alienation is not nihilism but a positive role, a detachment which guards one against being submerged in any cause, or accepting any particular embodiment of community as final. Nor is alienation deracination, a denial of one's roots or country. Some unofficial ideologues fear that a critical view of America would influence intellectuals in Asia and Africa to be anti-American, or to reject democratic values. This is a parochial view of the intellectual life. A society is most vigorous and appealing, when both partisan and critic are legitimate voices in the permanent dialogue that is the testing of ideas and experience. One can be a critic of one's country without being an enemy of its promise.[33]

The accusation that the intellectual left helped to destroy the Republic is made only in the dubious light of historical hindsight. Only because of the triumph of National Socialism is the indictment of the left given some plausibility. It has now become fashionable among conservative circles in Germany to maintain that not only did Tucholsky help to destroy democracy, but he made way for fascism as well. This is a more serious charge than "corrosiveness," for it implies that in some way Tucholsky was an enemy of democracy itself. Such criticism, of course, tends to confuse the innocent with the guilty, to place the blame for the demise of the Republic upon the left and to exonerate the right. In 1933, Tucholsky wrote his friend, Walter Hasenclever: "I am slowly going crazy from reading how I have ruined Germany. For twenty years I have been pained by one thing—that I have not been able to succeed in removing one policeman from his post."[34]

Tucholsky was asking what power had he had to destroy the Republic or to ruin Germany. His enemies controlled the police, the army, the bureaucracy—the means of power. Yet the accusation continues that Tucholsky made the task of the Nazis easier by not supporting the Republic's leadership. It is said that while he and the other *Literaten* did not actively destroy the Republic, they also did nothing to aid its survival. As with most simplifications, this was partly true—but it was also true of everyone else. No one really loved the Republic. For the Communists, it was "bourgeois"; for the conservatives, it was

"Marxist." The moderate parties feared radicalism and were timid in the face of anti-republican threats from the right. The moderates were largely embarrassed by the Republic, for it was connected with the defeat and the Versailles Treaty. Tucholsky coined the word "*jein*" for the middle parties, since they could say neither "*ja*" (yes) nor "*nein*" (no). Tucholsky wanted them to give a resounding "no" to the traditions and forces of the past:

> The Republic does not want to recognize that only an unconcealed struggle against the old monarchy can be of any aid. It must not in any way be connected with the foul tradition of ·the Wilhelmine epoch with its cruel barracks efficiency, its insolent arrogance, its deep mendacity and its criminal use of the state to favor a small caste.[35]

The left intellectuals did not destroy the Republic. The Nazis and their right-wing allies destroyed German democracy. It is preposterous and unfair to expect Tucholsky and his friends to have foreseen the victory of National Socialism. They predicted only the triumph of the old reactionaries, not the radical right of Hitler. And by 1926, Tucholsky believed that the old reactionaries had by and large already triumphed. If he could have foreseen the advent of the Nazis, he would have supported the Republic against them. No more than anyone else was Tucholsky able to conceive of the power, which the Nazis would gain and wield. The accusations against Tucholsky and the left intellectuals are essentially a conservative argument against all opposition to the *status quo*. All criticism of things as they are runs the risk of making way for conditions, which are even worse. But the chance for improvement makes the risk worth taking. Tucholsky did not destroy the Republic; he did make a desperate and ultimately futile bid to transform it into a humane and democratic society. For Tucholsky it was not a question of the *survival* of the Republic, but of its *establishment* in the first place.

The contention still arises, however, that Tucholsky and his friends might have been more effective if they had bitten their lips and worked within one of the moderate political parties. Indeed, the left intellectuals at first glance appear to be curiously unpolitical. On the other side of the political spectrum, one of the primary reasons given for the failure of the conservative intellectuals to assume political responsibility in Germany was their distrust of politics. When Thomas Mann called himself an "unpolitical man" he joined a long intellectual tradition of contempt for politics.[36] Nietzsche eloquently stated the argument of idealism against the political:

> Culture and the state—one should not deceive oneself about this—are antagonists: "*Kultur-Staat*" is merely a modern idea. One lives off the

other, one thrives at the expense of the other. All great ages of culture are ages of political decline. What is great culturally has always been unpolitical, even *anti-political*.[37]

Nietzsche was, of course, expressing a very sympathetic contempt for the pretensions of the power state, but the simultaneous contempt for any politics at all has had unfortunate consequences. With their regard for politics as a "lesser reality" the conservative intellectuals unconsciously passed into bondage by politics. Ignoring politics in the name of culture, they abandoned government to the philistines interested only in power and force. They took seriously the false idealism of the Nazi spiritual rejuvenation-cant, which served only to mask Nazi statism and brutality. When the conservative intellectuals woke up, it was too late. When the time of testing came, the long tradition of aloofness from politics rendered the conservative intellectuals impotent to ward off the catastrophe or even to recognize it when it arrived. On another, broader level, the realities of power, chauvinism and racism were hidden from the German public mind by the conviction instilled by classroom and pulpit that the heritage of German idealism rendered all else superfluous.[38] Upon initial observation, because of their refusal to join any political party, Tucholsky and his friends appear to be as contemptuous of politics as their right-wing opponents. But on closer investigation, it is clear that Tucholsky believed that the transformation of Germany had to come within and through politics:

> Nothing is more painful to us [Germans] than thoughts and ideals that become concrete reality. You may do everything: make the most dangerous proposals, *in abstracto*; you may create paper revolutions, even displace God himself—but the tax laws—oh, they prefer to make those themselves.[39]

The conservative intellectuals rejected politics as corrupt by definition. Tucholsky rejected only certain political methods, not politics itself. He believed that the politics of Weimar had compromised the Republic. The Socialists through their lack of absolute rejection of the right had confused the political issues and were destroying, through politics, the very principles which the SPD had traditionally sought to preserve. He did not deride the Socialists because they were "dirty politicians," but because they were inept politicians. Tucholsky was not opposed to politics, but he did hold aloof from a political party that allowed any toleration of right-wing machinations against the Republic. He saw only disaster in a compromise with the right. By the same token, he rejected cooperation with the Communists because they were authoritarian and undemocratic. They were also imprisoned intellectually by their "dogma."

Tucholsky therefore could not find any party to join. (Only during the brief period from 1918–1922 was there an exception when he was a member of the USPD.) He thus remained aloof from parties not because he was contemptuous of politics. On the contrary, he believed that he could best help those in power to see clearer boundaries and definitions by remaining the outsider, the critic who points to the errors of the past and the dangers of the future. It is not the role of the social critic to join and try to reform from within that which he criticizes. His role is to inspire those who have talent for such practical activity. The critic's prerogative is to de-sanctify sacred cows; he does not have to become their herdsman in the process.

To be sure, Tucholsky stated idealistic, vague and even "hopeless" goals in articles such as "We Negativists," but he also tirelessly examined individual policies and actions on a practical level. In article after article he examined political events, pointing out errors of policy and suggesting ways whereby they might be rectified. He always held up the ideal of a more humane and democratic culture before the society, but he also descended to the level on which that ideal had to be accomplished—in the classrooms, in the ministries of government and behind the caged windows of bureaucrats.

Tucholsky believed that the spirit of a culture was intimately bound up with its public institutions. By reforming its political institutions the inner spirit of the society could also be changed. Abolish not politics, but bad politics and change would occur. The abolition of corrupt institutions and corrupt politics would be the first step toward a pure and honest culture.

The right wing also used terms such as "greed," "corruption" and "hypocrisy," but there is little doubt that Tucholsky's understanding of these words was different from the conservatives'. Unlike the extremists of both left and right, who are always to some extent puritans, Tucholsky did not expect government to enforce virtue. Tucholsky was little concerned with how a man conducted his private life so long as he did not infringe upon the rights of others. (Tucholsky had no love for the Nazis, but he defended Ernst Röhm against those who used his homosexuality to discredit him.) Tucholsky was concerned with public morality, not private sin. For him, greed was the dominance of one class at the expense of another.

It was "immoral" for the law courts to dispense unequal justice according to a man's political persuasion or social status. It was immoral to deny prison inmates sexual outlets other than the homosexual. It was hypocritical for government to proclaim the traditional moral virtues and then conduct murderous wars and tell lies to the people. It was hypocrisy for the upper classes to proclaim Christianity and then fester an unjust social and legal system. An "honest" society would be one in which all people would be equal before the law, in which there would be no condescension on the part of officials toward the "lower orders." It would be a society in which people would be free to dissent, free to go their own way, to develop as individuals—not free merely to conform to the pronouncements of government, no matter how benevolent. Honesty consisted of the opportunity for the individual to be true to himself, to develop his own identity in a free and mobile society. Because these conceptions of morality were different from and even undermined traditional definitions, the conservatives attacked Tucholsky himself as being immoral. Indeed they coined the phrase "cultural Bolshevism" for the reforming ideals of Tucholsky and his colleagues. In the eyes of the right, to be called a "Bolshevik"—even a cultural Bolshevik—was to be placed under the supreme anathema.

Tucholsky did not, however, expect democracy to abolish all greed and corruption. It is a truism that under democratic regimes, scandal is a constant occurrence. But Tucholsky believed that democracy created a predisposition in society for integrity and virtue. Conversely he believed that authoritarianism with its censorship, its secrecy and system of privilege created a predisposition for dishonesty and corruption. Democracy would not eliminate sin, but it would foster the "sense of decency." Authoritarian government, on the other hand, not only failed to eliminate sin, it heightened its probability.

The premises and goals of left and right intellectuals were profoundly disparate, but the two groups were superficially united in their hatred of that butt of all social critics—the middle class. The conservatives usually added the word "Jew" to the phrase, but the descriptions were much the same when they accused the bourgeoisie of being interested only in profits. But there the similarity ended. The conservatives hated the bourgeoisie because it was either not of the "Volk" or it was crass or simply déclassé. Tucholsky, on the other hand, held the middle class in contempt because he believed it was politically irresponsible and politically blind to its own best interests. It had been the class most corrupted by the triumph of the Bismarckian state. It had succumbed to military power after a long tradition of resistance. In its fear of the left after the war, the bourgeoisie tolerated, even welcomed, the tyranny of the right:

> They [the middle class] know no middle way between patriarchal overlordship and a bolshevism degenerated into robbery. They are not free. They bear all burdens as long as they are allowed to make money.[40]

Instead of forming the bulwark of democracy, the middle class had degenerated into the lackey of imperial Germany:

And we hate that Germany which can create this bourgeoisie: vapid merchants, compared to whom the old Forty-Eighters were titans—fat bellies which think only of business and are flattered if they may place a "by appointment to the Count" sign on the store. They still bow to the empty royal coach and regard with awe the very manure of the imperial horses...[41]

For Tucholsky, this had been the ultimate *coup* of the Empire, to gain the adulation of the middle class while holding it in contempt. In his criticism of the bourgeoisie, Tucholsky did not stop with its political conservatism. It has always been fashionable among the left to deride the middle class for its stolidity, its smugness, its pretensions, piety and philistinism. Tucholsky also joined this chorus and implied that bourgeois political blindness was caused by (comic) social aspirations and (stupid) economic fears. The bourgeois was a universal type to be found in every country and in every age:

In no country is the bourgeoisie very edifying. National characteristics can tone down specific qualities or illuminate them; it seems that precisely this sphere of income and property determines a mentality that makes people shallow and hard, chauvinistic out of anxiety, heartless out of narrowness of horizon, and rude out of lack of imagination. There is not much to distinguish a Belgian Philistine from an American Babbitt, or a German Philistine from his French counterpart. People who earn more than the bare necessities of life, but not enough to meet the aspirations they accepted without understanding them when they chose to be bourgeois, simply are that way.[42]

The bourgeoisie had not been the same at all times. Its "armor of prejudice" differed with the age and the fashion, but however it might change, the armor was worn until death. The middle class was myopic, never able to emerge from the "lowlands of its dim cognition." But it was worse in modern times because the bourgeoisie had become subject to arrogance, a demon who "whispers in their ears that he who has technology needs no soul (and, besides, has got one already)." To demonstrate the qualities of the Weimar bourgeois, Tucholsky selected two plants from the German herbarium and pressed them in the book of his satiric wit:

Frau Emmi Pagel from Guben, Lower Lausitz. Wife of Paul Pagel, bookkeeper, who in his papers lists himself as a "works official." Frau Pagel is of medium height; her legs are a bit too fat; she has wide hips, a fresh complexion, is well-scrubbed but not well-groomed; she has fat, manicured fingers, with a signet ring and an ornate wedding ring. Hair cut short. By no means a provincial woman, but just a woman who lives in a small town.

These are her ten articles of faith:

I. Under the Kaiser everything was better.
II. A head bookkeeper is more than a bookkeeper.
III. A letter mustn't start with "I... "; that is impolite.
IV. The Jews are to blame for all the misery. The Jews are dirty, greedy, materialistic, voluptuous, and dark. They all have such noses and want to become ministers, if they aren't already.
V. Of course there are no ghosts. Yet, it is uncanny to walk in a cemetery at night or to be in a big dark house alone (Mice).
VI. Servants are a race apart from the propertied, but they don't feel it.
VII. If you put sugar in rhubarb, it turns sour. (This belief is quite senseless; it stems from a misunderstanding and thus is ineradicable).
VIII. Communism means that everything is cut to pieces. In Russia the women are raped; they murdered a million people there. The Communists want to take everything away from us.
IX. What everybody, including myself, likes is pretty; what everybody, excluding myself, likes is beautiful.
X. The whole world is against Germany—out of envy.

So much for Frau Pagel.

On the other hand, Frau Margot Rosenthal, a lawyer's wife, is rather tall, a trifle too thin to be called slender, very well-groomed, but doesn't always look that way. Her hair isn't oily, but people think so. As for her complexion... "You wouldn't believe what all I've tried for my..."

I. Christians are more stupid than Jews and that is why they are called "Goyim."
II. Of course there are no ghosts. Still one doesn't have to go to a churchyard alone at night... I don't have to try everything.
III. A man who is able to buy and collect French engravings is cultured.
IV. Communism means that everything is cut to pieces. The Communists want to take away everything we have so carefully bought, piece by piece. Of course, there have to be workers and one should treat them decently; the best thing is not to pay any attention to them.
V. The whole world is against the Jews—out of envy.
VI. Art must not be exaggerated.
VII. When someone sits in an elegant hotel, he is elegant himself.
VIII. During a thunderstorm one must turn off the gas (Cf. Frau Pagel, VII: Rhubarb).

IX. You can't send any husband alone to Paris, least of all mine. The axe in the house...
X. My husband is too good-natured.

So much for Frau Rosenthal.
And who will pick the other plants?[43]

However much they might despise and distrust one another, the Gentile and Jewish bourgeoisie were united by the common fact of their prejudice, smugness and ignorance. Tucholsky believed that the Jews were particularly blind to their own interests and for this reason he perhaps held the Jewish middle class in even greater contempt than the anti-Semitic Gentile bourgeoisie. He thought that both were fatal for the Republic. In his attempt to demonstrate the myopia and pettiness of the German bourgeois, Tucholsky created a caricature, Herr Wendriner.

As famous in Germany as Babbitt was in America, Herr Wendriner was Tucholsky's archetype of the self-made German businessman. (He was also Jewish, a more complicated aspect of his character discussed in a later chapter.) Wendriner is interested only in money, but believes himself to be cultured. He is a monarchist, but is despised by the aristocracy. He prospers under the Republic, but hates it because it tolerates the "reds." He is expansive and voluble with his friends; with his family he is egocentric, petty and cruel. He is a true schlemiel, the person who bumbles around, seeking his own best interest, but really promoting that of his rivals.

The descriptions of Wendriner, his personality, his speech habits, and his unconscious assumptions demonstrated Tucholsky's brilliance as a cultural critic. The Wendriner sketches—sixteen in all—through their nuance of tone, through what was left unsaid, were more effective indications of the philistinism of German bourgeois culture than all of the manifestoes. The scenes are varied. One time Herr Wendriner has insomnia and we hear his thoughts about his health, his wife's habits and his business. When he tells of his trip to Paris, he boasts of the prices, the girls, and the weather. At other times, he has company and complains of the cost, or he deceives his wife and we hear him telling his little woes to his mistress. The subject matter of the Wendriner stories is the usual cliché of the vulgarity, the insensitivity of the newly rich middle class. What is unusual and brilliant is Tucholsky's capturing of the tone of speech, the cadence of dialect and the banal train of thought. It sounds so authentic that one is almost forced to say, "Yes, that's the way it is." Everyone knows a Wendriner. A good example is "Herr Wendriner Tells a Story." In this sketch, Wendriner is entertaining his friend, Herr Welsch, at Sunday dinner:

It's ready! We can begin. But what is this? You called us and the food is not on the table. I've told you a hundred times that I want the food on the table when I sit down to eat. The maid—! The maid—! Excuse us, Welsch, but we have a new girl—well, I refuse to be annoyed on Sunday. Now then, what I wanted to say—I wanted to tell you about what happened to me the other day. I was coming out—oh, the soup at last! Bat up!—I was coming out of the theater, I think it was the Playhouse, no—it was definitely the German Theater—I came out and was walking along the street—not so many dumplings for me. They are excellent, but I'm not supposed to eat them. The doctor says I'm getting too fat—I came out and a strange man spoke to me. Very young, a very young man— Walter! Can't you watch what you're doing! You've gotten everything all over yourself again. We'll have to tie a bib around you! Such a big boy too! White or red, Welsch?

I like the red better too—a very young man, I didn't know him—give me a little salt—and spoke to me. He said he had nothing to eat. I said, dear friend, I said, I also sometimes have nothing to eat, but I don't go right out and tell everybody on the street about it! And why choose me! As if richer people than me weren't coming out of the theater—ridiculous. Welsch, what my wife puts before you, you can eat! There is no embarrassment here—help yourself—well, I said to the young man, now listen to me, I said, you look respectable enough. How is it that you have nothing to eat? Welsch, now do me a simple favor and don't be so dainty! Help yourself! Take a little more fish! Take some! Help yourself! It's not necessary to ask here. So, the young man said he was from Breslau and naturally I pricked up my ears—Walter, you should not eat so much butter sauce! Don't eat so much! You won't get any more. Recently he vomited! Don't eat so much butter sauce! Can't you hear? Take the butter sauce away from him! You help yourself to a little more, Welsch. Last Sunday, Regierer was here and he ate enough to last him for three weeks! A healthy appetite! Have something else, Welsch! You have forgotten the chopped egg. You must pay attention to these things. What did you say, Welsch? The decision of the people? I don't know. I'm not for it. I have such an uncomfortable feeling. They begin with that and end with an auto. And I want to say to you—the Jews should now—*La domestique*—yes, yes, the meat is very good. I'll say more later. Not now. So the young man said he was from Breslau. I interrupted myself. It's not necessary for the girl to hear everything. They run around afterward and tell who knows what. Take some of the fruit compote. Compote is very healthy. Do you also take salts—I mean so much salt—it's not a proper laxative. Hilde, do you see your parents picking their noses at the table? You don't pick your nose at the table. Welsch is right, you should never pick your nose. To return to the young man—he said he was from Breslau and when he was a small boy he had known my dead father. He sometimes gave him candy. I naturally acknowledged nothing. It was already late and the streets were a bit dark—I couldn't know who the young man really was. Is there no bread? Look, there is no bread again—you know that I want bread on the table at meals. Well, dress yourself earlier! And that picture is crooked. What do you do the whole day? Nobody cares when I'm not looking. Yes, it is a good picture. I do a little collecting. Impressionists naturally. I don't think much of modern art. Well, he said he was unemployed and had no place to live—oh, so dinner is over. You are excused, Hilde! Excused, Walter! Come, Welsch, let's have a little coffee and liqueur in the other room. And a cigar. Here is a light one—no take this one, it's better. Have a light. Now to return to the story. Do you—my wife has left the room—do you know the joke about the old count who got married and in the hotel before the wedding night went quickly into the bar? He wanted a Pilsner. The bartender said, Herr Baron, don't drink a Pilsner. It will slow you down, it's better to take a glass of sherry. And so he did. The next morning he came downstairs and said to the waiter: Know what—give me two glasses of sherry and send my wife a bottle of Pil… Ah, you are back. I was just saying to Welsch that somehow rent control is going to have to be regulated differently. Is the coffee ready? Yes? Come, Welsch, we'll drink some coffee. One or two lumps of sugar? Milk? I never take milk. The doctor forbids it. He has also forbidden coffee, but you can't do everything the doctors say. Now listen to what happened with the young man. He asked me for my address—which I did not give him. I will not give my address to a stranger—when so many swindlers are running around Berlin. Oh it just occurred to me. Did you really sell Oberbedarf? I don't know—I have no real faith—What! You aren't leaving! Your sister-in-law can just wait a while. You are always there early enough. Ridiculous. Stay a little while longer! Stay—well, if you want to. Wait, I'll see you out. Here—this is your topcoat. That is mine. Yes, I have things made by Kropat. I'm very satisfied—he gives me special prices. The master always serves me himself. Welsch, did you throw this paper down here? Oh, that was from your flowers. Walter! Take away this paper! Hilde should not make so much noise. Tell her that Papa doesn't like it. And tell the maid to come out here. So, good-bye, Welsch! A safe trip home!

Where are you? I don't know—I don't like Welsch. The man is nervous! I wanted to tell him a story. You know the one about the young man I've already told you about—recently at the theater—it is very interesting. But you can't tell Welsch anything. You know why? He doesn't listen![44]

What Tucholsky most despised about the middle class was its adulation and emulation of the Prussian military. It was this idolatry which made the continuation of the Prussian ethos possible and which made it so difficult to destroy. The middle class had been corrupted and the greatest source of the corruption was the army. For Tucholsky there was one paramount reason for Germany's poverty of civilization: "It depends on you. Kill the German military—then you will have a German civilization."[45]

Militarism was the poison which had infected the German soul. Only through its extraction and destruction would it be possible to have a Germany in which a humane life was possible. It was militarism that festered the spirit of lordliness, which cast a meanness and narrowness on every aspect of German public life. It was the triumph of the military ethos that made Germany nothing but a vast "barracks" with "subjects" to be ordered around rather than "citizens" to be governed. Militarism was the Ungeist that poisoned the German social and political atmosphere:

> This is the heart of the matter: militarism stands there; we stand here....
> And our hearts cry out with the dead, "*Ecrases l'infame*"![46]

In 1919 Tucholsky began a campaign to discredit the military and diminish its influence in the Republic. His hatred of militarism became an obsession and it was this hatred through which he always viewed the Republic. Tucholsky believed in 1919 that there was every probability that the generals would both destroy the Republic and begin a new war of revenge. They would be successful, because militarism with its patterns of subservience and brutality was the strongest trait of the German national character. Somehow, Tucholsky believed, the awe in which the individual German held the military would have to be eliminated if the Republic were to be truly established.

Tucholsky realized that the task of discrediting military values in the eyes of the masses would be difficult, for the long Prussian tradition of pride in the army had been intensified by war propaganda. Germans at large knew little of the true conditions of battle, of the human indignities and the barbarities. The image of the German army and especially of the Officer Corps remained heroic and noble. During four years of war, the controlled press made no criticism of the army or of its leadership, just as it gave the German masses little inkling of the impending defeat in 1918. Even the loss of the war did little to diminish the prestige of the army. The monarchy was identified with the atrocities of the war; the monarchy was blamed for the defeat. The generals were praised and the populace greeted the returning soldiers with garlands and music.[47]

To be sure, no nation disparages its army in time of war, but in no other nation, in either war or peace, was the Officer Corps praised as highly as in Germany. An officer was a superior being; a model of nobility for children to emulate. Criticism of the officers was almost unthinkable in Germany and Tucholsky's attack upon them brought him to the notice of the military establishment and earned for him its undying hatred.

Tucholsky began his polemic upon the evils of the Officer Corps with an expose of what he believed to be its poor and at times criminal behavior during the war. Using a kind of "now-at-last-the-truth-can-be-told" tone, Tucholsky published a series of articles in 1919 in *Die Weltbühne* under the general title of *Militaria*. Each of them seized upon the virtues for which the Officer Corps was noted and attempted to demonstrate how the actual behavior of the officers in the field belied the pristine reputation. In his articles, Tucholsky used the techniques of shock and overstatement. It was a general attack more upon the *élan* and spirit of the officer than upon the individual. He was trying to say that Prussian officers were like other soldiers in that they too could be cruel, venal and dishonest. His attack necessarily lacked precision, for it dealt in generalities in order to create an impression of decadence and corruption. With their strident quality, the articles were somewhat less effective than many of Tucholsky's more subtle, satiric writings. Yet, antimilitarism represented the core of his struggle against reaction and the army command remained the focus of his fears for the future.

Tucholsky began the series with an essay entitled "*Offizier und Mann*" ("Officer and Man"), which dealt with the relations between the officers and the enlisted men during the war. Tucholsky maintained that contrary to popular opinion the officers had been arrogant toward the enlisted men. During the war, they had lived in another world and had come into contact with the common soldier only when absolutely necessary. The so-called "comradely cooperation" between the troops and their officers had occurred only in moments of the most extreme danger. Tucholsky contended it was this contempt for the small soldier that demonstrated the bankruptcy of the old Prussian spirit:

> ... The officer swaggered around the front with a bored look, saluted indolently or not at all when he met a *Kerl* and carefully cultivated that contempt which superiors always showed for the German soldier. To be sure, there were many exceptions—but here we are speaking of the spirit that ruled the German Officers' Corps and it was bad.[48]

It was the alleged pettiness of the officers toward the men, which Tucholsky hated most. He gave the contrast in wages as an example. The enlisted men received thirty-three *Pfennige* per day while according to Tucholsky it was well known that the officers were able to save money out of their salaries—

salaries whose exact amount was never revealed for reasons of "discipline." Tucholsky, however, denied the barbarism which Allied propaganda attributed to the German officer, rather "it was much more a question of a furtive and silent agreement among the officers to tolerate moral corruption."[49] Above all, Tucholsky was disgusted by the spectacle of an army propaganda, which had preached the superior virtues of the Prussian officer to the men while individual officers behaved in a contemptible manner.

In the second article, "Verpflegung,"[50] Tucholsky continued in the same bitter vein, but concentrated more on the poor treatment of the enlisted men. He contended that most of the needless sufferings of the common soldier were due to the corruption of the officers. He gave food as an indication. The portions of food allotted to the enlisted man were carefully calculated, but he seldom received the full amount. In Tucholsky's picturesque phrasing, food fell from above through the ranks, which acted as a giant sieve, until finally only marmalade and bread were left for the common soldier. Tucholsky told of instances in which officers shipped home whole trucks full of provisions for their families—provisions intended for the fighters. There were cases in which milk for the wounded was seized in order to make pastry for the commanding officer. According to Tucholsky, it was a corruption, which spread through the whole of the army, although the enlisted men did not have the opportunities for crime, which were open to the officers. The theft of food was not of the venial sort in which a man holding a candle crept up to the sausage chest while everyone else was sleeping—no, it was much more efficient. "The lords ate and sent the rest home. The men went hungry."[51]

In succeeding articles Tucholsky continued his attack. He described the stealing of artwork from private homes by German officers, while they punished the enlisted man if he sent a pound of butter home to his family. Tucholsky reported that the officers seized not only works of art, but women as well. They reserved the prostitutes on the bases and in the occupied cities for themselves and ordered the nurses to remain aloof from the common soldier.

It was indiscriminate accusations such as these that vitiated the effectiveness of Tucholsky's campaign against militarism. He offered no documentation. He failed to distinguish between the professional officers who were almost all killed in 1914 and the inexperienced parvenus who were hastily appointed to take their places. He refused to admit that anything could be said in favor of the military and thus he presented a demonology, rather than a reasoned analysis. Even those persons who were inclined to favor his views questioned Tucholsky's reckless generalizing from individual instances. Tucholsky could never answer such criticism properly, for it was almost impossible to prove the truth of generalities concerning "type" or "spirit." The usual recourse was to employ more generalities.

In 1920, the *Weltbühne* exhibited its flexibility when it published a reply by an anonymous staff officer who, in reasoned and liberal tones, refuted Tucholsky's attack upon the military leadership. Tucholsky answered by contending simply that the two worlds of the civilian and the military could never be reconciled and thus a dialogue was impossible:

> I think that with the staff officer and myself, it is the same as with all polemicists when they meet one another. Bach speaks beyond the other. We do not speak the same language. You must choose between us.[52]

For Tucholsky the military in every state was a parasite upon society. It was *the* factor, which prevented mankind from achieving humanity and civilization. Tucholsky's intransigent attitude caused many of his most sympathetic admirers to fail to listen when he spoke more reasonably, as in the same series of articles when he dealt with the evils of official propaganda during the war. He attacked the press ministry, which had deceived the populace and the field papers, which had lied to the soldiers on the front. In horrified tones, Tucholsky described the participation of the intellectuals—the professors, writers and philosophers—in the fabrication of propaganda. The field papers, which the soldiers read, had engaged in the most open lying, as they became dominated by rightist factions. Tucholsky reported it had been "understood" that reporters would present the point of view of the right-wing "Fatherland Party." Tucholsky also spoke of the anti-Semitic overtones of the official journals. U.S. President Woodrow Wilson had been caricatured with Semitic features, thus associating Jews with "the enemy."[53]

Tucholsky's extreme attack upon the officers also mitigated the effectiveness of his appeal to Germans to accept the disarmament clauses of the Versailles Treaty. The treaty was anathema to almost all Germans of every class. Tucholsky, however, considered it a blessing in disguise. The Entente had performed a positive service for Germany by insisting upon her disarmament. Tucholsky admitted that the Entente had no monopoly upon morality, but in spite of the ill will behind the treaty provisions, they were best for Germany because they opposed militarism:

> With imperialistic power the Entente for reasons of malice wishes to force from the German government the very things that we desire to drive from it for reasons of good will in our spiritual struggle.[54]

The treaty stipulated that the army be reduced to 100,000 men. The great German General Staff was dissolved. There could be no compulsory military service and enlisted men were to serve for twelve years. The number of officers was reduced proportionally and their term of service was to be twenty-five years. Germany could possess no tanks, armored cars or military aircraft. It was seemingly impossible for Germany to ever again amass military force sufficient for waging war.

Tucholsky however warned that the army leaders would try to circumvent the treaty terms. In an article entitled "Neuer Militarismus" ("New Militarism"),[55] Tucholsky remarked that the government would ostensibly comply with the treaty provisions, but it would undermine them by the simple expedient of creating special "police units." The old organization and the old leaders would be transferred to the new unofficial military organizations such as the Free Corps. In Tucholsky's opinion, it would be an inevitable process. Since Gustav Noske, the minister of war, had relied upon the officers of the monarchy for protection, they would naturally demand something in return. The compensation would be control of the new "police troops." The officers had served the monarchy, then the Social Democrats, and now they would serve the "mixed system" until they were in a position to exert complete control. The paramilitary units would insure the continuation of the old ways:

> We see in preparation the conservation of the thrice-cursed military spirit. If we consider that all of the larger German cities will have such military formations, then we shall have, in addition to the permitted hundred-thousand-man army, yet another hundred thousand men who in their drill, behavior, mentality and crudity will be indistinguishable from the old army. The old spirit will be preserved in all its purity—but it must and shall be eliminated.[56]

In his attempt to discredit the military, Tucholsky was most effective when he used satire. One of the best examples is a piece written early in 1920 entitled "Der Preussenhimmel" ("The Prussian Heaven").[57] The scene opens in heaven with St. Peter ordering about a column of angels. He shouts such things as, "Chests out! Dress right! In the names of all the saints, stop quivering your wings!" God enters, speaking with a heavy Prussian accent. After inspecting the angels, God dismisses them and enters the chancellery with St. Peter in order to admit the new arrivals. The first is a worker, beaten, bleeding and wearing torn clothes. He says good morning and Peter rebuffs him for speaking before being addressed, remarking loudly, "You're not in a Social Democratic Party office." After being told to address the old saint as "Sir," the worker inquires politely if he is indeed really in heaven. Peter ignores the question, orders him to be quiet and finally asks the worker what he wants. "The man replies: 'I was murdered in Marburg. My body lay on the street. My death is un-atoned.'"

God has been listening silently all the while. Upon hearing the worker's reply, he raises himself to his full height and asks in horrified tones if the worker thinks he is in a nest of Communists. As to the question of Marburg—when the murderers arrived, they would be accepted, but the worker would have to leave. God then explains in his heavy Prussian dialect that a new order prevails in heaven:

> You know—things have become very different since Willem declared me to be the dear God of Prussia.… Too bad he lost the war! Everything was so well organized… ! Well, he didn't actually lose the war—the others merely won it!

The worker is no sooner taken care of than another person enters and states that his name is Arco-Valley. (He murdered Kurt Eisner, the first and only short-lived socialist prime minister of Bavaria, on February 21, 1919.) When asked what he does, he replies that his occupation is "Bavarian National Hero." Asked for his heavenly qualifications, he raises a bloody hand and says in solemn tones, "Eisner, Excellency." Peter inquires if he does not know of the prohibition against killing. Arco-Valley replies (his patriotic jargon equally as untranslatable as God's Prussian dialect):

> I have made use of my national right of emergency and shoved aside an alien damaging element, as my conscience commanded me to. The thanks of everyone of good will is certain, not to mention the secret police.

He is, of course, admitted and the sketch closes with God's saying that he has adopted the Imperial red, white and black colors for his own and soon all of the German soldiers will be in heaven with him. Then he will feel truly wonderful. Whereupon is heard "So will we, Excellency! So will we!" from the chorus of workers below.

Such was the mildest form of Tucholsky's satire. On other occasions, he expressed greater bitterness, as when he characterized the military as the "monkey in uniform." It was satire of the following manner that particularly infuriated the German War Office:

> Toss down a *Groschen*! There stands an organ-grinder, wounded, blinded and ruined for the rest of his life. But upon his music box there sits an animal, grimacing, picking lice and fleas and gnashing its teeth—a monkey in uniform.[58]

With their generality and exaggeration, Tucholsky's attacks upon the military leaders are unimportant as an analysis of the nature of the German army. But in spite of the irrationality of his completely negative attitude toward anything even remotely connected with the army, Tucholsky's insights into future military developments in Germany were essentially correct. The paramilitary forces did become the bane of the Republic and were, in effect, a circumvention of the Versailles provisions. Because he believed that the old army posed the greatest threat to democracy,—it was, in his opinion, absolutely necessary to conform to the letter of the treaty if the Republic were to survive.

The revolution, in Tucholsky's view, had made the army even more dangerous, for although the military organization had not changed, it was nevertheless called "republican," a title, which obscured its reactionary purposes. Tucholsky believed that Wilhelmine Germany had been an openly militaristic and oligarchic state ruled by the army, the bankers and the industrialists. The revolution had not destroyed those rulers. It had given them a democratic facade behind which they could operate to create an authoritarian regime, which, with its greater injustice and cruelty, would be a distorted caricature of the old Empire. Tucholsky believed the Republic must not be allowed to provide that facade. The old guard had to be uncompromisingly exposed for what it was, the enemy of democracy and "decency." He believed that without the complete destruction of every remnant of the old regime, the new could not be born. Or, it might be born, but the old men would capture and kill the child—worse, they would educate it and use it for their own designs. Thus, the Republic only served to mask the disease infecting German society and culture, not to destroy it.

NOTES

1 See the unpublished dissertation (Columbia, 1964) by Istvan Deak, *The World of Carl von Ossietzky, Germany's Homeless Left in the Weimar Republic.*

2 The twenties were truly golden years for the German newspaper industry, for it was the period when great mass circulation really began and when the newspaper had little competition from other mass media such as radio and film. An interesting and informative history of German journalism is Peter de Mendelssohn, *Zeitungsstadt Berlin, Menschen und Mächte in der Geschichte der deutschen Presse* (Berlin, 1959), which, with its many illustrations and facsimiles of Berlin newspapers, is a magnificent example of the modern book publisher's art. In Berlin alone in 1930-31, there were forty-five morning papers, fourteen evening papers and two afternoon papers (de Mendelssohn, p. 306), not to mention magazines. For a specific history of the great Ullstein press, see the anniversary volume: George Bernhard, et al., *50 Jahre Ullstein, 1877-1927* (Berlin, n.d.). A lesser work is Hermann Ullstein, *The Rise and Fall of the House of Ullstein* (New York, 1943). For abrief ssay upon the general political influence of the mass media of the twenties in Germany, see Emil Dovifat, "Die Publizistik der Weimarer Zeit, fresse, Rundfunk, Film," in Leonhard Reinisch (ed.), *Die Zeit ohne Eigenschaften. Eine Bilanz der zwanziger Jahre* (Stuttgart, 1961), pp. 119-136.

3 Kurt Hiller, "Aufstieg, Glanz und Verfall der Weltbühne," *Konkret*, 3-7 (Hamburg, March-July 1962), No. 4, p. 19.

4 Alf Enseling, *Die Weltbühne, Organ der "intellektuellen Linken"* (Münster, 1962).

5 Kurt Hiller, "Aufstieg," p. 19. In addition there were other eminent writers such as Erich Kästner, Lion Feuchtwanger, Manfred Georg, Hermann Kesten, Richard Lewinsohn, Walter Karsch, and Arnold Zweig.

6 Kurt Tucholsky, "Die Rolle des Intellektuellen in der Partei," G.W., III, 13; K.T., *Front*, 9 (1929), 250.

7 Kurt Hiller, *Köpfe und Tröpfe* (Hamburg, 1950), p. 274.

8 Kurt Hiller, "Aufstieg," No. 3, p. 7.

9 Ibid., No. 4, p. 19.

10 Enseling, p. 32. It is difficult to determine the number of issues printed, for the records of the *Weltbühne* were confiscated by the Nazis and have been lost. The information, which is available, is found in letters of Jacobsohn to Tucholsky.

11 De Mendelssohn, p. 304, 258, 260

12 Hiller, "Aufstieg," No. 4, p. 19.

13 Golo Mann, "The Intellectuals, Germany," *Encounter*, IV, No. 6 (June, 1955), 43. See also Ralf Dahrendorf, *Gesellschaft und Demokratie*. In: *Deutschland* (München, 1966), especially the chapter, "Deutsche Intellektuelle, Politik und Status," pp. 308-326.

14 For an excellent discussion of the transformation of "culture" into "religion," see Fritz Stern's article, "The Political Consequences of the Unpolitical German," in *History*, No. 3 (New York, 1960), 105-134.

15 Kurt Tucholsky, "Wir Negativen," G.W., I, 372, 375-377; K.T., *Die Weltbühne*, XV/12 (March 13, 1919), 279.

16 Fritz Stern, *The Politics of Cultural Despair, A Study in the Rise of the Germanic Ideology* (Berkeley and Los Angeles, 1961), p. 98.

17 H. Stuart Hughes, *Consciousness and Society, the Reconstruction of European Social Thought, 1890-1930* (New York, 1958), p. 338.

18   Kurt Tucholsky, "Meinen Freunden, den Idealisten," G.W., I, 239; I.W., *Die Schaubühne*, XIII/3 (February 1, 1917), 107.

19   Kurt Sontheimer, "Antidemocratic Thought in the Weimar Republic," *The Path to Dictatorship, 1918-1933, Ten Essays*, translated by John Conway (New York, 1966), pp. 32-49.

20   Kurt Tucholsky, "Wir alle Fünf," G.W., I, 1041-43; K.T., *Die Weltbühne*, XVIII/34 (Aug. 24, 1922), 204.

21   Ibid., G.W., I, 204.

22   Friedrich Nietzsche, *The Twilight of the Idols, The Portable Nietzsche*, translated by Walter Kaufmann (New York, 1954), p. 506.

23   Kurt Tucholsky, "Militaria," G.W., I, 591; I.W., *Die Weltbühne*, XVI/4 (January 22, 1920), 106.

24   Kurt Tucholsky, "Kadettenliteratur," G.W., I, 726; I.W., *Die Weltbühne*, XVI/35 (August 26, 1920), 236.

25   Nietzsche, *Twilight*, pp. 506-507.

26   Kurt Tucholsky, "Gesicht," G.W., I, 1182; K.H., *Die Weltbühne*, XX/27 (July 3, 1924), 33. English translation "Face of a German," by Harry Zohn in: *Germany? Germany! The Kurt Tucholsky Reader* (Berlinica, New York, 2017), pp. 28-29.

27   Kurt Tucholsky, "Der Kontrollierte," G.W., I, 88-89; Anonym., *Vorwärts* (Sept. 18, 1913).

28   Kurt Tucholsky, "Militaria," G.W., I, 592; I.W., *Die Weltbühne*, XVI/4 (January 22, 1920), 106.

29   Thomas Mann, *Betrachtungen eines Unpolitischen*, Stockholmer Gesamtausgabe (Frankfurt/M., S. Fischer Verlag, 1956).

30   Nietzsche, *Twilight*, p. 541.

31   Kurt Tucholsky, "Preussische Studenten," G.W., I, 410; I.W., *Die Weltbühne*, XV/20 (May 8, 1919), 532.

32   Golo Mann, *Deutsche Geschichte des neunzehnten und zwanzigsten Jahrhunderts* (Frankfurt/M, 1960), p. 708.

33   Daniel Bell, *The End of Ideology* (Glencoe, Ill., 1960), p. 16.

34   Kurt Tucholsky, *Ausgewählte Briefe*, 1913-1935 (Hamburg, 1962), p. 259.

35   Kurt Tucholsky, "Die zufällige Republik," G.W., I, 996; I.W., *Die Weltbühne*, XVIII/28 (Sept. 13, 1922), 25.

36   See Leonard Krieger, *The German Idea of Freedom* (Boston, 1957), for a discussion of aloofness from politics.

37   Nietzsche, *Twilight*, p. 509.

38   See Fritz Stern, "The Political Consequences" and "Introduction," *The Path to Dictatorship*.

39   Kurt Tucholsky, "Wir Negativen," G.W., I, 372.

40   Ibid., p. 373.

41   Kurt Tucholsky, "Wir alle Fünf," G.W., I, 1043.

42   Kurt Tucholsky, "Die Glaubenssätze der Bourgeoisie," G.W., II, 1253-1256; P.P., *Die Weltbühne*, XXIV/40 (October 2, 1928), 522.

43   Ibid.. Full English translation by Harry Zohn in: *Germany? Germany! The Kurt Tucholsky Reader* (Berlinica, New York, 2017), pp. 58–60.

44   Kurt Tucholsky, "Herr Wendriner erzählt eine Geschichte," G.W., II, 449; K.H., *Die Weltbühne*, XXII/21 (May 25, 1926), 824.

45   Kurt Tucholsky, "Militaria," G.W., I, 592.

46   Kurt Tucholsky, "Die lebendigen Toten," G.W., I, 419; I.W., *Die Weltbühne*, XV/21 (May 15, 1919), 564.

47   See Walter H. Kaufmann, *Monarchism in the Weimar Republic* (New York, 1953), pp. 229-230.

48   Kurt Tucholsky, "Offizier und Mann," G.W., I, 329; I.W., *Die Weltbühne*, XV/2 (January 9, 1919), 38.

49   Ibid., G.W., I, 330.

50   Kurt Tucholsky, "Verpflegung," G.W., I, 332; I.W., *Die Weltbühne*, XV/3 (January 23, 1919), 87.

51   Ibid., G.W., I, 334.

52   Kurt Tucholsky, "Schlusswort," G.W., I, 596; I.W., *Die Weltbühne*, XVI/7 (February 12, 1920), 219.

53   Kurt Tucholsky, "Vaterländischer Unterricht," G.W., I, 339; I.W., *Die Weltbühne*, XV/7-8 (February 13, 1919), 159.

54   Kurt Tucholsky, "Wir Negativen," G.W., I, p. 374.

55   Kurt Tucholsky, "Neuer Militarismus," G.W., I, 484-486; I.W., *Die Weltbühne*, XV/41 (October 2, 1919), 405.

56   Ibid., G.W., I, 485.

57   Kurt Tucholsky, "Der Preussenhimmel," G.W., I, 577-79; K.H., *Freie Welt* (1920). Full English translation by Cindy Opitz in *Berlin! Berlin! Dispatches From the Weimar Republic* (Berlinica, New York, 2013), pp. 83–85

58   Kurt Tucholsky, "Der Affe auf dem Leierkasten," G.W., I, 837; I.W., *Welt am Montag* (May 10, 1921).

Gustav Noske, German Minister of War (left), with Reichspräsident Friedrich Ebert (middle). Both were long-time targets of Kurt Tucholsky.

V.

BATTLES OF THE WEIMAR REPUBLIC

Tucholsky had many disagreements with the Weimar Republic, but his bitterest disappointment was the Social Democratic Party, for it appeared to have been *the* agency that could have introduced a true spirit of democracy into Germany. Instead he watched the Socialists cooperate with the military and order the army to put down the Spartacists. Tucholsky was never able to forgive the Socialists for their pact with the army leaders. The worst offender in his mind was the Socialist Minister of War, Gustav Noske. Noske entered the government of the Social Democratic President Friedrich Ebert on December 27, 1918, after the withdrawal of the Independent Socialists.

Noske had always been associated with the right wing of the SPD and after his actions of the following year, many Socialists began to wonder if he belonged to their number at all. With the statement, "Somebody has to be the bloodhound," Noske took to his task with a relish that earned him the epithet, *Mörder Noske*. He gave his full cooperation to the generals during Spartacist Week in January and with his assent, official sanction was given to the right-wing Free Corps mercenaries—a triumph for the forces of reaction.

In March 1919 further Spartacist uprisings occurred in Berlin and Noske alienated almost all leftist opinion when he announced that anyone who was found resisting the government was to be shot upon capture. The Free Corps responded with zest and in all some twelve hundred workers were killed. Noske had been given the double commission of defending the Republic and destroying the revolution. His success in the latter helped to insure the eventual demise of the former. To be sure, Noske and the Socialists believed they were presented with an agonizing dilemma—bolshevism or compromise with the old guard. By choosing the second of the alternatives, they lost their trump card of the continuing threat of popular insurrection. The army needed the support of the Socialists to keep the masses in line, but after the defeat of the Spartacists, the threat of revolution from the left became minimal. By that time, however, there was little the Socialists could do to stem the tide of reaction. The success of the army had been too striking.

Tucholsky recognized after 1919 that the army had recovered its lost prestige, largely because of Socialist cooperation. He conceded that the SPD might truly have believed in the necessity of cooperation, but he questioned why the party continued to cooperate with the army so enthusiastically. If the Socialists could not repudiate the army, Tucholsky wanted them at least to repudiate militarism. Tucholsky believed that only the civilian leadership could destroy the militarist spirit in the masses. He admitted that it could not be done in a day, but at least a beginning had to be made. The tragedy in his opinion was that Noske had been chosen to make that beginning.

Tucholsky finally came to believe that the Socialists were incapable of providing a democratic leadership. They were too inept politically. They seemed to miss every opportunity to recoup their losses, for they continued to see danger only on the left while exhibiting a fatal blindness to the threat of the right.

Yet in spite of his public pose of despair, Tucholsky did not give up hope for the Republic until almost the very end. He believed that the Socialists had missed the great opportunity in 1918 to effect a truly democratic revolution, but a chance might reoccur if the right overplayed its hand and behaved stupid. In Tucholsky's opinion, the great second chance for Social Democracy to reassert its authority came with the Kapp Putsch, or Kapp-Lützwitz Putsch, an attempted coup by members of the Reichswehr to replace the Weimar government with a military dictatorship. It was named after the men behind it, Wolfgang Kapp and Walther von Lüttwitz, an army general.

On January 20, 1920, almost two months before the putsch, Ignaz Wrobel warned that the military were making fools of the Social Democrats and especially of Noske.[1] Tucholsky asked how Noske, a "former" Social Democrat, could fail to see the dangers of militarism and the surviving elements of the old system. Tucholsky warned the Socialists that their cooperation with the Nationalists would drive the masses into the arms of the Communists, a bit of wishful thinking since the masses had shown no great revolutionary fervor in the past. On March 13, the putsch came and Tucholsky's warnings were justified. He wrote on March 25, 1920:

> Sixteen months of inaction have taken their revenge. On the thirteenth of March 1920, the German militarists thought their hour had come and they set to work. Remarkably the catch escaped them... [2]

The crisis came with the attempt of the republican government to comply with the treaty provision that the army be reduced to a hundred thousand men. The core of the regular army was not directly involved in the insurrection, but it did nothing to aid the regime of Friedrich Ebert and Gustav Bauer, a Socialist who became Chancellor, with Ebert being the President. The Republic survived only because of the success of the general strike. With the putsch squashed, there is no doubt that the army lost prestige and Tucholsky saw the period immediately after as providing an excellent opportunity for the republicans to take up the reins of revolution once again. By dealing severely with all those who had been in the least implicated in the putsch, the government would be able to strengthen itself against its rightwing enemies by speaking their own language of strength and ruthlessness. But the Republic missed what Tucholsky believed to be its second chance to consolidate its power.

After the failure of the Kappists, Tucholsky published a series of articles in the *Weltbühne*, which lamented the political naiveté and blindness of the Socialists, and, at the same time, pleaded with them to grasp the .new opportunity given them. He inquired how anyone could possibly have been surprised by the putsch and remarked sarcastically that only the government could have been, since it read no opposition newspapers.[3] According to Tucholsky, the Ebert-Bauer government had "slept" for sixteen months despite of all warnings. As the old officers returned from the war, they had begun to fear the dissolution of the Officers' Corps. No longer having an external enemy, they created an internal one for purposes of self-preservation. In such manner they justified the paramilitary organizations and, Tucholsky contended, the government stupidly let itself be convinced by them. Again the person who bore the greatest responsibility, who should have taken the army in hand, was Gustav Noske.[4]

In exasperated tones, Tucholsky pointed out that the Republic had failed to heed even the most obvious warning signs. In 1919 and 1920, the Kaiser's birthday was officially celebrated in the Reichswehr. Noske did not make the slightest protest. In addition the government failed to heed the danger posed by the soldiers returning from the Baltic campaigns, a dangerously reactionary enclave.[5] He concluded that only the most radical journals had warned of the impending danger to the Republic. The large daily papers, even the most liberal, had had only words of praise for Noske, the "strong man."

Tucholsky ended his analysis by stating that the right-wing political parties would, of course, deny having had any part in the putsch, but he maintained that they were nevertheless its "spiritual fathers." Yet now the right-wing was in disgrace and the Republic had the opportunity to reorganize the whole of the society from the Officers' Corps to the school system. Tucholsky reiterated that the opportunity to create a "real revolution" was at hand.

In April 1920 Tucholsky presented in the *Weltbühne* a list of demands to the government.[6] He asked for compliance with Article 160 of the Versailles Treaty, the provision that demanded that the German Army be reduced to one hundred thousand men. He demanded the immediate dismissal of all officers upon whom the slightest shadow of disloyalty to the Republic had fallen. Tucholsky called for the dissolution of all paramilitary organizations. In the main, Tucholsky's proposals merely asked that the civilian government assert its control over the military and that those guilty of treason be punished by the law. Tucholsky's demands were far more sober than those incorporated into the pact between the trade unions and the Weimar coalition parties. The workers had literally saved the Republic by means of the general strike. Before they would return to work, they demanded through the voices of trade union leaders that certain guarantees be made. As a result, a nine-point pact was agreed upon on March 20, 1920. In addition to the disbanding of illegal military organizations, the pact agreed to amplify existing social welfare schemes and to nationalize certain industries. The most radical provision was that new governments would take office only after the trade unions had approved of them. Only slightly less revolutionary was the demand that laws be enacted that would guarantee social and economic equality to the working class.

In the light of this actual agreement, Tucholsky's proposals were modest. However, the fact that Tucholsky considered it necessary to make his demands a month after the trade union pact demonstrated its fate. The politicians paid no more attention to the pact than they did to Tucholsky.

Noske's resignation was accepted on March 22, 1920, but Tucholsky believed the new defense minister to be little better than his hated predecessor. Otto Gessler, who remained in office until 1928, was overawed by the generals and became their willing tool in the civilian government. In 1921, Tucholsky recognized Gessler's obsequiousness before the army command and regarded with horror his contention that the army should remain "unpolitical." Tucholsky believed that the army "had to be republican".

> The new Reichswehr Minister wants the army to be unpolitical. That is wrong. The army must be political through and through. The question is not—Republic or monarchy—the question is democracy or despotism.[7]

To be sure, during the Kapp Putsch the core of the army had remained "loyal," but it was fickle. Tucholsky maintained that if the Kappists had succeeded, the army would have lost no time in rushing to their support:

> The soldiers rode through the city in their trucks and were loyal... yes, after the end of the operetta, we saw the slogans on the tanks: "We stand behind the Ebert-Bauer regime." Fortunately, the words were written with chalk so they could easily be washed off. It was an exchangeable loyalty.[8]

Gessler's subservience to the generals became increasingly depressing to Tucholsky. By July 1922, he was predicting another putsch for the coming winter. Tucholsky believed that this time the militarists would be smarter than the Kapp people had been. They would close the roads, take over the press and telegraph and kill their known opponents. He stated that one night they would simply come, rouse the people out of their beds and the Republic would die with hardly a whimper.[9]

> Today we republicans stand naked and exposed. And I do not think much of the slogan "Masses to the streets!" Where will they go? Do we have a fighting organization that we can employ to defend us in the case of a putsch? Do we have weapons? What are the workers going to fight a putsch with? Their pocketknives?[10]

Again Tucholsky implored the democratic regime to awaken and protect itself with concrete action. In 1922, he sharpened and reformulated the suggestions he had made shortly after the Kapp Putsch:

Here are our proposals:
1. Transformation of the Reichswehr into a people's militia. The dismissal of all superfluous and counter-revolutionary generals and officers.
2. Demilitarization of the civil police... forced pensioning and control of all unreliable elements, especially in the provinces.
3. Reform of justice—especially among the state attorney's offices which are still in a process of definition. A ruthless cleansing of all monarchical elements from justice.
4. Democratization of the regime. A thoroughgoing investigation of every republican grievance, the dismissal of all officials whose anti-republican politics can be proved—with withdrawal of pension...
5. The strengthening of the central government over the states.
6. Complete reordering of the teaching bodies of the schools and the high schools. Immediate abolition of all coercive methods, including the indirect measures that propose to enforce a new military drill under the cover of "physical exercise."
7. Immediate amnesty for political prisoners of every kind, in so far as they are republican.... .
8. Suspension of paragraph 360 of the civil code, number 8. This ordinance prosecutes the unauthorized wearing of orders and medals. It serves nothing to forbid this monarchical nonsense—its value must first be withdrawn. Since titles are no longer given, this deeply anti-republican caste has more value than before—the value of scarcity. This foolishness of the monarchy must succumb to the worthlessness of the ordinary.
9. Above all: explanation and propagation of the new ideas of a new Republic.[11]

These proposals of 1922 show clearly that Tucholsky was an advocate of moderate republican democracy. There was little that was radical about them. There was no call for socialization, no demand for the outlawing of the right wing. Tucholsky simply asked for a forthright and intransigent opposition on the part of the Republic's leadership against its enemies.

In his nine proposals Tucholsky touched upon all of the major problems facing the Republic. Justifiably he headed the list with a request for the formation of a republican army and the dismissal of reactionary generals. Technically the army command was always loyal to the Republic, but it was not republican. The army formed a separate entity and in time of crisis, the democratic regime could never be sure of support from the military. The preservation of the Prussian army organization was one of the crucial mistakes of the Republic's founders. The failure of the regular army to lend the Republic the support of its enormous prestige was a misfortune. Even the election of General Paul von Hindenburg to the presidency did not alter the basic antipathy of the army to the Republic. The army became a symbol if not the embodiment of reaction, and the Officer's Corps became an even more exclusive enclave of the aristocracy and the wealthy than before the war.[12]

An army which remains a neutral, apolitical force may be desirable when there is general agreement concerning the virtues of democracy. However when there are many powerful enemies of a democratic order, a politically neutral armed force can be dangerous. Tucholsky was correct in maintaining that the Republic could never be stable until the army leadership was thoroughly republican. It was true that General Hans von Seeckt, commander in chief of the Reichswehr supported the constitution and the democratic state, but his concept of the army as a "state within the state" made it possible for it to turn against the Republic when another man became leader. The danger was well illustrated by Seeckt's attitude in 1923 during the Hitler Putsch. Ebert called Seeckt in to determine the posture of the army. When he inquired whom the army would follow, Seeckt replied, "The army will follow me."[13]

Tucholsky called for the dismissal of all anti-republican officials. Certainly the government bureaucracy played a dubious role in the Republic. Tucholsky hated bureaucrats for their arrogance and contempt for citizens and their worship of the state. Yet the contribution of the bureaucratic structure to the weakening and eventual demise of German democracy is difficult to define. Because the bureaucracy professed to be above politics, it is doubly difficult to determine its effect upon political life. On the other hand, there is little doubt that the administrative apparatus which the Republic inherited from the Empire helped to make the way smoother for the full establishment of Nazi power, since the Weimar bureaucracy was also transferred virtually intact to the Hitler regime. And in general the German bureaucracy divorced its conception of the German nation from the actuality of the Weimar state.

A bureaucracy is important because neither an absolutist state nor a mass democracy can function without an efficient, centralized administrative structure. Yet bureaucratic values may not coincide with democratic values. As mass democracy becomes more complex, with its welfare schemes and other public obligations, so does bureaucratic regimentation necessarily increase, thus coming into conflict with the ideal of individual freedom. Moreover, as the forces involved in competitive capitalism grow larger through cartels, mergers, trade unions and trade associations, they tend to form large private bureaucratic bodies from which the public interest can be protected only by governmental interference and control. The power of the state bureaucracy again increases.

The state bureaucracy in the Bismarckian Reich had grown stronger with the development of an industrialized, pluralistic society. But unlike England and France, the growth of German bureaucratic regimentation was unbalanced by a tradition of liberal democracy that held governmental interference to be anathema. Thus when Germany was converted into a mass democracy in 1919, the paradox of the bureaucratic collectivized state—i.e., greater equality but less freedom—was compounded by the autocratic tradition of the German past. Therefore, the Weimar Republic was subject not only to the internal contradictions of any modern welfare democracy, but also inherited an administrative bureaucracy, which did not feel guilt because of its authoritarian tendencies, but was proud of them. The only possible saving grace was that the German bureaucracy also prided itself on independence from political rivalry and from the outward political structure of the state. But, in the end, the state bureaucracy in the Republic proved to be very "political" in the sense that it augmented antidemocratic forces. The author Franz Neumann made a strong indictment of the bureaucratic structure:

> The ministerial bureaucracy is a closed caste. In the Republic its personnel was ostensibly neither anti-democratic nor pro-democratic and cared little about the forms of state and government. The upper civil servant regards the state more or less as a business undertaking to be run efficiently... Political problems are reduced to technical administrative problems... Essentially, of course, it is an anti-democratic and authoritarian outlook. It values success more than right or social justice. Power is revered because it guarantees efficiency. Efficient and incorruptible in the ordinary sense, the ministerial bureaucracy was the center of every antidemocratic movement in the Weimar Republic.[14]

While it may not have been a center of every antidemocratic movement, there is no doubt that the ministerial bureaucracy was not the neutral, apolitical force it advertised itself to be. Rather, the bureaucracy formed a third "organ of state" along with cabinet and parliament. During times of acute crisis, as toward the end of the Weimar era, the administration was the one stable element. If at those times key bureaucratic functionaries were not democratically oriented, then it is clear that much harm could be done. Article 130 of the Weimar constitution stated that members of the bureaucracy were to serve the commonalty, not a party; but then the article almost Contradicted itself by saying: "All officials are guaranteed freedom of political opinion and freedom to join organizations." Thus, in public it was possible for a bureaucrat to claim political neutrality while in private he belonged to organizations dedicated to the destruction of the Republic. In effect, he became a representative in the government of an antidemocratic faction. The republicans committed a great error when they failed to demand some small proof of democratic loyalty from their appointed officials—officials who were contemptuous of the "party state" where "bosses" ruled, officials who looked upon Germany as "their state" to be ruled as "efficiently," not as democratically, as possible.[15]

Tucholsky was especially concerned that republican and democratic values be taught in the schools. He knew what a center of chauvinism and reaction the school system had been before the war and he doubted that it would be able to produce a democratically oriented youth without sharp changes. Only the firm intervention and surveillance on the part of the republican regime would assure those changes. In 1919 Tucholsky reported that the Free Corps was recruiting students from the high schools. Representatives from the army were often invited to address school assemblies.

Tucholsky claimed that this failure to attempt to instill the values of democracy was especially serious in regard to upper-class youth, for it was they who would be the future lawyers, teachers, cabinet ministers and theologians of the Republic. Their parents would insure that they were drilled with the old teachings and the old values. But very early Tucholsky realized with dismay that the Entente, the Allies would lend their support to the German reactionary forces because they were anti-Communist. To be against the Communists was to be forgiven of all other sins.[16]

In the proposals of 1922, Tucholsky also called for a greater subordination of the provinces to the central government. This may appear curious at first because it was an article of faith among the Allies after the Second World War that Hitler triumphed rapidly because the provinces were weak vis-à-vis the regime in Berlin. For Tucholsky it was exactly the opposite. In his view the provinces were centers of resistance to the republican government. They allowed the growth of private armies; they tolerated the hatching of plots against the government; and they prevented the central government from effectively advertising itself among the population at large.

Provincial autonomy had been one of the greatest problems of the Empire. The power of the Imperial Chancellor had been derived mainly from the fact that he was simultaneously the premier of Prussia, a state that comprised two-thirds of the area and population of the Reich. Superior Prussian power had been the only factor that had given the excessively federalized Second Empire any semblance of unity and strength.[17]

Hugo Preuss, the framer of the Weimar constitution, had wanted to abolish the federalism which had crippled the Empire. He proposed simultaneously to strengthen the central government and eliminate the Prusso-German problem by creating eight new states from the territories of Prussia and the small states of northern Germany. But federalism proved too strong. Local pride and tradition in the smaller states, always the strength of German particularism, would not countenance merger into larger units. In Prussia, the Social Democrats who now controlled the state government were just as unwilling to relinquish their local powers as the Junkers before them had been. Germany thus retained a federal structure with state representation in one of the houses of the bicameral legislature.

Still the central government did have far more power than under the Empire. The individual states or *Länder* could not pass laws in contradiction to federal statutes. They also had to have a republican government elected in conformity to national election procedure. The *Länder* were also required to enforce the laws of the Reich or they would be forced to do so by the federal armed force. The central government had control of national defense, public welfare, communications and foreign relations. It also possessed for all practical purposes supreme authority in matters of taxation.

The Berlin government was thus dominant, but Tucholsky believed that it did not assert its authority forcefully enough. It tolerated reactionary and anti-republican governments in Bavaria. Tucholsky often called upon German tourists to boycott Bavaria because of its dictatorial regime and anti-Semitic incidents.[18] In his eyes, the Republic did nothing to put forth its own case in the provinces.

Almost a year after the German Revolution, Tucholsky took a tour through several provincial towns to determine what effect the revolution had. He was not encouraged by what he found. For Tucholsky it was most remarkable that the people he talked with seemed to have little conception of the changes, which had occurred around them. The small revolution had taken place without their participation; in fact, against their will. Tucholsky found that they knew nothing about the war except what the War Press Office had told them. They spoke only in the clichés concerning the heroism of WWI-General Erich Ludendorff, the humane qualities of the German soldier and German purity in general. Tucholsky found it extraordinary that the republican regime after ten months had found no time to spread its own propaganda in the provinces—the inhabitants might as well have been living in Bismarck's Germany for all they knew about the Republic:

> It is a thoroughly post-Bismarckian species which lives and breathes there: subjects of that master who, with a singular talent, alienated, undermined and destroyed German civilization. Now we have the consequences.[19]

Tucholsky further wrote that the years of authoritarian government had given the people in the provinces the strange gift of being able to think in a double fashion—privately and officially. No matter what their private opinion might have been about politics or culture, once the imperial government had spoken, official propaganda became absolute truth.

The problem that Tucholsky observed was that the Republic seemed unwilling or unable to advertise itself in the country at large. It had no educational programs; it devised no stirring themes with which to attract the youth. It was dull. In 1922, Tucholsky complained that the Republic did not appear to understand the most elementary principles of human psychology, for the reactionaries attracted thousands with their meetings, their movies and festivals. The republicans, on the other hand, used none of the modern techniques of propaganda at their disposal.[20] In addition, the Republic failed to exert its rule forcefully in reactionary provinces such as Bavaria and East Prussia. Tucholsky concluded sarcastically: "Bavaria raves in the mountains—East Prussia celebrates beside the sea—in the middle the Republic rules: *Unter den Linden*."[21]

Equally as pressing as the problem of the army was the need for reform in law enforcement and judicial procedure. The dissemination of "political justice" was one of the worst scandals of the Weimar era. Because of his legal training, Tucholsky spent much time in courts listening to trials. He maintained that an observer could tell much of the character of a country from its legal procedure. For his readers, Tucholsky constantly compared the treatment by the courts of left- and right-wing offenders. Liebknecht's followers received prison sentences of 519 years and nine months. "The Kappists were let go free."[22]

Tucholsky reported that men who revealed the hiding places of secret arms were arrested while those in possession of the weapons went free. Reactionary students who trampled the republican flag were left untouched, while tramplers of the imperial colors received three months.[23] Tucholsky came to believe that the behavior of the courts toward the right was tantamount to giving it free rein to behave as it wanted, no matter how criminal the action.

Such was certainly the effect, for during the era of political murders from 1919 through 1922, approximately 376 persons were killed for political reasons. Among them were the prominent figures Karl Liebknecht, Rosa Luxemburg, Matthias Erzberger, Walter Rathenau—the (Jewish) foreign minister of the Weimar government—and a pacifist army officer, Hans Paasche. Of the 326 murders committed by the right wing, only one was expiated by a conviction. Of the twenty-two murders perpetrated by the left wing, all but five were expiated. Seventeen leftists were convicted; of these, ten were executed.[24] No wonder Tucholsky often repeated Karl Kraus's phrase that Germany had become the land of *"Richter und Henker"* ("judges and hangmen") instead of Madame de Stael's *"Dichter und Denker"* ("poets and thinkers").

Tucholsky continued to tell the story of legal injustice throughout his career, but it was not until 1927 that he determined to expose the German judges as a type. In that year he wrote three articles for the *Weltbühne* criticizing and describing the behavior of the members of the German judiciary. His conclusions were that judges as a class were uninterested in the protection of the innocent; they were concerned only with the rights of the state. In the minds of the judiciary, the mere appearance of someone before a court made him *ipso facto* a suspicious character. And instead of rejoicing in the release of a defendant proved legally to be innocent, Tucholsky contended that the judges regarded each acquittal as a defeat of the state.[25]

There is no doubt that the judiciary of the Republic became more of a public prosecutor than the dispenser of impartial justice. Under the Empire and the Weimar Republic, German judges formed a separate class, specially educated and trained for its task. The judicial system was based upon the idea that judges should make a life profession of their work. A candidate for membership in the judiciary had to undergo a training of six years, three of which were spent in formal legal study at a university. At the end of the university course, the candidate took a difficult examination, after which he began a three-year period of practical training spent observing and assisting officials in various branches of the legal system.[26]

An assessor who desired to become a judge usually was first appointed a deputy judge and then he began a slow climb upward in the profession from district court to state court and perhaps to the national *Reichsgericht*. Judges were appointed for life. They were independent from all organs of government including the legislature—while they were constrained to observe laws, the legislative authority was not allowed to influence the administration of justice. They could not be removed from office except by court proceeding following a form established by law. No official had any right or power to influence a judge's decision. In short, the German judiciary was the most independent on earth and should have been the fairest.

However, the closed quality of the training and the very independence itself became a detriment. During the republican period, when the judiciary became a bastion of reaction, it became all but impossible to replace anti-republican judges with men more favorably disposed toward democratic forms. The apprenticeship and examination system insured that new appointees would conform to the beliefs and methods of the incumbents. In the instance of the blatantly unequal treatment in the courts of leftist and rightist partisans, the legislature was powerless to force the judiciary to change its methods.

By and large, the judges of imperial Germany performed well as administrators of equal justice, but their commitment was to the state form of the Empire, not to the "state" as a general abstraction. When the Republic was created, those same judges found it impossible to transfer their allegiance to the new organization of the state. The framers of the Weimar constitution might have done well to follow the example set in France during the beginnings of the Third Republic. For a brief period the French set aside the law prohibiting the removal of judges and thereby they attempted to insure that only men who were not hostile to the Republic remained in office.

The Weimar republican leaders, however, hesitated to remove the offending judges because the judiciary represented a link between the old and the new regimes. It provided the stability of a continuing legal foundation. In their view, the preservation of the old judiciary was a factor that gave legitimacy to the republican state form. It made the Republic seem less the product of a revolutionary seizure of power and more the result of a legal transfer of authority.[27] Yet the undermining of the principles of equal justice as well as those of democracy by the "political judiciary" did far more harm to nation and Republic than a thorough reform of the whole legal apparatus could possibly have done. Through their sabotage of republican law, the judges of the Republic undermined the very base of law, i.e., equality and due process.[28]

Tucholsky believed that in the system as it stood was no hope for reform since only upper-class lawyers were admitted to the judicial ranks. The only possibility for change was a revolution. He demanded at least that those judges with a known reactionary reputation be forced to resign. He proposed that the old judiciary be destroyed and a new one created with raised salaries to help maintain loyalty to the Republic. His warnings had as little success as his earlier campaign against the military. Just as with the officers, Tucholsky believed that the judiciary had too pure a reputation in German society. He sought, therefore, to expose the shortcomings of the judiciary as a class:

> ... If one can endure the test of nerves required to visit a court trial—with the overbearing tone of the judges, the contemptuous behavior of the defense attorneys, the prima donna role of the prosecutor and

the impudence of the clerks… The moral maxims asserted there occupy the level of the mediocre instruction given for religious confirmation… The victim of theft always bears a part of the guilt "because frivolous leaving around of his things" made the task of the thief easier… One has to hear how state prosecutors refer to a woman not as Frau Grassmann, but always as "Grassmann." One has to hear how judges address the accused, in order to grasp from what kind of source flows this stream of justice. One must see how some judges encourage police officials to treat the public as poorly as possible. One must hear the implications that resistance is not a crime, but sacrilege. One must hear the delicate or brutal influencing of witnesses by means of suggestive questions… These judges no longer consider the basis upon which they act. Small functionaries bend life around the concepts of the criminal law. It is often asked in Berlin how these men spend their free time and whether they indeed do not know what goes on in the outside world and what is the custom of the land. A glance at the clock-twelve thirty! Court's adjourned, court's adjourned.[29]

As with his earlier attack upon the Officer's Corps, Tucholsky's critique of the German judiciary had its limitations. In their attempt to characterize the "typical judge," to convey impressions of atmosphere, Tucholsky's criticisms were often vague. Tucholsky was aware of this flaw in his critical approach; nevertheless he justified it:

Collective judgments are always unjust and they should and ought to be unjust. For the critic of society has the right to regard the lowest type in a group as representative of it, for the group tolerates that type, does not exclude it and thus positively incorporates it into the group spirit.[30]

This is one of the clearest statements by Tucholsky concerning his method. The spirit of any group was defined by its lowest common denominator, a method of analysis which lacked precision. Tucholsky's generalizations are oftentimes appealing because he fought for the good causes, but they were nevertheless subject to unfairness. When describing individual cases of injustice, however, Tucholsky could be specific with shattering effect. He wrote of the many instances in which the courts allowed themselves to be used as instruments of press censorship by the military. The War Office could sue a writer or artist whose work contained antimilitary themes. The charge was usually slander.

In 1921, Tucholsky himself was called before the Criminal court in Berlin-Moabit and prosecuted for his article, "Offiziere", which appeared in August 1920. The article was an amusing, sometimes childish, piece of sarcasm, which any institution with confident leadership would have ignored. It was ironic that Tucholsky was acquitted when so many of his colleagues had been convicted on flimsier "evidence." A few lines serve to illustrate the ridiculous quality of the military's program of prosecution:

> The officers are a factor in our cultural life that is like the heavy, insoluble dregs of a decomposing body in water.... The effect of common civilian life upon the dethroned officers may provide amusing material for the poetic creator of a tragic-comedy. [they show] the resentment of old lions whose teeth and claws have been withdrawn... They are no longer able to understand the world, yet they must live in it. And now we see clearly what they have always been: unproductive, useless, superficial... [31]

Also George Grosz, whose caricatures of the German ruling class are justifiably famous, was arrested on such a charge. In 1920, the police confiscated a group of Grosz drawings that satirized the military. The authorities prosecuted Grosz and his publisher, Wieland Herzfelde, in the so-called "Da Da trial." Both men were convicted of defaming the reputation of the army. The court fined Grosz three hundred marks, Herzfelde six hundred marks—"about what it costs to murder a pacifist," Tucholsky retorted. In his article on the trial he remarked that opinion, not crime, was being punished by the courts:

> It is easy to establish that this procedure has nothing to do with justice. I have never grasped why the accused is not simply brought into the courtroom and forced to say, "My name is Grosz—major criminal." And the judge says then, "Very good. Three hundred marks fine!" That would save much time and work. But with the general education and outlook of our judges, we cannot demand that they handle those things as we expect them to. We no longer have faith in the political justice of this country. In all of these cases, a crime is not being punished. According to the best knowledge and conscience, it is a way of thinking that is being punished. [32]

In 1922, more than opinions were prosecuted when the grisly alliance of political murder, anti-Semitism and the law was exposed in the farcical trial of the assailants of Maximilian Harden. Even Tucholsky, who had few illusions, was aghast at the proceedings in Moabit in December 1922. Harden, brilliant publicist and gadfly of Wilhelmine Germany, saw his influence, but not his enemies' hatred, diminish after the war. He had been born a Jew and after Rathenau's murder, he believed his own life to be in danger. On July 3, 1922, he was so concerned that he wrote an American friend of his fears. [33]

Harden went to the post office to mail the letter and as he returned to his home in Grunewald, two assassins beat him on the head with an iron rod. Hearing Harden's cries for help, a neighbor rushed out and captured one of the would-be killers, Herbert Weichardt. Lieutenant Ankermann, the man who had actually wielded the rod, escaped. The neighbors bandaged up the sixty-year-old man's wounds and dispatched him to the hospital where surgery saved his life. After his recovery, Harden pressed charges and Germans witnessed the unusual spectacle of an intended victim living to confront his assailants. A lengthy investigation was made. Tucholsky remarked when he read the results, "The stench of a whole world is there."[34]

It was a story typical of German assassination plots of the period. Albert Wilhelm Grenz, twenty-five-year-old Oldenburg bookseller and pornographer, had hired the two assassins as a middleman for a "patriotic organization in Munich", the ultra-nationalist Organisation Consul, which also plotted Rathenau's murder. Weichardt was a country bumpkin who was involved mainly for the money. Ankermann was a disgruntled ex-officer. Grenz had hired the men in March, but they spent over three months living it up in the bars and with the prostitutes of Berlin. They continually demanded more and more money from Grenz until he was finally forced to go to Munich to seek instruction. After Rathenau was killed on June 24, 1922, Weichardt and Ankermann were spurred on by example to take their job more earnestly. Nine days later they made their attempt in Harden.

All of the details of the plot came out at the trial, but they did not have the effect which would be expected. Tucholsky reported that the proceedings began "like a friendly five o'clock tea." He then compared the treatment of Weichardt and Grenz with the methods used upon workers brought before the courts:

> In no other room of this building, be it above, below or beside-in no room has the accused experienced such treatment. I consider it praiseworthy not to treat defendants like recruits and to address them as "Mister." In Moabit, this is not the usual custom. One must see the little pieces of proletarian misery in those countless, anonymous trials, where the press is absent and about which no one cares. Only a few law students attend in order to warm themselves in the court building. One must see the bristling mustaches and the inevitable certainty with which the judgments fall as the judges and lawyers in lovely cooperation chop up their victim. "So, you no longer remember where you were that night? Well, perhaps we can refresh that memory a little!" Nothing of that could be detected in this court. Fear? That would have been unthinkable.[35]

In the end, it appeared that Harden was more on trial than they. In amazement, Tucholsky reported that the world had never before witnessed such a proceeding. The judge and the two lawyers for the defense were Jews, a fact, which may have accounted for their excessive concern for "objectivity" and "detachment." The jury was all Gentile because the lawyers claimed they wanted no prejudice to be expressed against their clients. There was never a more clear-cut case—a victim in bandages confronted his assailants. Never were so many irrelevancies brought into a courtroom. What a grim comedy it was. The defense tried to prove that the men had been incited to their actions by the unpatriotic character of Harden's writings. Weichardt said that he took part in the plot because he wanted to reconcile himself with his estranged family and he told Harden that he was sorry. Grenz was not apologetic. He said in his defense that he had never seduced a German girl and that fifty percent of the German people stood behind him in his action against Harden.[36]

The judge asked very few meaningful questions. He did not inquire how Grenz had obtained the money to make the payoff. He accepted Grenz's story that he had gone to Munich merely "to see the Alps" when the whole world knew that Munich was the headquarters of the plotters. Furthermore, Tucholsky reported that the judge interrupted a witness's testimony before she could answer, by saying: "But, of course, you don't remember."[37] In short, it was a hopeless comedy. On the third day, Harden was at least allowed to speak in his own behalf. Tucholsky called it the best speech ever made in Moabit and he wrote down his impressions of Harden's oration:

> Our last professional European was speaking. A man was speaking through whom a silenced world rose up once again. He was the representative of an almost forgotten epoch, an epoch which still believed in justice, in "fair play" [in English in the original], in morality and principle, even when it was a question of conflict of opinions. "I have always fought the Emperor, from the first day on—but I was not killed under his rule." As he spoke, he rose above his personal complaints, speaking above the heads of the petty bourgeois who surrounded him. He spoke the language of the world, not the language of this Germany... He challenged the jury at least to agree upon acquittal if they were of the opinion that annoying intellectuals—especially Jews—should be killed. He spoke of the murderous incitements in the Nationalist newspapers, of the misfortune that the parvenu in Doorn had brought about—he spoke with a warm heart and a cool mind.[38]

In addition, the defense constantly referred to Harden's Jewish origin with subtle innuendo and reference to the fact that he had changed his name.[39] In his address to the court, Harden concentrated upon the anti-Semitism expressed in the trial. He maintained that the court acted in an arbitrary fashion dangerous to the concept of law when it allowed his Jewish origin to be a part of the evidence in the trial. Harden said that it was not yet against the law to be a Jew and until then, justice should be upheld in the courts according to the existing law or else anarchy would result. Harden asked what possible hope there could be for the German future if the Germans continued their solidarity with their murderers and concluded with the prophetic statement:

> Then take care that all men who were born as Jews receive the yellow patch, and that they not be allowed to publish magazines and books. But you will not be able to control this terror! Do you not see how far it would reach? Do you intend to wait until it establishes itself in the courtroom?[40]

The speech had no effect. Each of the defendants was sentenced to one year in prison. It would have been better if Harden had not bothered to press charges. Although the trial was poorly attended and aroused little interest, it was one of the most important legal proceedings of the Weimar era. Not only did it show that the republican law against terrorism was ineffectual, but it also demonstrated that the courts were destroying the foundations of a state power based upon law, not the arbitrary will of individual men. The *Rechtsstaat*, pride of the Germans, no longer existed. Well might Tucholsky write as his closing words for 1922: "Tear away the false blindfold from this figure of Justice! We no longer have any justice."[41]

No one in power paid any attention to Tucholsky's proposals of 1922. Afterward he slowly began to lose hope that a real German republic would ever develop. In the following years he returned again and again to an analysis of the early days of the revolution trying to see how matters might have been different. He was like a man who had witnessed a disaster and was condemned by its indelible horror constantly to contemplate how it was possible for the tragedy to occur. Tucholsky's career was a series of anguished reappraisals of the past and vain outcries for reason in the future.

Tucholsky had harsh words for all of the institutions of the Republic, but his bitterest invective was directed toward the Social Democrats. They had been in his opinion the main hope for the establishment of the sense of decency. The whole succession of Socialist miscalculations, missed opportunities and blunders came to a maddening culmination for Tucholsky with the sudden death of the Socialist President of the Republic.

On February 28, 1925, Friedrich Ebert died of appendicitis. No other man in public office had been the object of so much vilification by the ultra-nationalist press. The Nationalists accused him of activities extending from sexual perversion to treason. Ebert filed suit for libel in the case of the latter accusation and in order to pursue the trial he postponed the abdominal surgery necessary to alleviate his illness. The court sentenced the accused to three months in prison, but incredibly enough, the judge stated that the President of the Republic had technically committed treason by his participation in the Socialists' strikes in 1918. The judge continued that from a moral or historical standpoint, Ebert was not guilty, but technically he had betrayed the government. Ebert had begun prosecution and ended in being the real defendant.

Five days before Ebert died, Noske paid him a visit and, shocked by his physical condition, urged him to go away for a rest. Ebert's reply was a pathetic comment upon the low esteem in which the presidential office was held:

> I cannot go away. My honor is at stake. Or rather the honor of the head of state. Do you know what is happening today? In the Barmat Committee they want to establish today whether I have had sexual relations with one of my office secretaries. What I haven't suffered under this pressure! I've never shown it and I've said even less, but I can go on no longer. They slander me like a criminal. That they aren't ashamed of their moralistic slime—they who proclaim the spiritual and moral revival of Germany—that is my pain. The filth that surrounds me! Disgusting![42]

Tucholsky hated the despicable accusations of the super-patriots, but he felt no sympathy for Ebert who he believed had brought his misery upon himself through toleration of the reactionaries. Tucholsky had never approved of Ebert's methods, but for a while after the President's death, Tucholsky held his peace. He devoted only a few paragraphs to Ebert in which he accused him of being a traitor to the very working class he had been chosen to represent. But in January 1926 he attacked Ebert in one of the bitterest polemics he ever wrote. Entitled "Die Ebert Legende" ("The Ebert Myth"), the piece was a reply to a defense of Ebert which appeared in the *Weltbühne* and which was written by one of the President's former press agents. In his article, Tucholsky presented a catalogue of all of the frustrations, disappointments and dashed hopes of the left-wing intellectuals.[43]

In "Die Ebert Legende," Tucholsky's main point was that the leftist extremists had posed no real threat in 1918. He maintained that at the end of the war, there had existed a democratic spirit of reform in Germany that had not been Bolshevist. In fact, the workers themselves had possessed a bourgeois outlook and had been in any event powerless to effect a program of socialization. But Ebert, the "traitor," had stifled the latent democratic spirit by his actions; he had missed all of the incomparable opportunities presented on November 9. Tucholsky maintained that in 1919, no one would have wondered at vast changes. The estate owners had expected expropriation; judges had awaited dismissal. But nothing had happened because Ebert "insanely" had restored to life precisely those same burdens under whose weight the state had first collapsed. Tucholsky declared false the argument that Ebert had had no choice because a Communist revolution had been imminent. Out of a "groundless fear," therefore, Ebert had missed the chance to implement the most simple of reforms. He had insured the triumph of reaction:

> It is untrue when maintained that the ninth of November could provide no opportunity for decision. A decision was made and resulted in the complete triumph of German reaction. And that is Ebert's guilt, which no one can wash away.

Tucholsky recounted all of the events, which most shocked the intellectual left. In the name of "order," the Social Democrats had murdered the workers whose welfare they had been pledged to defend. As a result, under Socialist auspices, the right wing enjoyed an influence greater than under the monarchy. To support this contention, Tucholsky pointed out that the Emperor would not have dared to violate the rights of the individual states as had the Republic in 1923 when its troops marched into Saxony and Thuringia and unseated the legally elected Communist governments there. Never under the monarchy had the lives of the opposition been in so much danger as under the Republic. And when the Socialists had the opportunity to gain the allegiance of the common soldiers as well as of the workers: "Herr Scheidemann at the Brandenburg gate flattered the lowest movie-house instincts of the returning men. He greeted them as 'undefeated.' In truth, they were as defeated as he was."

Tucholsky concluded the "Ebert Legende" by saying that the sad truth was that the Socialists were ashamed of their role in the revolution. They should have been proud to bear the title of "treason" when given by the Nationalists. Little had really been expected of the Socialists in 1918, but they had failed to accomplish even the most minor reforms:

> The men of November did not accomplish what could have been accomplished: a reform of all branches of the state, abolition of militarism, democratic education of the youth and, above all—the support of a new spiritual atmosphere which was in its beginnings. Instead, they destroyed it… Do we have class justice? Yes or No? Do we have an anti-republican army? Yes or No? Do we have reactionary despotism? Do we have shameful education in the universities?… Something from the French Revolution still exists today: its victory. Something from Ebert still exists today: his defeat, his lack of courage, his betrayal of comrades…

This is one of the bitterest examples of left-wing disillusion with Social Democracy. But in his bitterness, Tucholsky's judgment became somewhat clouded and subject to oversimplification. He was absolutely unable to sympathize with the idea that the Socialists had faced a real dilemma at the end of the war. On the other hand, Tucholsky was correct in saying that a genuine willingness to try democracy existed in Germany in 1918. Although their expectations might be different, both the workers and the middle class had looked to the Republic for the fulfillment of their hopes for the future.[44]

But the Socialists failed to capitalize upon this support. They turned instead to the powers of the old order and followed a policy based upon force and repression. By their cooperation with the generals, by their support of the Free Corps, by their timid behavior vis-à-vis the remnants of the old regime, the Socialists had made the implementation of the ideals of bourgeois democracy highly improbable. Tucholsky correctly judged that the majority of workers were not extreme in political outlook and thus the Socialists missed the chance for which they had long been waiting. In Tucholsky's eyes Ebert had betrayed the hopes of fifty years of German Social Democracy.

When, however, Tucholsky said that leftist extremism had posed no threat, he was writing eight years after the fact. When Ebert and his colleagues in January 1919 watched two hundred thousand armed men in the Berlin streets, the threat seemed real enough. It is true that the Social Democrats tragically overestimated the strength of the Spartacists, but they were terrified by the model of the October Revolution in Russia. Ebert believed he was the Kerensky of the German Revolution— Alexander Kerensky, an early, moderate minister of Soviet Russia was forced into exile by the Bolsheviks in 1917— and Ebert was determined not to suffer a similar fate.[45]

One of the great weaknesses of Tucholsky's polemic was its ambiguity and inconsistency when speaking of the German masses. He wrote of the "spirit of democratic reform" which existed in 1918, but in other writings he lamented the hopeless reaction that characterized people in the provinces.[46] Tucholsky thus exaggerated and underestimated the revolutionary fervor of the German masses at large. The behavior of the people in 1918 led Tucholsky to believe they had possessed a genuinely revolutionary outlook, but their acceptance of the "meager" results of the revolution, as exemplified in the elections to the National Assembly, led Tucholsky to call them "reactionary." Tucholsky could not see that most Germans in 1918 believed that a true "social revolution" had taken place. The masses were not "revolutionary," they were war weary and they wanted the society to be stabilized as quickly as possible. The Social Democrats thus merely bowed to majority will when they refused to carry out a full program of political, social and economic revolution. This was the crux of the Social Democratic problem.

The greatest weakness of the Socialists was that they were good middle-class Democrats. The SPD had become a parliamentary party, bourgeois in spirit and thoroughly patriotic in its commitment to the German national state.

This was inevitable as Socialist leaders became professional parliamentary politicians, associating more with other politicians than they did with workers, as R. N. Hunt had pointed it out in the 1960s:

> Even before the Weimar period the party leadership was completely *verbürgerlicht* in the objective sense. This had come about in two ways: through the influx of middle-class elements into positions of importance and through the social ascent of originally proletarian leaders. The percentage of SPD Reichstag fraction members with middle-class backgrounds increased from sixteen percent in 1903, to thirty-four percent in 1912, to thirty-five percent by 1930. Thus in our period the proportion of such leaders had leveled off at about one-third. But the remaining two thirds, who had working-class origins, could no longer be called proletarians for they had all, almost without exception, taken salaried white-collar positions of one sort or another.[47]

The Socialists had become dedicated to an evolutionary program of reform to be achieved within the context of the existing society. Much as they might pay lip service to Marxism, they were embarrassed by revolution. When 1918 came, the Social Democrats were as horrified by the defeat as anyone else. They did not see the armistice as the defeat of Prussian militarism. On the contrary, they regarded it as the defeat of the nation to which they belonged. The SPD in 1918 approached being than merely a nineteenth-century liberal, nationalist party, than a nineteenth century Marxist, internationalist party. Tucholsky could not forgive them for this devotion to the state in general; he was even more horrified by their support of the Wilhelmine state in particular.

Rather unimaginatively, the Socialist leaders had believed that 1918 presented them with only two alternatives; the maintenance of the society essentially as it was or Bolshevism. In choosing the former, they preserved their old enemies without maintaining the restraints that a politically tolerant monarchy had placed upon those enemies. Paradoxically, William had been the emperor of the Socialists as well as of the Junkers and there was thus a kind of political neutrality on the part of the monarchy. In 1918, the SPD was unable to assure for itself the same protection, which the theoretically hostile monarchy had given it.

For Tucholsky the choice that had faced the Social Democrats in 1918 was broader. He believed the alternatives were reaction, Bolshevism or middle-class democracy: That he [Ebert] was unable to accomplish a revolution of the fourth estate may have been his historical misfortune. That he did not create a revolution of the third is his guilt.[48]

Yet the Socialists believed that middle-class democracy had been established and their actions after November 9 were designed to preserve it. They came to believe that the Republic which they had established would provide the best means whereby true social justice could be realized. This is illustrated by a statement in the Heidelberg Program of 1925: "The democratic republic is the most favorable basis for the struggle of the working class for liberation, and thereby for the realization of socialism. Therefore the Social Democratic Party guards the Republic and seeks to perfect it."[49]

But it was astonishing to Tucholsky that they could believe the November revolution had changed anything. In his opposition to the Socialists, Tucholsky rejected the one party that was the continuing hope of democracy and his position appears to have become merely "negative." Tucholsky himself was not unaware of the difficulties of his opposition. In 1926, Hermann Schützinger wrote rather spitefully in the *Berliner Volkszeitung* that the writers of the *Weltbühne* seemed to have little practical effect. He asked what official recognition the left intellectuals had received; which members of the Reichstag represented them. In his answer to Schützinger, Tucholsky stated his conception of his negative, politically "homeless" role—the "sowing of seeds":

> "Upheavals have always so begun—with almost unnoticed conventicle meetings. Everything that has later become a party was at first a sect. We are sowing seeds. One of them will certainly sprout.[50]

What Tucholsky did not add is that for every sect which becomes a party, there are a thousand others which are either so exclusive or strike so few responsive chords within the society that they disappear without a whimper. That was precisely what the left intellectuals formed—a sect, which the society at large greeted either with indifference or hostility. Not only were those seeds sown on infertile ground, but there were few gardeners to tend the feeble sproutlings. But that did not mean that Tucholsky should either have given up the struggle or compromised his principles. He saw no possible victory for democracy or "decency" as long as the SPD tolerated the influence of the old, corrupt forces. Therefore opposition to both the Socialists and the right-wing parties was the only answer for Tucholsky.

NOTES

1 Kurt Tucholsky, "Militaria," G.W., I, 590.
2 Kurt Tucholsky, "Kapp-Lüttwitz," G.W., I, 614; I.W., *Die Weltbühne*, XVI/12-14 (March 25, 1920), 357.
3 Kurt Tucholsky, "Militärbilanz," G.W., I, 630; I.W., *Die Weltbühne*, XVI/17 (April 22, 1920), 464.
4 Kurt Tucholsky, "Kapp-Lüttwitz," G.W., I, 616.
5 The Baltic campaigns of the Free Corps in 1919 are confusing, for they were promoted by both the victorious Allies and by German reactionary interests. The victors hoped to use the Germans against the Bolsheviks and the German reactionaries hoped to gain Baltic territory as a permanent German possession. In the end, the Free Corps adventurers in the Baltic were disastrously defeated by the Latvians and the returning embittered volunteers became for a time the core of the anti-republican movement. See Robert G. L. Waite, *Vanguard of Nazism: The Free Corps Movement in Postwar Germany 1918-1923* (Harvard, 1952), pp. 94-139.
6 Kurt Tucholsky, "Militärbilanz," G.W., I, 634.
7 Kurt Tucholsky, "Die zufällige Republik," G.W., I, 994; I.W., *Die Weltbühne*, XVIII/28 (July 13, 1922), 25, and "Militärbilanz," G.W., I, 633. A post-war study, F. L. Carsten, *The Reichswehr and Politics, 1918 to 1933* (New York, 1966) supports Tucholsky's judgment that the army was too neutral and thus contributed to the Republic's instability.
8 Kurt Tucholsky, "Kapp-Lüttwitz," G.W., I, 618f.
9 Kurt Tucholsky, "Der trockene Putsch," G.W., I, 1001; I.W., *Freiheit* (Berlin, July 16, 1922), and: "Was wäre, wenn... ?" G.W., I, 976; K.T., *Die Weltbühne*, XVII/25 (June 22, 1922), 615.
10 Kurt Tucholsky, "Die zufällige Republik," G.W., I, 996.
11 Ibid., 997.
12 Jean F. Neurohr, *Der Mythos vom Dritten Reich* (Stuttgart, 1957), p. 56.
13 Friedrich von Rabenau, *Seeckt—aus seinem Leben 1918 bis 1936* (Berlin, 1945), pp. 341-42.
14 Franz Neumann, *Behemoth, the Structure and Practice of National Socialism* (New York, 1942), pp. 77-80, 370
15 Karl Dietrich Bracher, *Die Entstehung der Weimarer Republik* (Hannover, 1963), p. 16, 56; and *Die Auflösung der Weimarer Republik* (Stuttgart, 1955), pp. 184-91.
16 Kurt Tucholsky, "Preussische Studenten," G.W., I, 410; I.W., *Die Weltbühne*, XV/20 (May 8, 1919), pp. 407f. and *passim*.
17 See Arnold Brecht, *Federalism and Regionalism in Germany, the Division of Prussia* (New York, 1945).
18 Kurt Tucholsky, "Reisende, meidet Bayern," G.W., I, 784; I.W., *Die Weltbühne*, XVII/4 (January 27, 1921), 114. And G.W., I, 1144; I.W., *Die Weltbühne*, XX/6 (Feb. 7, 1924), 164.
19 Kurt Tucholsky, "Eindrücke von einer Reise," G.W., I, 496; I.W., *Die Weltbühne*, XV/43 (October 16, 1919), 473.
20 Kurt Tucholsky, "Monarchie und Republik," G.W., I, 970; I.W., *Die Weltbühne*, XVIII/24 (June 15, 1922), 609.
21 Kurt Tucholsky, "Die Geschäftsreisenden," G.W ., I, 968; I.W., *Die Welt am Montag* (Berlin, June 12, 1922).

22   Kurt Tucholsky, "Das Buch von der deutschen Schande," G.W., I, 823; I.W., *Die Weltbühne*, XVII/36 (Sept. 8, 1921) , 237.

23   Kurt Tucholsk:y, "Gegen die Arbeiter? Allemal- !" G.W., I, 868; I.W., *Die Welt am Montag* (Berlin, Dec. 5, 1921).

24   For statistics, see the various publications by E. J. Gumbel, of which his magazine, *Die Menschenrechte*, and his book, *Vier Jahre politischer Mord* (Berlin, 1922), are the most fruitful. For many of the same statistics, see the briefer post-war work, *Vom Fememord zur Reichskanzlei* (Heidelberg, 1961), especially pp. 45-46.
The numbers for political murder from 1919-1922 by right-wing perpetrators were: accidentally killed (184); arbitrarily shot (73); shot while fleeing (45); alleged breaking of martial law (37); alleged self-defense (9); lynched in prison or transit (5); alleged suicide (1); **altogether 354**. The numbers for political murder from 1919-1922 by left-wing perpetrators were: shot out of reprisal (10); arbitrarily shot (8); alleged breaking of martial law (3); alleged self-defense (1); **altogether: 22**.

25   Kurt Tucholsky, "Deutsche Richter," G.W., II, 771-783; I.W., *Die Weltbühne*, XXIII/15, 16, 17 (April 12, 19, 26, 1927), 581, 619, 663, 773-776.

26   See Frederick Blachly and Mirian E. Oatman, *The Government and Administration of Germany* (Baltimore, 1928), pp. 436f. for a complete description of the legal apprenticeship.

27   Of course, the idea of "legal transfer" was aided by the fact that Ebert had been appointed Chancellor of the Empire by Max von Baden shortly before the outbreak of revolution. Thus, the last Chancellor of the Imperial Reich and the first President of the Republic were one and the same person. See Bracher, *Die Auflösung*, pp. 15-21.

28   The present Federal Republic, however, has attempted to deal with those former Nazi judges who continue in the courts. The problem is how to oust the offending men without violating the independence and sanctity of the judiciary. Any tampering with the judicial branch of government by the legislature would set a dangerous precedent. The government has managed to invent an ingenious solution: the retirement age has been lowered to the age of the youngest undesirable judge and pressure placed upon all of the men with questionable backgrounds to resign with full pensions.

29   Kurt Tucholsky, "Deutsche Richter," G.W., II, 775f.

30   Ibid., G.W., II, 773.

31   Kurt Tucholsky, "Offiziere", (G.W., I, 721-724),

32   Kurt Tucholsky, "Dada-Prozess," G.W., I, 801; I.W., *Die Weltbühne*, XVII/17 (April 28, 1921), 454, 802

33   Harry F. Young, *Maximilian Harden, Censor Germaniae, the Critic in Opposition from Bismarck to the Rise of Nazism* (The Hague, 1959), p. 246.

34   Kurt Tucholsky, "Prozess Harden," G.W., I, 1070; K.T., *Die Weltbühne*, XVIII/51 (Dec. 21, 1922), 638.

35   Ibid, G.W., I, 1073, 1075

36   Ibid, G.W., I, 1077.

37   Ibid., G.W., I, 1074.

38   Ibid, G.W., I, 1074. The "Parvenue in Doorn" was Emperor Wilhelm II who had fled to Doorn in the Netherlands after World War I.

39   Harden was often referred to in rightist journals as "the Jew, Isidor." Isidor had never been his name; he was born as Felix Ernst Witkowski.

40   Quoted by Young, p. 254.

41   Kurt Tucholsky, "Prozess Harden," G.W., I, 1078.

42 Max Peters, *Friedrich Ebert, sein Werden und Wirken* (Berlin, Grunewald, 1954), p. 163. The Barmat Committee was appointed to investigate the "Barmat Scandal" of 1923. Barmat was a wholesale merchant of questionable character who directly after the war had brought large quantities of food from Holland to starvation-wracked Germany. He made a large amount of money, but his action was, nevertheless, of service. Therefore, when he asked for an interview with President Ebert, it was granted without question. But Barmat's real purpose was to become friendly with Ebert's office staff. Thereafter, he often used the government's official telephones to conduct shady business deals abroad. When Barmat was caught dealing in food profiteering and was arrested, the scandal broke. The rightist press accused Ebert of having connections with Barmat and of sharing profits from his deals. Ebert was innocent, but the trials and investigations were carried on for years and acted as a continuing source of discredit to the presidency.

43 All following quotes from: Kurt Tucholsky, "Die Ebert-Legende," G.W., II, 321; I.W., *Die Weltbühne*, :X:XII/2 (January 12, 1926), 52, 322ff. See also: "Abreißkalender," G.W., II, 287; I.W., *Die Weltbühne*, XXI/50 (December 15, 1925), 891.

44 Klemens von Klemperer, *Germany's New Conservatism, Its History and Dilemma in the Twentieth Century* (Princeton, 1957), p. 72. A more careful examination of the early years after the revolution indicates that, at that time, the Republic served to focus the hopes of the majority of Germans. While the workers, for their part, expected a millennium through socialization, large segments of the middle classes emerged from the war and revolution looking to the Republic for the reestablishment of national greatness and unity as well as for the setting up of a new social order. The historian, therefore, cannot maintain that the Republic was doomed by the lack of backing by the populace.

45 Richard N. Hunt, *German Social Democracy, 1918-1933* (New Haven, 1964), pp. 29f.

46 Kurt Tucholsky, "In der Provinz," G.W., I, 647; I.W., *Freiheit* (May 16, 1920).

47 R. N. Hunt, *German Social Democracy, 1918-1933* (New Haven, 1964), pp. 142-43). Angress describes how also the Spartacists overestimated the revolutionary fervor of the masses: "The expectations of Luxemburg and her associates, implicit in the demands they set forth, revealed the curious absence of a sense of reality and of proportion. They chose to ignore the true state of mind of the masses to whom they appealed, an attitude which was to become a chronic feature of German Communism. They failed to appreciate the fact that the German people in 1918 were convinced that the revolution had already established a new order of society, and that the people, after four years of war which had ended in defeat, were tired of strife and chaos. In; Werner T. Angress, *Stillborn Revolution, the Communist Bid for Power in Germany, 1921-23* (Princeton, 1963). The Spartacist Program was published in: *Die Rote Fahne*, No. 29, December 14, 1919, pp. 17f.

48 Kurt Tucholsky, "Die Ebert-Legende," G.W., II, 322.

49 R. N. Hunt, German Social Democracy, 1918-1933, p. 33.

50 Kurt Tucholsky, "Was brauchen wir?" G.W., II, 351; K.T., *Die Weltbühne*, XXII/7 (February 16, 1926), 239.

Karl Liebknecht and Rosa Luxemburg, two Communist leaders who were killed by rightwingers. Above is Luxemburg speaking to sailors in 1918; below is a poster by Army Veterans calling for their murder.

Arbeiter, Bürger!

Das Vaterland ist dem Untergang nahe.

Rettet es!

Es wird nicht bedroht von außen, sondern von innen:

Von der Spartakusgruppe.

Schlagt ihre Führer tot!
Tötet Liebknecht!

Dann werdet ihr Frieden, Arbeit und Brot haben!

Die Frontsoldaten

VI.

THE RISE AND FALL OF THE COMMUNISTS

For Tucholsky, the Communists at the other extreme of the leftist political spectrum offered as little hope of reform as the Socialists. There was literally no organized political faction or party which Tucholsky believed himself able to join. And certainly nothing better illustrates both Tucholsky's ideological convictions and his political dilemma than his relationship with Communism. Tucholsky was never a member of the Communist Party and he did not describe himself as a Communist, but the issue is confused both by Tucholsky's frequent use of Marxist terminology and by the accusations of his right-wing enemies. Toward the end of his career, he wrote many poems and essays for Communist journals and his famous book, *Deutschland, Deutschland über Alles*, was published by a Communist house. Tucholsky often wrote that the only hope for Germany lay in a working class movement. As the crisis in German political life deepened, the KPD (Communist Party) appeared to Tucholsky to be the only party which represented the true interests of the worker. Yet, as most of the other members of the intellectual left who flirted with Communism, Tucholsky was unable to join the party. The reasons for Tucholsky's simultaneous acceptance and rejection of the Communists go far in explaining why the intellectual left could not find a political home in the Weimar Republic. Of all of the parties on the left, Tucholsky and his friends stood closest to the Communist, yet because of its doctrinaire dogmatism, they were unable to find in that movement the solutions which they sought.

Social reformers often postulate or select an ideal man who either symbolizes or will fulfill the hope for a changed society. For some, it has been the peasant; for others, a member of a racial or ethnic minority. For Tucholsky, it was the worker. In his mind, the working class formed the only group which had consistently resisted the tyranny of the Empire and in turn had been exploited by it. The worker provided the only possible foundation for a democratic order. With these ideas, Tucholsky became a part of the "prolcult" of the twenties, a part of that group of intellectuals who constantly sang the praises of the downtrodden proletariat. Because they appeared to compose that part of the society that suffered most from the inflation, civil disturbances and international incidents such as the Franco-Belgian occupation of the Ruhr, the workers assumed a dignity and strength in the eyes of the leftist intelligentsia. As one writer has phrased it: "It was Rousseau's Noble Savage all over again, only in a different setting."[1] For example, in 1929 Tucholsky wrote that the middle class and the party functionaries might reject the intellectuals, but the workers accepted them. Although he resisted the temptation to say "the good workers," his working class, nevertheless, seemed almost too pure as opposed to the self-seeking directors:

> We are attacked by the bourgeoisie as "Bolsheviks." On the other hand, we are distrusted by the functionaries of the worker parties. But the workers have never distrusted us as long as we behave in a retiring and sympathizing fashion. Those who work along and do not talk too big have always been welcome to the workers.[2]

One of the reasons for Tucholsky's idealization of the worker may have been some vague guilt over his own middle-class origin. Tucholsky was the son of a wealthy merchant and banker. In his youth, he had the advantages of education and a gay [but straight!] bohemian period made possible by his financial independence. In 1929, Tucholsky wrote an article for *Deutschland, Deutschland über Alles* entitled "Das Volk" in which he clearly expressed an almost painful awareness of the differences between himself and the worker. Tucholsky's father had provided the money, which insured his son's success, but the worker could succeed only through "heroic" effort:

> In order to be able to write this picture book the following conditions are necessary. I must be well fed. I must have a roof over my head. I must have the leisure and time to look at the pictures, which the publisher has given me. In my youth, my father must have given me the money to learn more than my ABC's and the multiplication table—that is the most necessary. Occasionally a heroic proletarian, through gigantic exertions, is able to break through these barriers. In spite of hunger, cold and half-education, he is able to achieve, through nightly work and severe willpower, what the merchant's son accomplishes much more easily.[3]

This is clearly a mild statement of Tucholsky's uneasiness about the advantages that he enjoyed as a youth. Surely the "merchant's son" is a reference to himself.

Tucholsky believed that background distinguished between workers and others. The sufferings and privations of the working class could not be experienced vicariously. They had to be lived. Tucholsky thus never styled himself as an adopted son of the proletariat. He believed his middle-class origin limited his role in the working-class movement to that of a sympathetic helper. He looked upon himself as an intellectual with a bourgeois background who could offer advice, but not lead. Unless the intellectuals were willing to offer personal sacrifices by mounting the barricades, Tucholsky maintained he could not hold a leadership position in a worker party.[4]

Tucholsky always distinguished between the working class and the organizations that represented it. In other words, he did not believe the aims of the Communist Party always to be synonymous with the best interests of the proletariat. Tucholsky, in fact, never regarded left-wing extremism as the answer to the needs of the workers. His political position is best revealed by the fact that the only party he ever joined was the Independent Socialist. He believed the Independents offered the best way between the hesitant Majority Socialists and the violent Spartacists. But his tenure with the Independents was brief, lasting only two years. In 1920, Tucholsky joined the USPD mainly because it opposed the Majority Socialists' dealings with the old military. He was not attracted to the radicalism of the Communists and he was repelled by what he believed to be the betrayal of the workers by the SPD. Therefore when the Independents officially reunited with the SPD in 1922, Tucholsky found himself unable to accept the principles of either the Communists or the Socialists and he joined no political party thereafter. However he looked upon the former with more sympathy than the latter.

Tucholsky was generally disappointed in the leadership that the radical left gave the workers. To be sure he was horrified by the killing of Spartacists in January 1919 and the torture of Karl Liebknecht and Rosa Luxemburg by right-wing Freicorps in the streets of Berlin, but he was also just as horrified by the senseless sacrifice of workers in the streets. He was disturbed that the workers' cause had provided the occasion for mob violence and he believed the riots had occurred in part because of poor leadership. Actually the KPD was more the victim than the cause of the disturbances, for the riots grew spontaneously out of street brawls, which the Communist leaders were unable to control.[5] The decision by Luxemburg and her cohorts to lend editorial support to the riots in the *Rote Fahne* made the chief blame fall upon the Communists.

The loss of Luxemburg's leadership was a terrible blow for the KPD. Her successors were by and large mediocre. After her death, the party began to shed its idealism and trust in the masses and give way to an irresponsible putschism.[6] By 1920, Tucholsky became so disgusted with the young extremists who styled themselves as leaders of the proletariat that he wrote a scathing attack upon them. Entitled "Führer?" ("Leaders?"), it was probably the strongest statement he ever made against the far left. He opened the article by asking who were the thin, nervous, "cheese-white" super-radicals found in all organizations? He maintained that such young persons looked upon themselves as the culmination of the historical process and found a thrill in their power to convince the masses:

> It is monstrously inexpensive to step before a gathering and thunder away that after today there must be a complete revolution in the form of society, of love, of civilization, of pacifism and a soviet dictatorship must be established. Bravo, bravo! For whoever is hungry and has a torn shirt sees salvation in everything and is inclined to believe. This radicalism is for sale everywhere.[7]

Tucholsky remarked that the real work always began after such speakers left the platform. It seemed that everyone wanted to be a leader, but no one wanted to help. Tucholsky expressed his distrust of such reformers:

> There are too many architects and too few plasterers... I must say that I have a strong distrust of these countless world reformers who want to destroy cosmic structures, but are incapable of placing a stamp on a letter.[8]

The above statement may at first appear confusing in the light of Tucholsky's constant call for revolution and change. Upon closer investigation, however, it clarifies the matter. Tucholsky clearly wanted nothing to do with theories of violence or of dictatorship by any group. As we have seen earlier, "revolution" for Tucholsky meant the establishment of true parliamentary democracy and the full provision for social welfare. He believed that the Communists sometimes betrayed those goals more than they fulfilled them, for he constantly complained about the poor leadership of the KPD.

In 1925, Tucholsky wrote, "If only the KPD had leaders, then every one of the 365 days next year would be a commemoration day."[9] Understandably, he complained, for seldom has a party been less able to sense the proper moment for action or for refraining from action. Between 1918 and 1923, the Communists attempted to seize power four times and each time they failed. The great problem of the Communists was their inability to recognize their lack of popularity with the workers. They continued to build upon grandiose dreams of a mass following and spontaneous revolution. Instead of making them more realistic, their defeats only caused the Communists to withdraw further into their sectarianism and their comforting historical explanations that the future insured their inevitable triumph. In addition, the party was weakened by the insistence upon ideological conformity. The Spartacists period's free exchange of ideas gave way to rigid, official directives whose truth could not be questioned. This is not to say that policies did not change, on the contrary, they changed frequently. Each alteration was followed by the expulsion of those connected with the old line. The new line then became absolute truth.[10] Expulsion from the party became so frequent that in 1932, Tucholsky was led to say in one of his *Schnipsel* short texts: "KPD. 'Too bad that you aren't in the party—if you were, we would be able to expel you.'"[11] Such a process did not help to create the sense of proportion and flexibility needed for astute political decisions.

The causes of the Communist misjudgment lay in Moscow as much as in Berlin. Beginning informally under Lenin and Trotsky and becoming formal under Stalin, the policies and purposes of the KPD were dictated by the Executive Committee of the Communist International. It soon became apparent to all but the German Communists that the Comintern's decisions served Russian national interests more than those of the KPD. The abruptly changing courses of action were often reflections of the changing fortunes of power factions in Russia. For all intents and purposes, the German Communist Party lost all independence and became the puppet of Stalin and the Comintern.[12]

With increasing apprehension, Tucholsky watched the slavish conformity to Moscow's directives. In 1928, he wrote that the KPD needed intellectual leaders who did not think that Germany was called Russia and who had some insight into actual German conditions. After the senseless May Day riots in 1929 in which twenty-five people were killed, Tucholsky wrote:

> I have always considered it correct and good that the German workers receive money and instructions from Moscow. It is regrettable that of recent these instructions have been lamentably poor.[13]

Most of Tucholsky's criticisms of the follies of the KPD leadership were hesitant and usually ended with an expression of hope that the future would be better. There was nothing resembling the bitter vicious attacks that he made upon the Social Democrats. It was almost as though Tucholsky simply could not bring himself to attack the only party that he believed offered any good promise. In 1928 and 1929 he seemed almost to plead with the party to become more flexible and, indeed, to accept the good services of well-wishers such as himself. In 1928, he wrote:

> The German Communists are unable to see the very real aid that the intellectuals could give them. They make strange selections, for they are ridden with poor, doddering, fourth-rate intellectuals... In most cases, the motive for their behavior is a well-grounded fear of competition.[14]

Tucholsky asked if the KPD intended to emulate the Social Democrats and sink into mediocrity by excluding the best minds? He ended the article with a plea to the KPD to use the talents of men like himself—talents, which were "standing idle."

The Communists attacked Tucholsky and his colleagues on the *Weltbühne* staff because they refused to join the party, because they refused to subscribe to the line from Moscow. The leftist intellectuals were denounced as tools of the right wing and as bourgeois traitors. These accusations pained Tucholsky. In January 1929, writing for the Communist journal, *Front*, he attempted to define the proper role of the leftist intellectuals in the proletarian cause and justify their position outside of the party. He first expressed his conviction that only through a free exchange of ideas could truth be reached:

> The *Weltbühne* is a tribune in which the whole of the German left, in the broadest sense of the term, has a voice. From our coworkers, we demand clarity, personal cleanliness and good style. Whether or not this is a. correct principle is another question, but it was the foundation of this journal when I assumed control of it after the death of my teacher, Siegfried Jacobsohn. And it was still so when I handed it over to Carl von Ossietzky, who has not departed a finger's breadth from this direction. The *Weltbühne* consciously renounces any kind of strict dogma; we are interested in discussion.[15]

Tucholsky then made one of the clearest statements of the frustrating inability of the leftist intellectuals to find a political home. He wrote that in 1913, the *Weltbühne* had stood "somewhat left of the Socialists." When the revolution broke out, it was unable to assume a leading role because it had no definite program. But it was precisely this lack of definition that Tucholsky believed gave the leftist intellectuals their greatest value. Because they were not party leaders, because they were not party members, they did not have to restrict themselves to the discipline of the party. They could be more objective and thus, through their discussions and free exchange of views, offer the leaders a choice of alternatives. He wrote, "We have never pretended to be the leaders of the working class." The intellectuals could only fill the function of "sympathetic helpers" who make their insight and intelligence available to the proletarian cause.

As in 1928, Tucholsky asked why the party intellectuals exhibited such a distrust of him and his colleagues? Why did they engage in the insufferable "snobbery of the calloused band" when none of them actually worked in factories? He warned that if the "small functionaries" of the KPD continued in their distrust, they would lose the sympathy of those members of the intellectual left who were lukewarm to the workers' struggle. Tucholsky complained that the party made his position difficult and asserted that the intellectual atmosphere of the party stifled originality and truth:

> There must be discipline, but in actuality, the intellectual enjoys greater freedom in the bourgeois journals—within their framework—than he does in the working-class press.

Again Tucholsky concluded by asking the KPD to accept the aid of the intellectual left in serving a common goal.

The Communists would, of course, have no dealings with Tucholsky and his ideas of "free discussion." The answer to Tucholsky's plea for cooperation was given in the very next issue of the Front. The article, signed "Carolus," was most likely written by the magazine's editor, Hans Conrad. He tried to emulate Tucholsky's sharp, incisive polemical style, but instead was brutal and vulgar:

> Tucholsky and the people around him à la Hiller "have never pretended to be the leaders of the working class." So writes that Tucholsky who with his peppery language smashes the ugly faces of the reactionaries with their own filth. With brutal derision, he is the one who has exposed the shameful role of Social Democracy, who calls the workers to the *Internationale*. That is leadership, leadership in a definite direction. And thus the question arises—why does Kurt T. write? Does he consciously place his ability at the disposal of the working class in the struggle for the proletarian revolution? If yes—he is consciously trying to lead?
> But that is not of utmost importance. It is interesting that Tucholsky speaks of worker parties—or of a worker party without having the courage to express openly what he stands for in his upright, but typically intellectual works: there is only one way for the liberation of the working class—the proletarian revolution and it is being organized only by the KPD! Therefore, there is today only one worker party, and to work for the proletarian revolution means nothing other than being closely bound to the KPD!... We are not Social Democrats. We are Bolsheviks and we say with Marx: "Who is not for us is against us!" Even to Kurt Tucholsky.
> "This side or that side of the barricades?" That is the question today. And on this side of the barricade stands the revolutionary working class led only by the KPD. We revolutionary proletarians want a meaningful, unswerving answer from your side, Kurt Tucholsky.[16]

Tucholsky and Conrad were, of course, worlds apart. It was intransigence and single-mindedness such as that expressed by Conrad that finally proved to be the undoing of the Communists after 1930. In the face of all evidence to the contrary, the KPD was convinced that it was the true mass party. Its leaders held to the belief that the true enemies of the working class were the Socialists, not the Nazis. With help from Moscow, the KPD leaders somehow convinced themselves that a fascist government was necessary before the proletarian revolution could take place. They maintained that once Hitler was in power and the Social Democrats out of the way, the masses would rally to the Communists and effect the revolution. To support this contention, they said that history assured their eventual triumph. Alan Bullock comments concerning the KPD's belief in historical inevitability: "Rarely has the distorting effect of a determinist philosophy of history on the political judgment of a party been more clearly demonstrated."[177] In spite of Socialist pleading for cooperation, the KPD voted with the Nazis in the Reichstag and Prussian Landtag and aided in the destruction of democracy. When Hitler assumed power, the KPD was swept away with hardly a whimper.

After 1929, Tucholsky gradually lost faith in the efficacy of the Communist Party, but he did not write any substantial criticism until after the Nazi triumph. In a letter to the leftist writer Heinz Pol written on April 20, 1933, Tucholsky expressed his disgust at the stupidity of the KPD:

> From front to rear, the KPD was stupid in Germany. It did not understand its own followers and it certainly did not have the masses behind it. And how did Moscow behave when things went badly? After an alliance with the Reichswehr, only a cold shoulder because something wasn't "correct"? I can't go along with that. I do not need to write to you that I have not joined a textile trust. I have not changed—I am as free as ever. But that never again. I don't care whether it is "correct" that the German Communists were swept away. And then, do the Russians have the courage to learn from *their* defeat—for it is their defeat? After bitter experience, even they will realize some day that nothing comes from:
> absolute power of the state;
> vulgar, one-sided materialism;
> the impudence to denounce the whole world for something, which Moscow dislikes.
> What a lack of instinct!... advise any KPD functionary not to tell me I am only an intellectual. I will answer that he is a renegade intellectual and an ass to boot. For my prophecies were fulfilled, but not those of the Rote Fahne. Leaf through it; it was wrong. It did not predict this fascism because every day it changed its predictions to something differ-

ent. What weakness! How insensitive! How ignorant! No more for me.[18] Tucholsky expressed his total disillusionment with the international Communist movement. He had tolerated its clumsiness and lack of insight, but after 1932—"no more." Russian leadership had proved itself bankrupt. Actually Tucholsky's skepticism about Russian intentions began shortly after Lenin's death and progressively increased until he repudiated Soviet policies completely in 1933. Tucholsky's changing attitude toward the Soviet regime demonstrated the political realism of which he was capable.

After the Russian Revolution, Tucholsky resisted the temptation to which some leftist intellectuals succumbed; that is, to believe that the new Russian regime could do no wrong, that a paradise on earth had suddenly been created. In 1920, Tucholsky denounced such silly beliefs when he reviewed Alfons Goldschmidt's book, *Moskau 1920*.[19] Tucholsky wrote it was clear that Goldschmidt, like most people, had seen only what he wanted to see. From Goldschmidt's report, it appeared that nothing had ever happened in Moscow. The women were beautiful, the cleaning women in the train stations happy, everyone was friendly, and, above all, the prostitutes were intelligent, politically informed and "smiled only as the female comrades of Lenin could smile." As he left the friendly "proletarian palace," Goldschmidt wrote: "I walked outside. The sky was blue. A butterfly fluttered by. A swallow soared. The sparrows chirped. The sun shone. Everywhere, one could see the influence of Lenin."[20]

Goldschmidt was, of course, all the more amusing because he was so serious. Tucholsky's comment was that it took far more courage to see things as they really are and he imagined what Goldschmidt's reaction would have been to the same condition in Germany:

> What a country! [Russia] There is little to eat, almost nothing to wear and a clearly nationalistic war is being fought—but that is all official and can be circumvented. If you bound the author's eyes, turned him around a few times and then told him that he was in Germany, he would say that the place was a pig sty.[21]

On the other hand Tucholsky attacked those people who denounced the Soviet government. He was a great admirer of Lenin and often compared his success to the "failure" of the German Social Democrats.[22] With the advent of Stalin and the purging of Trotsky, Tucholsky began to suspect the Russian claim to leadership of Communism. In 1928, he received an official Russian publication that contained an article on the founding of the Red Army. To his amazement, Tucholsky discovered no mention of Trotsky, the organizer of the army. Stating that such an omission was a sign of weakness and fear,

Tucholsky maintained that no one would ever be able to trust a publication that contained deliberate falsehoods. The Soviet government might believe its action justified, but censorship and lies were too much:

> Party discipline is a very good thing and we agree that the active politician needs it. Byzantine falsification of history, however, is always an evil thing, and the Russians should use every occasion to speak the truth.[23]

Again, however, it was not until after January 30, 1933, that Tucholsky became really outspoken against Stalinist tactics. As he wrote to Walter Hasenclever sometime in 1935:

> Stalin always served Russian policy and only Russian policy, which is certainly no offense. But it is a crime to sacrifice the European workers to these Russian interests...[24]

In 1927, Tucholsky wrote, "... Bolshevism... was never Communism."[25] Just as he separated the Communist movement in general from its Russian expression, so did he distinguish between the philosophy and the organization. The question arises as to what he thought of Marxism as an ideology. Did he believe it to be a valid historical system and a correct method for the pursuit of truth? Tucholsky often used Marxist terminology. He frequently wrote of the "class struggle" and exhorted the workers to a greater class consciousness. In 1934, Tucholsky wrote:

> ... I have never been a "Marxist." What the others say is nonsense. But I consider Marx's beginnings to be good, his teaching to be a necessary reaction to an idealism, which was just as idiotic as pure materialism. Whoever is able to think only in those two categories will continue to remain where he is—in the airless room of abstraction.[26]

Tucholsky was saying that he saw Marxism, not as a faith to be lived by, but as an event in the course of intellectual history. It was a reaction to the unreality of idealism, but only a reaction. To believe that only materialist explanations were valid, was to be as "unrealistic" as any idealist. Tucholsky believed that no single way of thinking, no extreme offered the way to truth. Not the abstractions, but the realities were important. Thus, for Tucholsky, Marxism was not "history" as it claimed to be—it was an historical event. In other words, Marxism was merely a way whereby the workers might be made militant champions of equality and democracy, but it was not an end in itself. It was not truth. Tucholsky thus spoke in the language of Marxist revolution, not because he was a doctrinaire, but because he saw in the working class the most likely bulwark against reaction, and the best hope for democratic equality. As he wrote in 1930: "I approve of the class struggle, but I don't think it should be a religion in disguise."[27]

Tucholsky thought the great problem of all intellectual movements, such as psychoanalysis or Marxism, to be their tendency to exceed their bounds and become religions in disguise. Tucholsky maintained that Marxism was a kind of tool in the struggle for human liberty. To believe, however, that it was a panacea that would change the nature of man and create a "new race of angels" in either Russia or anywhere else was false.[28]

Tucholsky was contemptuous of the orthodox Marxists who were convinced they knew the explanation to everything, who believed that they and only they knew the true course of the future.

"I no longer ·want to hear how the Communists know everything. I don't want to hear about the inevitability of history, how 'it' moves itself, how they know it all, how they have the whole of world history in their pockets,..." wrote Tucholsky on May 17, 1933. And the following year, he said to his brother that the naiveté of the Communists in believing they had the answer to everything reminded him of the little Polish Jewish boy that Heine spoke of: "He imagined that he had invented masturbation and wanted to go to Warsaw to have it patented."[29]

The crux of the matter is that Tucholsky was uninterested in ideology, in any single explanation of truth and reality. He was interested in results, not theories. "And I wish the daughters of the workers were free and could wind flowers in their hair—free from the Church and economic slavery. Free also from Communist theology..."[30] He did not want dogmas; he wanted a humane world with individual freedom. What Tucholsky really desired was an end to ideology and a beginning of humanity. "We must begin from the beginning (*von vorn*)— not listen to this ridiculous Stalin who betrays his people as much as the Pope—none of that will bring freedom. From the beginning, only from the beginning."[31]

These words were written in 1935 shortly before Tucholsky died. Five years before, he had written of a time in the future when humanity would be discovered again. Nothing better illustrates Tucholsky's non-ideological position than "Blick in ferne Zukunft" ("Glance into the Distant Future"):

And when everything is over—when it's all run dry: the horde madness, the joy of meeting in masses, screaming in masses and waving flags in groups. When this sickness is over, which exalts the lowest qualities of man. When the people have become, not smarter, but tired. When all the struggles for fascism have been fought out and when the last emigrants to freedom have departed this world—then will come a day when again it will be very modern to be liberal.

Then a man will come who will make a thundering discovery. He will discover the individual. He will say: there is an organism called man and he is of greatest importance. Whether he is happy—that is the question. That he is free is the goal. Groups are something secondary—the state is something secondary. It doesn't matter if the state lives—it matters that man lives.

This man, speaking in such manner, will have a great effect. The people will celebrate his thesis and will say: "That is something completely new! What courage! We've never heard that before! A new epoch of humanity is beginning! What a genius we have among us! Up, up! The new teaching—!"

And his books will be sold, or rather, those of his imitators, for the first one is always the fool.

And the effect will be that a hundred thousand black, brown and red shirts will fly into corners and on manure piles. And the people will have the courage to be themselves, without majority resolutions and without fear of the state, before which they had groveled like whipped dogs. And so it will go, until one day—.[32]

Precisely this lack of respect for ideology made the Communists and Nazis so fear and hate Tucholsky. Because he wanted no dogma, because he was unimpressed by deterministic schemes and abstract theories, Tucholsky was far more radical than either of those extremes. They detested Tucholsky because he dared to call for the establishment of the liberal, open society, which both the Communists and the Nazis feared and despised. The Communists hated his pragmatic idealism because of its rational flexibility, and its denial of their pseudo-scientific explanations. The Nazis hated his Jewish origin, his mockery of nation and race, and his belief in individual worth. Both Communists and Nazis believed in monolithic, simple solutions and thus neither could suffer Tucholsky's belief in tolerance, diversity and free exchange of opinion.

Tucholsky was a liberal and for that reason, he could find no political home. As he once said of the leftist intellectuals—they fell between two stools: the Communists called them right-wing sympathizers; the Socialists called them dangerous radicals. On the one band, they were rejected by the Communists, on the other, they themselves rejected the Socialists. The German political tradition offered them nothing but alienation.[33]

1   Werner T. Angress, Stillborn Revolution, the Communist Bid for Power in Germany, 1921-1923 (Princeton, 1963), p. 345.
2   Kurt Tucholsky, "Die Rolle des Intellektuellen in der Partei," G.W., III, 15; K.T., Front (1929).
3   Kurt Tucholsky, Deutschland, Deutschland über Alles (Berlin, 1929), p. 17.
4   Kurt Tucholsky, "Die Rolle des Intellektuellen in der Partei," G.W., III, 14.
5   See Brie Waldman, The Spartacist Uprising of 1919: A Study of the Relation of Political Theory and Party Practice (Milwaukee, 1958), pp. 161-197.
6   Angress, pp. 476f.
7   Kurt Tucholsky, "Führer?" G.W., I, 747; I.W., Berliner Volkszeitung, (October 16, 1920).
8   Ibid
9   Kurt Tucholsky, "Abreisskalender," G.W., II, 289; I.W., Die Weltbühne, XXI/50 (December 15, 1925), 891.
10   Alan Bullock, "The German Communists and the Rise of Hitler," The Third Reich (International Council for Philosophy and Humanistic Studies, UNESCO; n.d.), p. 505.
11   Kurt Tucholsky, "Schnipsel," G.W., 111, 1000.
12   See Angress, pp. 48-76, 478, Bullock, pp. 505f.
13   Kurt Tucholsky, "Das Märchen von Berlin," G.W., 111, 78; I.W., Das andere Deutschland (June 1, 1929).
14   Kurt Tucholsky, "Gebrauchslyrik," G.W., II, 1321f.; I.W., Die Weltbühne, XXIV/48 (November 27, 1928}, 808.
15   This and the following quotes from: Kurt Tucholsky, "Die Rolle des Intellektuellen in der Partei," G.W., II, 13., G.W., III, 16.
16   Carolus," Front, 11/10 (1929); found in the scrapbook.
17   Bullock, p. 509
18   Kurt Tucholsky, Ausgewählte Briefe, 1913-1935 (Hamburg, 1962), pp. 227f.
19   Alfons Goldschmidt, Moskau 1920 (Rowohlt: Berlin, 1920).
20   Quoted by Kurt Tucholsky, "Aus Moskau zurück," G.W., I, 745; I.W., Freiheit (October 13, 1920).
21   Ibid., G.W., I, 743.
22   See Kurt Tucholsky, "Gegen den Strom," G.W., II, 407-413; I.W., Die Weltbühne, XXII/15 (April 13, 1926), 567.
23   Kurt Tucholsky, "Dank vom Haus Stalin," G.W., II, 1132; I.W., Die Weltbühne, XXIV/19 (May 8, 1928), 731.
24   Kurt Tucholsky, Ausgewählte Briefe, p. 303.
25   Kurt Tucholsky, "Auf dem Nachttisch," G.W., II, 971
26   Kurt Tucholsky, Ausgewählte Briefe, p. 317.
27   Kurt Tucholsky, "Replik," G.W., III, 426; I.W., Die Weltbühne, XXVI/17 (April 22, 1930), 610.
28   Ibid., G.W., III, 424, 426
29   Kurt Tucholsky, Ausgewählte Briefe, p. 257.
30   Kurt Tucholsky, "Von den Kränzen, der Abtreibung und dem Sakrament der Ehe," G.W., III, 786.
31   Kurt Tucholsky, Ausgewählte Briefe, p. 338.
32   Kurt Tucholsky, "Blick in ferne Zukunft," G.W., III, 580f.; I.W., Die Weltbühne, XXVI/44 (Sept. 28, 1930), 580.
33   Kurt Tucholsky, "Die Rolle des Intellektuellen in der Partei," G.W., III, p. 15.

Kurt and Mary Gerold 1924 in Paris, where Tucholsky was a correspondent for Die Weltbühne. *The couple would split up four years later.*

VII.

THE PARIS YEARS

DURING THE early years of the Republic, Tucholsky had indefatigably devoted himself to his journalistic career, but suddenly in 1923 his writing activity was drastically reduced. Like most other Germans he was overwhelmed by the events of 1923, a year of horror for the Republic. Anyone might appropriately that if it could survive those ills it could survive anything: the occupation of the Ruhr, the separatist movement in the Rhineland, Communist troubles in Saxony and Thuringia, the Hitler Putsch, the astronomical inflation. The sufferings of 1923 undermined even further the shaky faith of the average citizen in the ability of the Republic to protect its own interests.

Understandably enough, 1923 was a particularly unproductive year for Tucholsky. He wrote less in those twelve months than he would in any year until the end of his writing career. Those few pieces that did appear were mostly wistful musings and reviews of books and films. One reason for the lack of literary activity was, of course, that the inflation made it necessary for Tucholsky to supplement his income with other work. For a brief period he found employment in the bank, Bett, Simon and Company, where he handled the giant bundles of currency that necessarily passed through a banker's hands when the mark was valued at four trillion to the dollar.

Still Tucholsky could have found time to write about the tragedies around him. It may have been that he was too depressed and exhausted by those events to be able to comment. Ten years later, when the roof not only cracked, but fell in, Tucholsky would remain silent for the rest of his life. Tucholsky well expressed the apathy and world-weariness of the Germans in 1923 in two short essays: "Die Nachgemachten" ("Imitations")[1] and "Das will kein Mensch mehr wissen" ("Nobody Wants to Hear That Anymore").[2] All joys seemed to be imitations of past ones. There was too much suffering for anyone to be able to enjoy himself. There were no surprises left, for everyone had experienced everything and known the worst. Everyone was too jaded to notice anything new. "Everybody is indifferent to everything. The capacity to react is exhausted. They are unable to continue."[3]

However, all of Tucholsky's writing that year was not a mere reflection of misery and sadness, for he also managed to produce some excellent humor. And Tucholsky seems to have begun the transition from the bitter, hard-driving polemic to the wistful, whimsical satire on culture and society for which he is noted. He began to perfect his talent for concluding a perfectly ordinary prose essay with a startling twist of words or an amusing twist of logic. We have seen an early example of this talent in his first published piece—"And what did the emperor do with his beautiful snuffbox? He sneezed at it." He also continued to develop his facility for employing risqué themes and ribald phrasings that in the mouths of his many imitators usually sounded coarse or vulgar.

Tucholsky's use of the surprise ending oftentimes was a mild satire upon his own poses and attitudes. An example was the satirical essay, "Ja, früher… " ("Yes, in the old times… !"), in which he berated the national obsession with the "good old days" when everything was inexpensive and therefore better. Tucholsky went on, petulantly asking for people simply to admit that the present was different from the past and then try to live in the present. He ended by describing the singular dreariness of German conversation in 1923 and then tacked on the paradoxical: "P.S. What are you saying? Do you mean that magazines use to pay for essays like this one?"[4]

In other pieces, written in 1923, Tucholsky satirized the national passion for work or described the long, beard-growing intervals waiting for a bureaucrat to answer a question on the telephone. In some of the essays, he paid tribute to his friends or imagined what their reactions would be when he died. In all of these writings, there appeared to be a gayer and, at the same time, a more mature Tucholsky. His convictions remained unchanged, but in his method he exchanged polemic for satire and exaggeration for more reasoned and convincing tones. In other words the youthful, belligerent, "let-the-chips-fall-where-they-may" attitude seemed to have mellowed into a more sophisticated attack, a more careful method.

During this process of maturing, Tucholsky became for a time almost uninterested in politics. In 1923, he thus made no mention of events—which now appear to so crucial—the occupation of the Ruhr by French troops and the Hitler Putsch. Perhaps the situation was so grave that it was ludicrous. Polemic in 1923 would have been boorish. Only laughter made any sense in such an impossible position. Tucholsky therefore closed the year, not with an analysis of political events, or a call of the republicans to arms, but with a eulogy of Charles Chaplin, whose art he called an "oasis" in a desert of political horror:

> Thank God you exist! Your heart matches your brain—you feel with your head and think with your heart! Enricher of life… We are grateful

to you, Charlie Chaplin, because you give us a presentiment that the world is not *teutsch* and is not Bavarian—but that it is very, very different. From the cellar, *de profundis*, we greet you—!⁵

During the course of 1923, Tucholsky became more and more restless in Berlin and he began to dream of being able to leave Germany for a time. Tucholsky needed a new atmosphere and new sights. His ideas were becoming stale and limited; he needed a different perspective. Above all, he needed a rest from the depressing surroundings in which he had lived for five years. All of this became possible with the stabilization of the currency in late 1923. Siegfried Jacobsohn agreed that Tucholsky should become the *Weltbühne's* Paris correspondent and Tucholsky managed to augment his income further by contracts with the *Vossische Zeitung* and the *Prager Tageblatt*, for which he was to write light social satire and descriptions of Paris.

This was disputed among his peers. Maximilian Harden criticized Tucholsky for writing for so middle-class a paper as the *Vossische Zeitung*, but Tucholsky replied that there was little else he could write for and maintain his freedom. His statement reveals something of his attitudes towards the various journals and his relationship with them:

> It is this way with the *Voss*: If to all of the newspapers for which I work, I applied the standards which I probably should, there would be none left for me. Naturally I must admit that a bit of weakness lies in that. But I know of no way out. Gerlach is not an especially intelligent editor, there can be no question about the *Tageblatt* and neither of us reads *Vorwärts*. Unfortunately *Die Rote Fahne* is not a newspaper. I can only again express regret that you are not going to carry out your old project of establishing a daily paper. That would be a real blessing.⁶

Tucholsky fell in love with Paris. Not only was he overcome by the beauty of the city and the hospitality of its inhabitants, but he was also stunned by the lack of crisis, the normality with which people lived their everyday lives. On April 22, 1924, he wrote Mary Gerold, who would soon be his wife:

> … women, pictures, wine, trees, theater. It is not any one of those things; it is not all of them together. It is the light, this enchanting light and then it is something else for which I fortunately have no words. It is also not joy—it is simply a heightened feeling of life. To walk around here is to be graced—it matters not where. I crept along an ugly old wall—and was blessed. It is a fairly tale.⁷

Enchanted, Tucholsky visited some of the less-frequented monuments and sights of Paris—Lafayette's tomb and a mass grave of 1300 persons guillotined during the Terror of the French Revolution of 1793/94. He sat in cafes with his old friend George Grosz, the artist, and discussed Berlin in comparison to Paris. Tucholsky was given a new sense of life, of the meaning of life. He confessed to Mary that one day in the middle of the street, he suddenly burst into tears:

> Do you know what a person does when he suddenly receives something for which he has waited fourteen years? He cries. For shame—I wept right in the street… It was because everything was there, because it again made sense to be in the world—because once again a cloud is a cloud, a rock a rock, the sun the sun. I go around in a state of enchantment.[8]

Tucholsky also expressed his joyous reaction in a poem which was later set to music. In its verses he mused while sitting in a Paris park—Parc Monceau—a favorite place to which he often returned when depressed or lonely.

PARC MONCEAU

Here it is pleasant. Here I softly dream.
Here I am a man—not just a civilian.
Here may I walk left. Here under trees of green
Is not a single sign to say what is forbidden.

A fat rubber ball lies under a rose,
In a nearby tree a small bird hovers.
A little boy is picking his nose
And is amused by what he discovers.

Four American girls look about:
"Is Cook correct? Yes, the trees are tall."
They turn Paris inside out,
They see nothing, but must see it all.

The children laugh with excitement,
On a house bright sunbeams play.
I bathe in the sun and am content,
I rest because my Fatherland is far away.[9]

Tucholsky's first impressions of Paris were in fact possessed of such a boundless enthusiasm that in 1926 he wrote of his gratefulness to Siegfried Jacobsohn for not publishing his first lyrical gushings.[10] Having just experienced the horrors of inflation-Germany, Tucholsky's reactions to France were at first too subjective and therefore false. But his objective evaluations referred again and again to the essential "humanity" of the French and used terms of praise which would do justice to the most home-loving Frenchman. In 1924, the joy of Paris for Tucholsky was its free spirit, and its unself-conscious atmosphere. "Paris works—Berlin slaves!!"[11]

With articles of praise such as "Das menschliche Paris" ("Humane Paris")[12] and of fond description such as "Die Rue Mouffetard,"[13] Tucholsky portrayed an ideal Paris whose image he might revise, but would never forget. In 1927 he published a travelogue about the Pyrenees.[14] The book ends with a description of his thoughts upon returning to France. Entitled "Dank an Frankreich" ("Thanks to France"), the section is a paean to France and to the embodiment of her spirit, Paris:

Thank you, France for letting me live in you. You are not my country... and yet I am at home in you... Sometimes I almost forget how good you are to me. I begin to take you for granted, to be unthankful. I must compensate for that.
I have not lost myself in your—I would have found myself again if I had been lost. You have given and given, lent and rewarded... I was so poor. I am so rich. And now there is no reservation, no criticism, no point of reference! Simply I stand on this bridge and am again in Paris, in the real home of us all. The water flows, there you lie. I throw my heart into the river, submerge in you and love you.[15]

During his first months in Paris Tucholsky was horrified to think that these were the people who only a few years before had been the "enemies" of Germany. Again he was reminded of the senselessness and horror of the war. He began again to write articles and poems about the sufferings of those years. When he spoke to his postman, he thought that only six years earlier they might have been forced to murder each other. Time and again, suddenly and involuntarily, a small incident, a word would plunge Tucholsky into despairing thoughts about the stupidity of the war.

Considering it both a duty and a necessity, Tucholsky made a pilgrimage to the battlefields of Verdun. It was a shattering experience. He realized how different, how much more deadly, the western war had been from the eastern:

You cannot imagine it. The corpses are no longer there—that is true—but you can see here what war is when it is waged with all of the power of giant industry. It is not like in Courland where it still retained something of the old romance. This was a factory of death... I have written about it—I don't know how it really was—in any event, I wept bucketsful while describing it. In Fort Vaux there is a dressing station. Anyone who goes in there and doesn't come out a pacifist is a swine.[16]

Tucholsky's visit to Verdun led to a special "war remembrance" number of the *Weltbühne* of August 7, 1924, for which he wrote three articles and a poem.[17]

Paris was a place of new beginnings in more ways than one for Tucholsky. Toward the end of July he returned to Berlin for six weeks to help put together the new Ullstein magazine, *Uhu*. He also took advantage of the occasion to marry his fiancée, Mary Gerold. Tucholsky then returned to Paris with his new wife. Many obstacles had been overcome since their first meeting in Courland and both had matured during the years in Berlin. But given Tucholsky's intense, mercurial temperament and Mary's practical, no-nonsense nature, it was certain that their future together would prove difficult.

The first years, however, were good and it was then that Tucholsky reached maturity as a writer, poet and critic. Although he wrote for other publications, the *Weltbühne* remained his primary forum for the discussion of politics and society. Tucholsky's multiple talents were demonstrated by the diversity of the articles he published while in Paris. Peter Panter wrote whimsical "impressions" of Paris, often drawing ironic comparisons with Berlin: " 'A metropolis?' said my friend, Lisa, as she returned from Paris, 'Berlin a metropolis? Children, the chickens cackle in Potsdam Square...'"[18] Panter also became an important literary critic. He was literally the first to recognize the importance of Franz Kafka. As he wrote on the occasion of Kafka's death:

> Kafka has died at the age of forty-one of tuberculosis. He was aware of it for years. I knew him—before the war—as a tall, thin, brown man, dark, very quiet, very shy and withdrawn. In contrast to Max Brod, who did not really please me and who was a great disappointment to me in Prague and Berlin, I loved Kafka—without having read a single line by him. He never wanted to publish—Brod had to pull things out of his chest of drawers. It is said that he destroyed a great novel. I see in his work the best classical German of our time. He was a writer for an insurance company.[19]

Tucholsky's reviews of the works of writers such as Sinclair Lewis, James Joyce and D. H. Lawrence, as well as the great German authors of the period, show the scope of his literary interests.[20] His review column, *"Auf dem Nachttisch"* ("On the Night Table"), was a catalogue of the important literary works of the twenties. But there were notable exceptions, Gide being among them. Tucholsky professed not to understand Gide and thus he did not review his works. Part of

Tucholsky's charm and value as a literary critic was his lack of pretension. In 1931 he wrote: "Because I try to write colorful and, if possible, scholarly criticism, my first concern has been not to play the role of a little literary pope."[21]

Peter Panter, of course, remained only one of the "five fingers on a single hand." Theobald Tiger continued to occupy himself with poetry and chansons. Kaspar Hauser achieved his greatest individuality with the Wendriner stories and a series of conversations in heaven entitled *"Nachher"* ("Hereafter").[22] But here we are mainly concerned with Ignaz Wrobel, which it must be remembered is to do an injustice to the wit of Peter Panter, the lyricism of Theobald Tiger and the irony of Kaspar Hauser.

When Tucholsky went to Paris, Ignaz Wrobel received something of a rest after his hard work of the six foregoing years, but his activity did not cease. Tucholsky signed a third of his articles with Wrobel's name between 1924 and 1926. Tucholsky continued to write mainly about and for Germans, but the French environment gave him a larger perspective upon German problems. And his general outlook became broader and more international in scope. An example was his change of view toward Raymond Poincaré, the President and on-and-off Prime Minister of France from 1913 to 1920. Poincaré was a conservative, anti-German, pro-Russian hardliner who had declared war against Germany in World War I and had ordered the occupation of the Ruhr. to enforce German reparation payments. In Germany, Tucholsky had upheld Poincaré's policies, but when he arrived in France he began to criticize the French premier severely. Maximilian Harden accused Tucholsky of seeking popularity. Tucholsky justified himself in a letter to Harden.

> (April 14, 1926). When I was in Germany, I defended Poincaré, but here I see all of the details and am of the opinion that his policy was not good. Understandable, but not good. Not because he was unable to carry out what he wanted either. It seems certain to me that in France itself he has created unending misery. His judgment of Wilhelminian Germany was correct, he never understood what enormous opportunities existed for France with us. His speeches are not pleasant and his behavior is cleaner than that of any Socialist minister—but I don't like him.[23]

At the same time, the political despair which had gripped him in 1923 diminished in Paris. In 1926, when Otto Flake in the *Weltbühne* despaired of any effective action by the left, Tucholsky replied: "I haven't consumed great spoonsful of optimism, but I don't see things in that light."[24]

Tucholsky had reason to become more optimistic, for in 1924 the Republic entered a six-year period of political success and economic stability. As Tucholsky wrote on May 22, 1924: "The political outlook has never been as favorable for Germany as in this moment."²⁵ This was true in the light of the French parliamentary elections held earlier in the month, because the victory of the left-wing coalition appeared to be in part a repudiation of Poincaré's Germanophobe policies. French foreign policy in 1923 had not had an unqualified success. The invasion and occupation of the Ruhr had been expensive. Poincaré's intransigent attitude toward German economic difficulties had caused a strain to develop in Anglo-French relations and had made Germany appear to be justified in her dissatisfaction with Versailles. The greatest impression on the French voter, however, had been made by the swift decline of the Franc. In April 1924 Poincaré appeared equivocal about his acceptance of the Dawes Plan; a recent proposal put out by the American Banker and politician Charles Gates Dawes—a Republican—, to restructure the German reparation payments after World War I with American loans. This sealed his fate. After the May election, Poincaré resigned and a member of the Radical Socialist Party, Edouard Herriot, combined the offices of Premier and Foreign Minister. Herriot repudiated the policies of the previous year and pledged himself to a program of conciliation.

The Germans naturally were heartened by the French election results, but Tucholsky's analysis was sober and admonishing.²⁶ He stated that even though the general outcome of the election had been expected, the vote against Poincaré did not especially denote a sudden love for Germany. Tucholsky correctly assumed that the German question had been peripheral to internal political considerations. He maintained that the Germans should not build up false hopes that the repudiation of Poincaré's Ruhr policy meant also the repudiation of the Versailles Treaty. Tucholsky believed that it was Poincaré's methods that the French had disapproved, not the sense of his German policy. Even the far left in France believed not only in the necessity of reparations, but that not enough had been paid. In short, the French still expected Germany to meet her obligations, but not at gunpoint.

In his analysis, Tucholsky advocated essentially the policy that the German Foreign Minister, Gustav Stresemann, was pursuing: fulfillment of the treaty provisions. But Stresemann regarded fulfillment as an expedient to be employed only until Germany was strong enough to press for revision, while Tucholsky considered the policy to be a simple necessity in the face of a defeat, which he believed to have been deserved. In Tucholsky's opinion, if only the Germans would accept their debt to the past, then the French election of 1924 could be interpreted as offering Germany a new chance for conciliation. Tucholsky stated that the French people were tired—tired of war and international confusion. There was thus a real opportunity for a peaceful future if the Germans would accept the defeat of 1918 and cease to agonize over the past. "No human being in the world is any longer concerned with this question [war guilt], which has long since been determined." Tucholsky admitted that terrible things had happened in the Ruhr, but he insisted that the Germans would gain nothing by denouncing Poincaré.[27] They could succeed only with the French as one democracy with another.

> For long, Germany has been able to say nothing to the world. Now there is a renewed opportunity to do so... France has extended a hand. It is not for us to make conditions—for they won the war, not we.[28]

The German voters also went to the polls in 1924. The Reichstag election of May 4 was a reflection of the foreign situation as well. Unlike the French, however, the German moderate parties declined. The hardships of the inflation and the Ruhr occupation had taken their toll to the benefit of the political extremes. For the first time, the Nazis were represented in the legislature, having received enough votes to give them thirty-two seats. The Nationalists increased from seventy-one to ninety-six, while the other extreme, the Communists, climbed from four to sixty-two representatives. The Socialists dropped alarmingly from 186 deputies to 100.[29]

Although the May election returns may now appear to have been an evil omen, they did not seem so to contemporaries, for the success of the extremists was short-lived. In the election on December 7, four months later, although the Nationalists remained the second largest party in the Reichstag, the Socialists were able to recoup most of their losses. The road to Franco-German accord appeared to be open (the May election was looked upon by many contemporaries as a kind of referendum on the Dawes Plan, for the Nationalists regarded it as a major campaign issue. In view, however, of its being approved by the Reichstag in August, it would appear that the election was far more a reaction to the poor domestic situation. In addition, the gains by the Communists, who also disapproved of the Dawes Plan, were made mainly because of the loss of the eight-hour day which drove thousands of workers to vote for the KPD.)[30]

Thus the elections of 1924 seem almost as though the German electorate threw off the mantle of responsible government in May only to assume it again in December. But for Tucholsky the gains of the moderate parties at the end of the year were more than offset by the election of the ultra-nationalistic General von Hindenburg as President in 1925, after Ebert had died. The presidential election was the one political event in these years, 1924–1927, which elicited extended comment from Tucholsky through the voice of Ignaz Wrobel.

Tucholsky believed that Friedrichs Ebert's occupation of the presidential office had been harmful, but he regarded the election of Hindenburg as an unmitigated disaster. There were two presidential campaigns in 1925. The constitution provided that unless a candidate received a majority of all the votes cast, there had to be a second election in which a simple plurality would be sufficient. In the first election, held on March 29, there were seven candidates. The Nationalists and the (liberal-conservative) People's Party supported the popular hero of the Ruhr, Karl Jarres, the long-term mayor of Duisburg who had been the unofficial leader of the resistance against the French occupation. The left was tragically split, for the Center, the Democrats and the Socialists supported separate candidates, with Wilhelm Marx, Willy Hellpach, and Otto Braun representing them respectively.

The smaller parties also took part in what became a political free-for-all. The Bavarian People's Party chose Heinrich Held as its candidate, the National Socialists supported Ludendorff, and the Communists rallied around the former Hamburg transport worker, Ernst Thälmann. Jarres received the largest number of votes. Second and third places were occupied by Braun and Marx, while Thälmann with less than 2,000,000 votes trailed far behind. The National Socialists received an insignificant 210,968.[31]

After the election, the obvious was finally perceived by the moderate parties and they began to coalesce. The SPD wisely decided to throw its support behind a middle-class contender, and the Weimar Coalition of Democrats, Centrists and Socialists put forth Wilhelm Marx as its candidate. The Communists stubbornly remained with Thälmann. The right-wing parties also combined forces, but they switched candidates, abandoning Jarres for Paul von Hindenburg. Stresemann, in his capacity as Foreign Minister, looked upon Hindenburg's candidacy as a mild misfortune since his election might lead the Allies to distrust Germany's intention of fulfilling her treaty obligations. Stresemann talked with Hindenburg and easily persuaded him to decline the candidacy. At the last moment, however, Admiral von Tirpitz, of all people, convinced the aged general that it was his patriotic duty to run for the highest office in the country. Tirpitz had led the German Imperial Navy until his dismissal in the middle of World War I and was, at that point in time, already seventy-five years old. On April 11, 1925, Hindenburg announced his candidacy and asked for the votes of all patriotic Germans.

Six days later, Tucholsky published an article in *Die Menschheit*, which expressed the horrified reaction of the Left in general to the possibility of Hindenburg's becoming president. He stated categorically that the election of the general would be a disaster for Germany:

> Hindenburg is Prussia. Hindenburg is: back to the manor house, away from the world, back to the barracks. Hindenburg signifies: to hell with the rest of the world, unceasing international difficulties, complete distrust by foreign powers, especially France, for Germany. Hindenburg is: the Republic in retreat. Hindenburg means: war.[32]

It was rare for anyone to attack Hindenburg in such a manner and to Tucholsky it appeared that the opponents of the old general were mesmerized by his fame and reputation. Instead of openly emphasizing their differences with the field marshal, Marx and his followers seemed only to point out similarities. They protested that they were as nationalistically oriented as Hindenburg, that they too wanted a place in the sun for Germany and other clichés of the patriotic jargon. Tucholsky believed such tactics to be folly and called upon the moderates to have the courage of their convictions. They should pay the general the respect due to any aged person, but they should not pay him homage. They should point out that the Republic did not need Prussian generals, that Hindenburg's army experience was hardly a qualification for leadership of a great and varied nation. Marx and his supporters would, thus, distinguish themselves absolutely from the other side. If, however, they continued to employ their "me too" tactics, Tucholsky contended the obvious conclusion of the voter would be to elect the genuine article—Hindenburg. Tucholsky asked the moderates to appeal to that large, but quiet group of Germans whom he believed wanted a moral revolution.

On April 26, 1925, Hindenburg was elected with 14,655,766 votes. Marx received 13,751,615 and Thälmann the small, but significant, 1,931,151. If the Communists had supported Marx, Hindenburg would have been defeated. In his analysis of the election, *"Was nun—?"* ("What Now?"), Tucholsky recognized that the Communists were largely at fault, but for reasons described earlier, he was unable to condemn them directly.[33] Instead, he lamely contended that their behavior was understandable in the light of their past treatment and thus they had wanted to "demonstrate" with a separate candidate. "Well, they had their demonstration," sighed Tucholsky, "and thus they insured the election of Hindenburg."[34] Tucholsky continued lamenting that his was an age in which the left seemed doomed to ineptness and impotence. If the Weimar Coalition had decided upon a single candidate in the first election, it could easily have won. And when the second campaign took place, it praised Hindenburg and urged the voters to choose Marx. But that was all in the past and Tucholsky asked, "What now?" In answering his question, Tucholsky expressed the foreboding of the entire left from the moderate democrats to the Communists:

> The imperial representative [Hindenburg] lives in the worst thinkable surrounding company. Will they advise him? They will rule. And he will do what he has done his whole life—he will underwrite their decisions.[35]

The general consensus of the Left was that the field marshal would be the creature of the right-wing monarchist groups. Through him they would throttle the Republic. Tucholsky could see only a dark future as a result of the election:

the last republican judges would be dismissed, the schools would drown in nationalism, army chief Hans von Seeckt (who did not favor army putsches) would relinquish his office, and critics of Hindenburg would be arrested on the basis of the law for the protection of the Republic. Whatever else needed to be done to kill democracy would be made possible by use of Article 48. As much as Tucholsky hated the tactics of the moderate left, be believed that with them there was at least some hope of a "moral revolution." With Hindenburg, he contended that all was lost. The "Tirpitz candidate" would take the oath to the constitution which he would destroy with Article 48. He would swear an oath, Tucholsky added contemptuously, "like his soldier's oath."[36]

Yet, Tucholsky spoke truer words than he realized, for Hindenburg took his oath to the constitution as seriously as he had taken his oath of allegiance to the Emperor. For seven years, the authoritarian field marshal upheld the spirit as well as the letter of republicanism. His faithfulness to the Republic was a surprise to everybody, not least of all the Monarchists and Nationalists.

Although Tucholsky at first lamented the narrow defect of the moderate parties, he and other writers of the left suddenly reversed themselves, maintaining that Hindenburg's election made no real difference since all political parties were essentially the same. Kurt Hiller, another *Weltbühne* writer, wrote a piece for the May 12 issue along these lines. He maintained that under Hindenburg internal policies would remain the same because it was impossible for them to grow worse. Since Hindenburg had not received a majority of the votes cast, he would be forced into a position of *Überparteilichkeit* (Being above party). Hiller continued, stating that the Socialists would survive Hindenburg's election and so would the reactionary officers, bureaucrats and teachers. He added wryly that they all would have survived under Marx also. Hiller closed with the bitter reflection that the difference between the Weimar Coalition and the right wing was practically nonexistent since the moderate parties supported the monarchy and the war.[37]

Tucholsky also assumed Hiller's position and went even further when he stated that perhaps it was for the best that Hindenburg had been elected, because thereby Germany had revealed her true nature for all to see. "For the first time in years Germany has made a political gesture which is not a lie."[38] Tucholsky declared that the republicans had never opposed Hindenburg's ethos or philosophy—they had only opposed his methods and thus in the end were indistinguishable. In a characteristic turn of phrase, Tucholsky quipped that with the moderates and the Nationalists, it was as though one favored the guillotine and the other the block, but both agreed upon the necessity for the death penalty.[39]

Tucholsky was correct in perceiving that Hindenburg probably represented the true mood of the nation, but it would appear as a double insult to accuse his opponents, who had lost the election, of really supporting Hindenburg in their hearts. Tucholsky, of course, knew that the moderates and the Nationalists were not really the same, but he believed that in the end the effects of their policies would be identical. He wanted nothing less than a cultural revolution and any policy which did not drive toward that goal ultimately gained his contempt.

Before the election, Tucholsky had demonstrated his practicality when he supported the moderates against Hindenburg, but he had had little hope that they would accomplish anything better. With Hindenburg, however, he believed there was no hope whatsoever. Tucholsky himself was not a "moderate." He lent his support to the middle parties not because they would maintain the Republic as it was, i.e., prevent its destruction by the Nationalists, but because they might transform it into a real democracy. In his view again, there was nothing left for the Nationalists to destroy. This was one of the reasons why his criticism of the Communists was so faint.

Above all—all of the German parties except the Communists were committed to the restoration of Germany to great power status in the international diplomatic game. This was what sickened Tucholsky. That was the way of the old world, the way that had led to destruction in 1914. Tucholsky wanted a repudiation of the old forms or nothing. In the mid-twenties he came to believe that the commitment of the German moderates to Germany's position as a great power had rendered a peaceful future impossible. In 1926, he wrote that the spirit of diplomacy had returned to pre-1914 conditions. France and Germany would continue to pursue the myth of hereditary enmity. All of the seeming progress in international relations from the Treaty of Rapallo between Germany and the Soviet Union to the Pact of Locarno between Germany, Britain, France, Belgium, and Italy was merely a sham for the preparations for war. And thus it was in the area of foreign relations that Tucholsky was his most prescient and prophetic. As he had written of the future in 1920:

> Where are we headed? We are no longer in control. We determine nothing and we lead no one. He who believes we do is a liar. Shadows and ghosts shimmer around us—don't touch them, they only give way, sink and collapse. A light is appearing, but we know not whether it is twilight or dawn.[40]

By 1926 Tucholsky believed that Europe had chosen the twilight.

NOTES

1 Kurt Tucholsky, "Die Nachgemachten," G.W., I, 1089; P.P., *Acht Uhr-Abendblatt, National Zeitung* (Berlin, March 21, 1923).

2 Kurt Tucholsky, "Das will kein Mensch mehr wissen," G.W., I, 1109; P.P. *Acht-Uhr-Abendblatt, National Zeitung* (Berlin, June 21, 1923).

3 Ibid., G.W., I, 1110.

4 Kurt Tucholsky, "Ja, früher… !" G.W., I, 1093; P.P., *Acht Uhr-Abendblatt, National-Zeitung* (Berlin, April 11, 1923).

5 Kurt Tucholsky, "The Kid," G.W., I, 1135; P.P., *Die Weltbühne*, XIX/49 (December 6, 1923), 564.

6 Kurt Tucholsky, *Ausgewählte Briefe*, 1913-1935 (Hamburg, 1962), p. 135). Hellmut Georg von Gerlach was a pacifist and a politician who ran the liberal *Welt am Montag*, for which Tucholsky briefly worked.

7 Ibid., p. 467.

8 Ibid.

9 Kurt Tucholsky, "Parc Monceau," G.W., I, 1152; Th. T., Die Weltbühne, XX/20 (May 15, 1924), 664.

10 Kurt Tucholsky, "Die Neutralen," G.W., II, 445; P.P., *Die Weltbühne*, XXII/20 (May 18, 1926), 777.

11 Kurt Tucholsky, "Paris," G.W., I, 1153; K.T., *Die Weltbühne*, XX/21 (May 22, 1924), 689.

12 Kurt Tucholsky, "Das menschliche Paris," G.W., I, 1170; P.P., *Vossische Zeitung* (Berlin, June 19, 1924).

13 Kurt Tucholsky, "Die Rue Mouffetard," G.W., I, 1179; P.P., *Vossische Zeitung* (Berlin, June 30, 1924).

14 Kurt Tucholsky (P.P.), *Ein Pyrenäenbuch*, G.W., II, 577.

15 Ibid., 705.

16 Kurt Tucholsky, *Ausgewählte Briefe*, 475-76.

17 Kurt Tucholsky, "Der Geist von 1914," G.W., I, 1200; "Vor Verdun," G.W., I, 1205; "Gebet nach dem Schlachten," G.W., I, 1211; "Vision," G.W., I, 1212. English translation by Peter Appelbaum and James Scott in *Prayer After the Slaughter* (Berlinica, New York, 2015)

18 Kurt Tucholsky, "Dorf Berlin," G.W., I, 1217; P.P., *Die Weltbühne*, XX/34 (Aug. 21, 1924), 293.

19 Kurt Tucholsky, *Ausgewählte Briefe*, 473.

20 See Gerhard Seidel, "Kurt Tucholsky als Literaturkritiker," *Sinn und Form*, XIV (Berlin, June 5, 1962), 937-946. Seidel notes that Tucholsky's criticism is valuable not only for what it says about Tucholsky, but also as a genuine contribution to German letters (pp. 940f.):… To the legitimate aids for our historical and theoretical observation and discussion of literature belong the reflections of the most manifold literary historical facts which are found in the critical judgments of Tucholsky—reflections of the literary works of the most diverse epochs, peoples, types, styles and authors. Just as a judgment of Goethe concerning Shakespeare is not only a statement about Goethe, but may also be used to elucidate Shakespeare, so do Tucholsky's assertions concerning literary matters merit our attention when these same matters become objects of our interest.

21 Quoted by Seidel., p. 942.

22   These stories have been translated into English by Cindy Opitz under the title *Hereafter. We Were Sitting On a Cloud, Dangling Our Legs* (Berlinica, New York, 2018)
23   Kurt Tucholsky, *Ausgewählte Briefe*, 137.
24   Otto Flake, *Die Weltbühne*, XXII/11 (March 16, 1926), 476. Reply in Kurt Tucholsky, "Was haben wir—?" G.W., II, 397; also: K.T., *Die Weltbühne*, XXII/14 (April 6, 1926), 524.:
25   Kurt Tucholsky, "Paris," G.W., I, 1156.
26   Ibid., 1152-57.
27   Ibid., 1157. During the occupation, French troops had killed approximately 130 German civilians and arrested thousands and also raped German women, although the numbers are disputed.
28   Ibid.
29   Election quotations taken from Wilhelm Dittmann, *Das politische Deutschland vor Hitler* (Zürich, 1945).
30   See the author's unpublished master's essay, "The Reichstag Election of May 4, 1924" (1958), on deposit at Columbia University.
31   The election results were: Jarres: 10,787,870; Braun: 7,836,676; Marx: 3,988,659; Thälmann: 1,885,778. Figures given by William Halperin, *Germany Tried Democracy* (New York, 1946), p. 316.
32   Kurt Tucholsky, "Der Kaiserliche Statthalter," G.W., II, 99; I.W. *Die Menschheit* (Wiesbaden, April 17, 1925).
33   See Chapter IX, "Tucholsky and the Communists."
34   Kurt Tucholsky, "Was Nun-?" G.W., II, 108; I.W., *Die Weltbühne*, XXI/18 (May 5, 1925), 645.
35   Ibid., G.W., II, 109.
36   Ibid.
37   Kurt Hiller, *Köpfe und Tröpfe* (Hamburg, 1950), p. 25.
38   Kurt Tucholsky, "Die Erstaunten," G.W., II, 118; I.W., *Die Menschheit* (May 8, 1925).
39   Ibid., G.W., II, 118.
40   Kurt Tucholsky, "Dämmerung," G.W., I, 611; K.T., *Die Weltbühne*, XVI/11 (March 11, 1920), 332.

Above: Secretary of State Walter Rathenau. The German Jewish liberal politician was assassinated by rightwingers in 1922. Soonafter, Tucholsky (below at Place de L'Opéra) would relocate to Paris.

VIII.

GAMES OF WAR

BECAUSE Tucholsky believed that General Paul von Hindenburg's election would create difficulties in German foreign relations, he began to devote an increasing amount of time to a consideration of European diplomacy, concerning himself in particular with the relationship between France and Germany. He developed an ever more pessimistic view of the future course of Franco-German relations and bluntly stated that German expansionism and desires for revenge would cause an outbreak of war in the near future.

In February 1925, Tucholsky elaborated upon his fears in an essay entitled "Zwischen zwei Kriegen" ("Between Two Wars") that was published in *Die Weltbühne*.[1] In the article, he maintained that the French and Germans were no closer to an understanding than they had ever been. All of the efforts of Édouard Herriot, French prime minister since 1924 and Gustav Stresemann, the Weimar chancellor and long-time foreign minister of Germany notwithstanding, the basic position of hostility of the two countries vis-à-vis one another would not change. Tucholsky added that the nations were again playing the same dangerous diplomatic games. They were not really interested in disarmament and international unity, even if protestations of such interest were made in the League of Nations and in the salons of international society. Tucholsky expressed the opinion that in spite of some hopeful signs, the European nations were not pursuing peace. He closed with a prophecy:

> We are not following the ways of peace. It is untrue to believe that friendly conferences by Lake Geneva [i.e. the Locarno Treaties] will sweep away the causes of future wars, namely: free economy, tariff boundaries and the absolute sovereignty of the state. The children of our best-known men all have the prospect of becoming unknown soldiers. It is not necessary for Germany to transform herself into a monarchy—this Republic will do it nicely enough. The philosophical

advocates of a black-red-gold liberation struggle are far more dangerous than the bearded worshipers of Wotan. We are standing where we stood in 1900—between two wars.[2]

It was, of course, an accident that Tucholsky was so amazingly accurate in his prediction. It was fourteen years after 1900 that World War I began. It was also fourteen years after 1925 that World War II began!

It is interesting that Tucholsky expounded the theory that the real danger to European peace lay with the "so-called republicans." In the past, Tucholsky had not ascribed overtly evil intentions to the moderates. He usually denounced them for a lack of courage, for timidity or stupidity. It was the forces of the ancien régime that he attacked as consciously plotting to destroy democracy and decency. But Tucholsky made a distinction between domestic politics and foreign policy. He claimed that the vociferous groups that attracted the most attention abroad—the officers, the Nationalists and the Junkers—were mainly in the internal politics of Germany. This was true because their desires for vengeance and an aggressive foreign policy were well known and could thus be guarded against.

The republicans, on the other hand, were more dangerous because they wore the mask of republicanism. Tucholsky claimed that they were just as revanchist and nationalistic in their attitudes toward foreign policy as any Junker. Their profession of republican ideals only served to conceal their true aims. Tucholsky was not speaking of the Socialists, but of the Democrats, the Centrists and those members of the German People's Party who claimed to be republicans. It was they who voted for the army budgets and it would be they who would approve the funds necessary for the next war. Tucholsky added that he had no doubt that the war of revenge would be fought under the colors of the Republic:

> Scratch a republican and you find a subject of William. The question is no longer republic or monarchy—that is a concern of yesterday. The question is imperialism or no. Germany answers, "Imperialism."[3]

Tucholsky thus believed that the Republic was pursuing the same goals as the Empire in the power politics of international diplomacy. In his eyes the republicans and the Nationalists were identical in regard to foreign policy— the Republic would eventually go to war for the imperialistic ideals of the Empire. Tucholsky naturally knew that there were differences between the extreme Nationalists and the moderate parties. The former would have embarked upon an ambitious and disastrous foreign policy as soon as possible. The moderates were more delicate, but Tucholsky was convinced that mere participation in the power game would lead to war. Hence the end result of the moderates' policy would be the same.

It is here that a weakness in Tucholsky's analysis is revealed. He so desperately wanted a revolution in German—and indeed in European—politics and culture and he so despised the ways of the power state that he was sometimes blinded to the finer distinctions necessary for everyday political life. He might hate the diplomatic game, but some of its players were less likely to make a war inevitable than others. The real differences between the moderates and the extremists of the right were apparent in issues such as the Dawes Plan and Germany's membership in the League of Nations. Certainly on the basis of those questions, no one could maintain that the goals of republicans and Nationalists were identical.

It may have been true that little separated the parties of the middle and the parties of the right as long as the Emperor was in power. But when those same middle parties were themselves thrust into power under the Republic and the right wing entered into opposition, the resemblance disappeared. Tucholsky found it difficult to recognize that the men who wielded power in the Republic were more interested in retaining that power for themselves than they were in handing it over to the forces of the old regime. The very fact of the Republic separated the moderates from the extreme right for all time. It is ironic that the intellectual left was one of the few groups in Germany that at times behaved as though the Empire still existed.

In 1925 Tucholsky predicted with amazing and uncanny accuracy the foreign policy that eventually led to World War II. Ironically, he chose Gustav Stresemann as the perpetrator of that policy. In Tucholsky's view it was Stresemann's attempt to revise the Versailles Treaty that would eventually lead to war. Thus, in the end, Stresemann was indistinguishable from the Nationalist revanchists and warmongers.

There is some ambiguity whether Tucholsky actually refers to Stresemann in "Zwischen zwei Kriegen", because Tucholsky does not mention the German foreign minister directly by name. Hans Prescher states in his book *Kurt Tucholsky* that the article refers to no particular person, but to a type of diplomacy. Mary Gerold Tucholsky has said in a personal letter to the author, that she believes the article refers to General Hans von Seeckt. Tucholsky probably had both Stresemann and Seeckt in mind when he wrote the piece, but the bulk of the article is an exact description of Stresemann's policies toward England and France. He could not have had Seeckt in mind since it was well known that the general did not favor agreements with France whom he believed could never be satisfied. Tucholsky's description of the eastern policy could with greater plausibility be applied to Seeckt, but since Stresemann finally came around to Seeckt's point of view concerning the east, Tucholsky's article is described here as referring solely to Stresemann. Nevertheless, Tucholsky's description of the eastern policy was a lucky guess since he could not know Seeckt's secret intentions and the reaffirmation of the Rapallo Treaty was not made until April 24, 1926.[4]

In spite of his polemical tone, it is doubtful that Tucholsky really believed that Stresemann was actively planning a war, but he did think that Stresemann's policies did help to make a future war more likely. And in this, Tucholsky was essentially right. He may not have seen clearly the danger posed by a fascist demagogue in Germany, but he correctly assessed the dangerous game that German diplomats were playing when they attempted to amend the treaty settlement. Although we may reject the vehemence of Tucholsky's invective in 1925, there can be little doubt that the Weimar Republic provided the basis for Hitler's foreign policy. It was in his judgment of the ultimate effect of Stresemann's policy that Tucholsky was most accurate in his description of the consequences of Germany's failure to undergo a true political and cultural revolution. Thus, we shall investigate in this chapter in greater detail Stresemann's accomplishments and Tucholsky's view of them.

Gustav Stresemann was the leader of the German People's Party (DVP) whose membership was composed primarily of business and industrial interests. During the war, he had been known for his ultra-nationalist and annexationist views, a fact which may account for Tucholsky's extreme suspicion of his motives in 1925. As a convinced Monarchist, Stresemann opposed the foundation of the Republic in 1918, but Stresemann had always been a realist and he came to believe that business interests could also prosper under a republican form of government. He acknowledged Germany's defeat and came to believe that she could regain her strength only by cooperation with the victors, who, because of a renewed friendship, would eventually lift the burdens imposed by the treaty. In Stresemann's view, a *détente* with France was absolutely necessary if Germany was to stabilize her position. If somehow French security could be assured, the Rhineland would be evacuated and Germany could concentrate upon a revision of her eastern frontier.

Stresemann had become Foreign Minister in 1923, but it was not until January 1925 that he was able to pursue a policy of friendship with France. It was then that he began the negotiations, which were to lead to the Locarno treaties of October between Germany and the victorious Allies of World War I, and the entrance of Germany into the League of Nations in 1926. Stresemann won international acclaim for his peacemaking activities. Germany was restored as a respectable member of the European family of nations and Norway awarded Stresemann the Nobel Peace Prize in 1927. For three years much was made of the "spirit of Locarno" by seekers of European union and cooperation.

The agreements signed at Locarno on October 16, 1925, consisted mainly of the recognition by Germany of her western frontier. They meant that Germany continued to agree to the demilitarization of the Rhineland and that she accepted the western frontiers established at Versailles, including the loss of Alsace-Lorraine. Little that was binding was said about the east since Great Britain refused to be a party to any kind of agreement guaranteeing the eastern frontier. As a result the significance of the pact was somewhat vitiated for France.

On the surface it appeared that France was the victor at Locarno, but Germany had not really given up anything that was hers. She had only recognized again the loss of territories that she was too impotent militarily to recover anyway. The advantages gained by the Germans were incomparable. The lessening of international tensions would make it easier for them to begin to rectify the eastern losses. The practical exclusion of the east from consideration at Locarno was a triumph for Stresemann. Having secured the west, he had opened the way for revision in the east. And Stresemann let it be known in 1925 that Germany could never accept the eastern frontier imposed upon her by Versailles; mainly, the border between Germany and Poland respectively Czechoslovakia. Yet in 1925 few persons were bothered by the unpleasant eastern questions. Instead they concentrated upon the "spirit of Locarno" and the precedent it had set for the peaceful negotiation of future European disputes.

Tucholsky, however, was unconvinced. As early as March 1925 he questioned the intent of Stresemann's reconciliation policy. Indeed, Tucholsky maintained that Stresemann was courting the west only to make war in the east. In other words, Tucholsky believed that a *détente* in the west would do nothing to halt the war whose approach he had predicted in "Zwischen zwei Kriegen." Tucholsky then outlined what he believed the future course of the Republic's eastern policy would be. In doing so, he gave an almost perfect account of Nazi foreign policy from 1938 to the outbreak of war in 1939.

Tucholsky maintained that Stresemann had subverted Versailles by helping to rebuild German industrial and military power. He wrote that beneath Stresemann's outer veneer of peace, based upon the order established by Versailles, lay the desire to restore the European position of the old Germany:

> You built quietly and you are not yet finished—but you have already accomplished something in common with the businessmen: imperialistic Germany has again become a European power.[5]

Tucholsky admitted that by accepting the western frontier, Stresemann had at least recognized *half* of the Versailles Treaty. The west could thus breathe more easily since it was assured Germany would undertake nothing against France. "But," Tucholsky asked, "if not against France, then against whom?" He answered his own question with "Poland." "There are ways to Paris in addition to those through Belfort—namely, through Warsaw."[6]

In his analysis, Tucholsky wrote that Germany's foreign policy for forty years had depended on a split between England and France. Now that the split no longer existed, the Germans would turn to the other side and "walk the road to catastrophe" by pursuing an aggressive eastern policy. Tucholsky maintained that it would be easy to trap the Poles into performing a provocative action since "as all small peoples, the Poles are possessed by a wild, provincial nationalism." Tucholsky then outlined in three paragraphs what he believed the future foreign policy of the Republic would be:

> At first everything will click. You will accomplish the *Anschluss* with Austria that is indispensable for you—the permeation of Austria with Prussian energy. Away with the republican army in Vienna; away with certain democratic tendencies that existed in that stump; away with the gentle deception of the Entente when the Austrians were able to say with a wink, "We are not as bad as our German brothers!!...
>
> ... Czechoslovakia will not be as easy to catch, but that is not really necessary. Filled with non-Czechs and often still shattered by nationality conflicts, but remarkably well led, that country poses for you no real danger since you think only in a military fashion. "We'll soon be finished with the Czechs." Finished yes—it is only a question of who is finished in the end.
>
> Poland remains. You calculate in this fashion: As a beginning, the Poles must be overrun. It is therefore necessary that you reach a previous understanding with Russia. The Russians may be trusted with all sorts of things—but not to make common cause with you against Poland and Romania, for each will believe he is able to deceive the other behind his back.... .[7]

Tucholsky stated furthermore that Germany would slowly squeeze out of paying reparations by agreement with America. Then in order to become the great power of Eastern Europe, Germany would attempt to extend her dominion to Asia itself. Tucholsky maintained, however, that the policy would fail because it would lead to war. The attack upon Poland would bring men from "Caledonia to California" in order to prevent a German hegemony in Europe. Tucholsky emphasized again that it would be the Republic, which would accomplish all of this.⁸ Tucholsky was, of course, astonishingly correct in his general outline. An aggressive eastern policy did precipitate World War II, but it was not Stresemann's policy directly.

There is much controversy among historians over the question of whether or not Stresemann was a "good European."⁹ Was he, as Tucholsky implied, guilty of duplicity in the negotiations leading up to Locarno? Did he know the generals were rearming while he pursued peace at Locarno? Was he acting in bad faith? These and similar issues have aroused heated controversy, but they are irrelevant if they involve the question (as they must) of whether or not Stresemann was remaining faithful to the spirit of the policy of fulfillment. Stresemann had never accepted the Versailles Treaty as being just and none of his statements, either public or private should have led anyone to believe that he had.¹⁰ Stresemann simply recognized that Germany was powerless to revise the treaty by any method except "cooperation."

There is no doubt that Stresemann knew of the secret rearmament of Germany, even though in November 1923 he denied to Lord Edgar Vincent d'Abernon, the British Ambassador to Berlin, that German armament factories existed in Russia (Abernon believed Stresemann, which later got the conservative politician and banker the reputation of being the "the pioneer of appeasement").¹¹ It would have been difficult for Stresemann not to know of Germany's circumvention of the treaty since almost everyone else did. Seeckt's biographer, Friedrich von Rabenau, says that in 1924 Seeckt believed it to be "a point of general knowledge… the fact that the Reichswehr's forces-in-being were slowly exceeding their legal limits."¹²

In 1930, the British chief of the imperial general staff, General Milne, indicated that the British had long known of "secret" German rearmament.¹³ But the most important point is that few persons really cared. This is shown by the decision to disband the Allied inspection commission in 1926, even *after* the *Manchester Guardian* had made its sensational disclosures about German rearmament. The *Guardian* had based his story on Philipp Scheidemann, the Social Democrat who had proclaimed Germany a republic from a window of the Reichstag in 1919. Even the issue of the *Guardian* that made the revelations also contained an editorial demanding an end to military surveillance in Germany.¹⁴ However, the issue is confused by those who say that by his knowledge of the secret rearmament, Stresemann was pursuing a war policy. In other words, he was only securing his defenses in the west in order to make war in the east. First, a general word about armaments.

Stresemann desired disarmament in the whole of Europe. Until that was accomplished, he believed there should be equality of arms. It is true that the purpose of armaments may ultimately be war, but in a world in which nations equate armed power with greatness, to countenance the development of weapons is not necessarily to pursue the course of war. A few generals may have had a war of revenge in mind. It is the business of generals to "have war in mind," but it is foolish to say that Stresemann's belief in German equality of arms was identical to belief in the necessity of war.

The very "spirit of Locarno" itself has created much misunderstanding of Stresemann's true position concerning rearmament. Locarno meant more than optimistic contemporaries were willing to admit. The Rhineland Pact was redundant since Germany had supposedly accepted all it contained when she signed the Peace of Paris. By allowing Germany to confirm her acceptance, of only a *part* of the treaty, the Allies threw the remainder of the Versailles agreement into question. Locarno was thus a circumvention of the treaty and the fact that Stresemann tolerated circumvention in other ways should have been a surprise to no one with his eyes open.

Stresemann's speech before the Council of the League of Nations on September 10, 1926, did not, of course, discourage pacifistic idealism. In it he stated that the German government was committed to peace, to international community, to individual freedom and to the equality of nations.[15] They were lofty phrases, but in them there was no acceptance, either implicit or explicit of the Treaty of Versailles:

> Of especial importance for the establishment of an ordered peace between the nations are the League activities in the direction of disarmament. The complete disarmament of Germany is indicated in the Treaty of Versailles as the beginning of general disarmament. May it be possible to make some practical progress towards general disarmament, and so prove that a strong and positive force inspires the great ideals of the League.[16]

Germany's signing the agreements at Locarno and joining the League did not mean that she was willing to be the junior partner in a new world of peace and friendship. Germany was not to be a messianic nation who in a mood of self-sacrifice and atonement would begin the new order by relinquishing military prowess and national sovereignty. Stresemann may have professed a faith in peace and unity, but he implied that equality must come first. "Equality" meant equal military power and the right to behave as irresponsibly as any other nation. Only when true equality was achieved could progress toward the community of nations be made.

Few had ears to hear, however, least of all the German ultra-Nationalists. It was ironic that they subjected Stresemann to a bitter tirade of abuse and vilification. The Nationalist press owned by Alfred Hugenberg (who later helped Adolf Hitler to power) violently opposed the policy of reconciliation because it seemed to mean acceptance of the shackles of Versailles. In actuality, Locarno gave Germany more freedom to maneuver than she had known since 1918. But Stresemann, the master of the old diplomacy, became the hero of the pacifists and the "Europeans," while he was despised as the archfiend by the Nationalists.

Tucholsky did not join in the applause since he believed that a strict adherence to the treaty was the best guarantee of the peace. But it should be clear that Stresemann did not conceal his dislike of the treaty and his unwillingness to help carry out its provisions. Tucholsky's charge of duplicity in so far as the Versailles Treaty was concerned had no foundation. However, even though his polemical style may have caused him to exaggerate, Tucholsky also accused Stresemann—or his kind of policy—of deliberately planning war in the east. It was a serious charge and it is not to be taken lightly, for although Tucholsky in his own time was one of the few members of the left to distrust Stresemann's intentions, similar accusations came to be widely accepted during World War II. Was there any truth in Tucholsky's belief that Stresemann's diplomacy was designed to produce war in the east?

Stresemann was far from satisfied with Germany's position in the east. As he wrote to ex-Crown Prince William on September 7, 1925, concerning the tasks of German foreign policy:

> The third great task is the readjustment of our eastern frontier; the recovery of Danzig, the Polish Corridor, and a correction of the frontier in Upper Silesia.[17]

The question is: was he willing to go to war to accomplish these goals?

Like most Germans of the period, Stresemann was prejudiced against Poles.[18] It was inconceivable to him that Poles should be allowed to rule over Germans and he believed with all his heart that they should be prevented from doing so. But there seems to be no real evidence that he ever considered war with Poland. If he had ever thought of war, it was no longer the case on April 16, 1926, when he wrote the German ambassador in London: "English collaboration is an absolute prerequisite to a *peaceful* solution of our eastern problem, and only *a peaceful solution* can be considered."[19] Furthermore, Stresemann appears to have believed that an economic collapse of Poland would aid him in achieving his goals peacefully.[20]

Was there then no basis for Tucholsky's harsh judgment of Stresemann? Certainly there was. Tucholsky did not have access to Stresemann's private letters and papers and thus could have no way of knowing the Foreign Minister's true intentions. There were many signs that Germany intended to do mischief in the east. She categorically refused to discuss the eastern boundaries in the Locarno negotiations. The rumor of Seeckt's military agreements with Soviet Russia made it seem highly likely that a plot for the partition of Poland was in the making. Tucholsky's suspicions of Stresemann's motives were not allayed when the *Manchester Guardian* and Philipp Scheidemann made their revelations of the German army's secret collusion with the Red Army. As Tucholsky wrote then, "If this continues, war in the east is a certainty." And Tucholsky was correct—not about Stresemann—but about the ultimate outcome of his eastern policies.

Stresemann had no warlike intentions, but when a man who was war-minded came into power, he found all in readiness. By the time Hitler appeared on the scene, the Republic had tolerated years of active anti-Polish propaganda. And Hitler used the army organization which had been clandestinely preserved and revitalized in the 1920s. In addition the reaffirmation of the Rapallo Agreement, the German-Soviet Treaty of Neutrality and Non-Aggression, signed in 1926 and renewed in 1931 and 1933, became the foundation of the Nazi-Soviet Pact of 1939. Stresemann may have wanted to pursue his goals only by negotiation, but when the Poles proved intransigent, his more brutal successor went to war. Thus in essence Tucholsky saw clearly the correct outline of the future, but his role was to be that of Cassandra.

NOTES

1 Kurt Tucholsky, "Zwischen zwei Kriegen," G.W., II, 38-43; I.W., *Die Weltbühne*, XX/6 (February 10, 1925), 185.

2 Ibid., G.W., II, 42f.

3 Kurt Tucholsky, "Zwei Sozialdemokratien," G.W., II, 85; I.W., *Die Menschheit* (April 3, 1925).

4 Hans Prescher, in *Kurt Tucholsky* (Berlin, 1959). See also: Kurt Tucholsky, "Brief an einen bessern Herrn," G.W., II, 67-72; I.W., *Die Weltbühne*, XXI/12 (March 24, 1925), 426.

5 Ibid., G.W., II, 68.

6 Ibid.

7 Ibid., 69.

8 Ibid., 71.

9 A substantial literature has arisen concerning Stresemann. Several important works are: Henry L. Bretton, Stresemann and the Revision of Versailles, A Fight for Reason (Stanford, 1953); Henry Ashby Turner, Jr., Stresemann and the Politics of the Weimar Republic (Princeton, 1963), which deals with Stresemann's involvement in German domestic policies and makes extensive use of the Stresemann Papers; and Antonina Vallentin, Stresemann (New York, 1931), an older biography which is much quoted, bot now out of date because of the release of the Stresemann Papers. See also Hans W. Gatzke, Stresemann and the Rearmament of Germany (Baltimore, 1954); and lastly, Gordon A. Craig, From Bismarck to Adenauer: Aspects of German Statecraft (Baltimore, 1958). Craig, in this excellent little study does not discuss Stresemann's status as a "good European." Instead he pursues the more relevant theme of Stresemann as a master diplomat. See also Harvey Leonard Dyck, Weimar Germany and Soviet Russia, 1926-1933: A Study in Diplomatic Instability (New York, 1966), which maintains that Stresemann approved of German-Soviet army collaboration.

10 See Eric Sutton (ed. and trans.), *Gustav Stresemann, His Diaries, Letters and Papers* (London, 1937), II, 59-253.

11 John Wheeler-Bennett, *The Nemesis of Power* (New York, 1954), p. 141.

12 Quoted by Erick Eyck, *A History of the Weimar Republic* (Cambridge, Mass., 1963), II, 46.

13 Ibid., pp. 214f.; see also *Great Britain, Official Documents, Documents on British Foreign Policy, 1919-1939, second series*, edited by E. L. Woodward and Rohan Butler (London, 1946), I, 603.

14 Eyck, II, 97.

15 For the text of Stresemann's speech, see Eric Sutton, ed., *Gustav Stresemann...*, II, 532-536.

16 Ibid., p. 535.

17 Ibid., p. 503.

18 Eyck, II, 30.

19 Quoted by *Ibid.*, from the Stresemann Papers, 7414H.

20 Gordon Craig, *From Bismarck to Adenauer*, p. 77n. Professor Craig adds: "That Stresemann thought of achieving his eastern ambitions by negotiation and not by force is supported by abundant evidence."

Adolf Hitler (left) and Reichspräsident Paul von Hindenburg. The World War I general would make Hitler Chancellor of Germany.

IX.

"PRELUDE TO SILENCE"

THE FINAL years of the Republic were years of disappointment and personal disorder for Tucholsky. Ironically they also comprised the years of his greatest public success. Yet as time passed he began to lose all hope for Germany. To be sure, he continued to write, to attack, but he appeared to be fighting out of despair and desperation, not because of optimism and faith. For a time his struggle became more and more furious, a wild-swinging attack upon everything he hated in the culture. In the final years, there was little system, little order to his crusade. He was a man fighting a last desperate battle, forced to strike out randomly against his enemies as they inexorably closed in upon him. As it became evident that the battle was lost, Tucholsky's fighting spirit ebbed, his final public silence proclaiming his admission of defeat.

Tucholsky's public despair was also mirrored in private misfortune and sorrow. The heightened sense of life, which he had experienced during the first months in Paris did not continue. In the closing years of the twenties, the death of friends, marital troubles and poor health began to beat him down and thrust him into mental depression. This period of despair and disorder had an incisive beginning. During the night of December 3, 1926, Siegfried Jacobsohn suddenly and unexpectedly died.

Profoundly shocked, Tucholsky returned to Berlin to take up the unfamiliar task of editing the Weltbühne. Jacobsohn's widow owned the magazine, but since Tucholsky had long been its most important contributor, it was unthinkable that anyone else should become its editor. Tucholsky did not find his new job easy. The journal had a circulation of only fifteen thousand and there were many financial problems inevitably connected with such a small enterprise. In addition, Tucholsky did not possess an editor's temperament. He found his necessarily didactic position uncomfortable. As early as mid-January 1927 he wanted to give it up. Not only did his editorial duties rob his creative energies for his own writing, but Berlin was so depressing that he found it difficult to accomplish any kind of work. In the end he solved the problem by hiring Carl von Ossietzky as editor-in-chief.[1]

Known for his writings in the *Welt am Montag* and Leopold Schwarzschild's *Tagebuch*, Ossietzky had already appeared in the *Weltbühne* for more than a year. He opposed the extremes of both left and right, but he saw the right wing as the greater danger. Although he criticized the KPD, he opened the pages of the *Weltbühne* to Communist writers in the common struggle against reaction. In brief, he upheld the standards of excellence of Jacobsohn, while making the magazine a more militant organ of leftist opinion.

It was, of course, impossible for anyone else to play Jacobsohn's role in Tucholsky's life. As Tucholsky said of his friend, "Our articles were really only letters to him."[2] Jacobsohn and Tucholsky had exchanged thousands of cards and letters containing quips, topical comments and, above all, editorial criticism of Tucholsky's writings. Theirs was an ideal author-editor relationship that transcended professional boundaries to become the closest friendship of Tucholsky's life. Ossietzky could obviously never fulfill such a function and his relationship with Tucholsky remained on a strictly professional level. Without a word, the new editor published whatever Tucholsky submitted—a strange and uncomfortable innovation for Tucholsky. Ossietzky understandably refrained from passing judgment on his older, more experienced colleague, but Tucholsky constantly complained of his aloofness and silence:

> Ossietzky—Ah, he is so distant. He almost never answers—it's been, I believe, two weeks since I've heard from him—irritations, proposals, jokes—nothing.[3]

Aloof or not, Ossietzky freed Tucholsky to leave Berlin and return to Paris. But France did not offer the solace and comfort, which he had expected. He remained restless and vaguely dissatisfied. He hated looking for a new house and his pattern of life seemed restricted and repetitive. Above all, his marriage was falling apart. Mary had begun to suspect that Tucholsky felt cramped by his legal bond to her. And although they never discussed the matter, she had a presentiment that he was indulging his attraction to other women. Mary was not the type to suffer ambiguity and she decided to return to Berlin in 1928. Tucholsky did nothing to reassure her and he sat sadly alone in Parc Monceau on the day she departed.

As in the past, it was only when Mary was irrevocably lost that Tucholsky realized how much she meant to him. He continued to correspond with her and even admitted at the end of his life that she was the one person he had ever really loved. It was a tragedy that two persons so profoundly attracted to one another found it impossible to live together. However, Tucholsky and Mary did not bother to obtain a divorce until 1933 when it became unsafe for her to live in Germany under his name. Tucholsky even offered to send her a letter saying they had separated for political reasons, if she thought it would make life safer. In his will, Tucholsky made Mary his "Universal Heir" (in the words of the German legal formula) and she inherited the rights to all his works.

Tucholsky did not marry again but he had liaisons with other women, none of which proved to be permanent. One of his mistresses, Lisa Matthias, did, however, provide the model for one of his most well-known fictional characters, Lottchen. Depicting a frivolous, gabbling, extravagant, thoroughly lovable gold-digger of a woman, the hilarious Lottchen monologues became as famous as the Wendriner stories. Wherever she is, Lottchen never stops talking. She constantly schemes how to get "Daddy" (as she calls Tucholsky—employing the English word) to buy her what she wants. She has no appreciation for intellect, but she understands economics well—the figures involved in buying fine cars, beautiful clothes and lovely trips. One of the best of the five Lottchen stories is "Lottchen Confesses One Lover." Lottchen doesn't speak; she chatters:

> There's something strange about me? What is that supposed to mean—something strange about me? There is nothing strange about me. Now come and give Lottchen a little kiss. Nobody's given me one little kiss the whole four weeks you've been in Switzerland. Nothing happened here. No—nothing happened here! What did you notice at once? You didn't notice anything at once—oh, Daddy! I'm as faithful to you as you are to me. No, that means—well, I'm really faithful to you! You fall in love with anything that has a woman's name in it. I am faithful to you—thank God! Nothing happened here.
> —Only a couple of times to the theater. No, inexpensive seats—well, the one time in the loge. How do you know that? What? How? Who told you that? Well, you, they were seats—through connections—naturally I was there with a man. You think I should go to the theater with a night nurse? Dear Daddy, it was harmless, completely harmless. Don't play the Camorra or Mafia or whatever they do in Corsica. In Sicily—all right, in Sicily! At any rate, it was harmless. Well, what did they tell you? What? Nothing happened.
> It was—it is—you don't know the man. No, I cannot do that—if I go with another man to the theater, then I will not go with a man whom you know. Really—I have not compromised you. Men are so impossible—they don't like it if you go out with their friends. And if it isn't a friend, the result is the same: Miss Julie! It is really not easy! Anyway

you don't know the man! You don't know him. Yes—he knows you—you're famous. It was quite harmless. Absolutely. Afterward we went to dinner. But nothing else.

Nothing. It was nothing. The man—the man is— I took him in the car because he looked so good beside me in the car—a magnificent escort. Oh, did Reventlow say that too? Well, I admitted it. But only as an escort. Oh the man was handsome. That is true. A wonderful mouth, such a hard mouth—just give Lottchen one little kiss. He was stupid. It was nothing.

Actually, he was not absolutely stupid. It is —I didn't fall in love with him. You know well enough that I only fall in love when you are around. A nice man, but I don't really go for the boys anymore. Not me. I don't really want all of that anymore. Daddy, he wasn't that good—looking. Anyway, he kissed well. So there was, I assure you, nothing more.

Tell me, what do you think of me anyway? Do you think of me what I think of you? You—I won't have it! I am faithful. Daddy, the man-well he was a kind of mood. Well, first you left me here alone, and then you didn't write much and you telephoned only once. And when a woman is alone, she is much more alone than you men. I certainly do not need a man—not I. And I didn't need him either; he must have no doubt about that! I only thought, I thought—when I saw him—I knew at once when I first saw him—but it was nothing.

After the theater there were still two weeks. No. Yes. Only roses and candy twice and the small soapstone lion. No. Give him my house key? Are you—! I would not give a strange man my key—! I'd sooner give him shelter. Daddy, I felt nothing for the man—and he nothing for me—you know that. Because he had such a hard mouth—and very small lips. Because he was once a sailor. What? On the Wannsee [a lake near Berlin]? The man went to sea on a gigantic ship—I forget the name. He knows all the commands and he has a hard mouth. Very small lips. He can't talk. But he kisses well, Daddy, if I hadn't felt so down, nothing would have happened—nothing really did happen. He doesn't count. What? In town. No, we did not eat at his place; we had dinner in town. Of course, he paid—are you mad? I should finance my acquaintances—that is too much—! It was absolutely nothing.

Tattooed? The man is not tattooed! The man has very clear skin, he has—no details? No details! Either you want me to tell you or you don't want me to tell you. From me you will not hear another word about the man. Daddy, if he hadn't been a sailor, then I want to tell you something. First. It was nothing. Second. You don't know the man. And third. Because he was a sailor and I gave him nothing and above all, like Paul Graetz says—barely once and it's ail the same—Daddy! Daddy! Leave

it—what is this here? What? How? What is that picture? Who is this woman? How? What? Where did you meet her? What? In Lucerne? Did you go on a little trip with her? In Switzerland they make little trips. Don't tell me anything—what? It was nothing.
This is a different matter. Me—once in a while I am attracted to a man. But you men?
You lose your heads!⁴

Humor was Tucholsky's greatest strength in the closing republican years. As he recognized, the time cried out for satire, for the Republic was so dogged by misfortune that its tragedy bordered on comedy.

The last years of the republican era were a study in political decline. The mid-twenties had seemed rosy enough. The German economy had recovered remarkably after the loans made possible by the Dawes Plan in 1924. The second economic scheme, the Young Plan of 1929, seemed to provide a method whereby the halcyon economic situation could continue. But the crash came too soon for the Young Plan to be implemented, and without its funds the German economic miracle proved to be a cheap conjurer's trick. By 1930, the state of emergency was so great that Chancellor Heinrich Brüning decided, perhaps mistakenly, that government by the ordinary processes was impossible. Government by presidential decree became the rule. The ranks of the Communists and the Nazis were swelled by the masses of unemployed laborers. In 1932 the clashes between these two implacable enemies took the form of violence and murder. As the economic depression grew in intensity, Germany succumbed to chaos.

The last, rather dramatic statement might cause a German who experienced these events to smile, for the idea that Germany was "gripped by chaos" became one of the great clichés of the time. So much so, in fact, that Tucholsky felt compelled to satirize it:

GERMAN CHAOS:

August 10
The chaos, which was announced would begin this morning at 8:30 has been postponed until tomorrow by an emergency decree of the government.

August 11
This morning at 8:30 chaos broke out (see last report). The chaos was begun by a speech of the Chancellor as well as by a brief, to the point statement by President Hindenburg. The Prussian Minister President,

Braun, asserted in his chaos address that Germany also was following the Prussian example.
Bavarian chaos first broke out at 9:10A.M. The National Bank is taking a wait-and-see position.

August 12

Today the National Chaos Agency began its work. Each chaos must have a special approval for Outbreak of Chaos obtainable from the National Chaos Agency. After which, there is an inspection by the National Chaos Inspection Office as well as by local state chaos officials. For the time being the National Bank is taking a wait-and-see attitude.

August 13

Chaos has now definitively broken out everywhere. A charming incident occurred in Esslingen [Württemberg]. The mayor there forgot to place the measures of the National Chaos Agency into effect and the good people of Esslingen knew nothing of the chaos until yesterday evening. They all went about their activities… with touching zeal. Only a radio announcement by the Württemberg chaos government put an end to this circumstance. Baking of *Chaos-Spätzle* is forbidden until further notice.

August 14

Today the German Social Democratic Party concluded the preliminaries of a significant resolution. The party has empowered its fraction to attempt to have the senior counsel of the so-called "Reichstag" make representations before the national government to the effect that the government, with all the means at its disposal, should ameliorate Paragraph 14 of the Chaos Law. Otherwise the party will enter into opposition.
The resolution is very significant because this is the first indication that a Social Democratic Party exists in Germany and that this party has ever stood in opposition to anything.
For the moment the National Bank will take a wait-and-see position.

August 15

The world economy, whose eyes are directed tensely upon Germany, needs peace and perseverance. We must hold out throughout the chaos! Chancellor Brüning will also continue to conduct business in chaos. … That the National Bank is taking a wait-and-see attitude needs no mention. …

August 20
The Berlin students, on the occasion of the tenth Chaos Day protested against the Peace of Westphalia as well as against all future peace agreements. Academic honor and four policemen were slightly wounded. The court was brought before Hitler.
Light chaos with a strong south-westerly wind.

August 21
The education committee of the SPD has protested the party-damaging products of the Asphalt-Literaten. In any event, the party, as such, has been dissolved.
Gerhart Shaw and Bernard Hauptmann, in order to cut advertising costs, have decided to celebrate their next birthday together. They will be 150.

August 23
The title of the Confusion Counselor, Dr. Schacht, has been changed to Senior Chaos Counselor.

August 24
Yesterday, in the streets of Schöneberg, a German mark was seen. This is obviously a case of public deception. We must emphasize that it is not in the national interest if such an incident occurs in Germany again. Even if the foreigners are not looking, we shall show them! The National Bank continues to wait and see.

August 26
Section 5 of Paragraph 67 of the resumption decree for the suspension of retro-activation of the prohibition of return transfer of old postal check payments to Haiti will be suspended in conformity to Paragraph 10, II, 17, of the General Legal Code—that is, it will be placed back into effect. Our prediction has been fulfilled: there is nothing to distinguish chaos from the present condition.[5]

Unlike his satire, Tucholsky's serious criticism began to assume an almost old-fashioned quality. In 1929 Tucholsky published his book *Deutschland, Deutschland über Alles*, a bitter, sometimes shocking attack upon everything that he disliked in Germany. The book consisted of separate articles and brief captions accompanied by John Heartfield's mocking and satiric photomontage—Heartfied, a famed visual artist who was number five on the Gestapo's most-wanted list, fled the Nazis to England in 1938. With the book, Tucholsky achieved a *succès de scandale*, which made him one of the most controversial writers of the time. But for all of its shock effect, the dominant quality of the book seemed to be a lack of timeliness. Ostensibly the critique was of Weimar culture, yet the book appeared to be far more a catalogue of Tucholsky's dislikes of the old imperial regime. Much of it was simply a cliché for Tucholsky in 1929. The majority of the articles, captions and pictures could have appeared in 1919.

Deutschland, Deutschland über Alles contains many diverse themes of varying importance, which follow each other in no apparent order. Many of the essays and poems had appeared before in the *Weltbühne*; others were written for a specific photograph in the collection. Part of the book consisted of Tucholsky's subjective reaction to what he considered to be minor cultural annoyances and shortcomings, such as the ugliness of mailboxes and the mental vacuity of sports fanatics. The main objects of attack, however, were the former monarchy, the army, organized religion, the judiciary and the Nationalists. One of the book's most effective techniques was the use of contrast. A series of photographs would show miserable poverty and squalor with the question, "Where is Germany's money? Here?" The reply was, "No, here," and then followed pictures of rich banquets, brimming shop-windows and costly army maneuvers.[6]

Another contrast was devoted to pacifism. The first of two photographs showed a crowd of happy school children playing in the snow. The second depicted a group of dead soldiers, one of whom is naked and mutilated. Another photograph, captioned "camouflage," showed a large machine gun and two men covered by a heavy net which renders them almost invisible. Tucholsky's comment: "This net is not a net. It is an allegory." Tucholsky derided the racist (*völkisch*) parties and their vulgar doctrines by showing a child washing a chamber pot in the gutter. There was much more of *Deutschland, Deutschland über Alles*, which appeared not to be Tucholsky's kind of satire. Sometimes it showed a surprising lack of taste such as in the article "Köpfe" ("Heads") . It showed two stern, rather characterless "Prussian" faces and described the cultural emptiness that Tucholsky believed they represented. On the overpage was a picture of a man's buttocks, with ears growing from each side, thus showing that certain faces "belonged in trousers." 14 But this and similar lapses of taste were exceptional in the light of the great body of Tucholsky's work, and the importance of *Deutschland, Deutschland über Alles* did not lie there. The book made many dramatic and poignant effects. Occasionally it provided great social satire or wise cultural criticism such as the poem "German Judges of 1940" which accompanied a picture of two fierce-looking youths, proudly posing after a bloody student duel. And there was the excellent article "German Judges" among whose pages was contained an equally superior satiric photograph of a judge with paragraph signs in place of his face and hands.

The parts of the book devoted to the Republic as such sought to make its institutions and leaders look ridiculous. In doing so, Tucholsky did not confine himself to generalities. For example, the President of the Reichstag, Paul Löbe, was pictured in a tasteless hiking costume—a photograph that Heartfield had dug up somewhere. For Tucholsky, Löbe was the example of the mediocre man who through simple perseverance, but no special merit, rises to the top. Tucholsky attacked Löbe for betraying the Socialist cause:

> And such are now the labor leaders! These are now those for whom a flame once blazed up to heaven. These are the successors to those men who made sacrifice upon sacrifice for a cause which was holy to them—Paul Löbe is one of the better people in his unspeakable party. He wears a clean vest and never betrays his principles, because he has none... .

This was a vicious, almost irrational attack upon a man who as President of the Reichstag was noted for his impartiality, his fairness and objectivity. To make Löbe look ridiculous and vilify his character was only to aid the cause of his rightist enemies.[7]

The Reichstag was described as a sleeping institution; Stresemann as an epigone, who was only a "star" when compared to the true dramatists of the past. One particularly evocative photograph mocked the alleged impotence of the legislature with an angry little cockatoo with ruffled crest and screeching beak. The picture was entitled "The Reichstag Representative" and the bird was shown as saying, "We shall force the government to... !" The picture, which perhaps became the most famous, displayed the best-known generals of the German past in montage. It was titled "Animals are looking at you" ("Tiere sehen dich an"). It is interesting that this sensational picture was Heartfield's idea, not Tucholsky's. In a letter to Jacob Wassermann, Tucholsky said that it was not his kind of satire, it was too rough, and he added, "Insulting animals doesn't appeal to me."[8]

All in all, *Deutschland, Deutschland über Alles* was an attack both upon the old monarchy and the new Republic. The only genuinely positive note was struck in a final section called "Homeland." It was a eulogy of the natural beauties of Germany:

> For 225 pages, we have said no—no, because of pity; no, because of love; no, because of hate; and no, because of passion. Now we want to say yes. Yes to the landscape and to the countryside of Germany.[9]

In contrast to the violent negativism of most of the book, a few concluding pages praising the countryside was a weak positive note indeed.

Tucholsky himself was aware of the book's shortcomings. In 1933, he described it as "clumsy": "As an artistic accomplishment, the book is clumsy (klobig). And weak. And much too mild."[10] In 1929, it was considered far from mild and even many sympathizers of Tucholsky repudiated *Deutschland, Deutschland über Alles* as being too brutal. Most of the reviews were unfavorable. Herbert Ihering's *Tagebuch* review was one of the best. He accused Tucholsky of writing the same old familiar material and upbraided him for not living in Germany and taking a personal part in the struggle:

> To me it seems to be a polemic without risk when Kurt Tucholsky again and again hammers away at the same old themes. He attacks the same military and the same justice, even if it is done with an often very telling, very amusing and effective characterization of type. However, in *Dt. Dt. über Alles*, it was necessary to say that the same tendencies are recognizable in other countries.... A polemic without risk—precisely, a man as gifted as Tucholsky, a satirist of his stature should be in Germany where he could be a part of things and participate in the struggles. He should not be a spectator in Paris or Sweden and observe things from a distant box in the theater. This kind of polemic from afar was possible at the time when Heinrich Heine was in Paris. But it is not possible today when events trip over one another, when each day witnesses a new corruption upon which one must take a position.[11]

Ihering hit Tucholsky in a sensitive spot and he felt compelled to reply. In a private letter to Ihering, Tucholsky admitted that the book had an anachronistic quality, that it attacked many things, which were long-dead issues. But Tucholsky took sharp issue with the accusation that he always harped upon the same old themes. He stated that the crimes, the indignities and the injustices were still the same and still demanded the same denunciation:

> And believe me, if I constantly write the same things, I do it knowingly. Perhaps it is boring year after year to take Salvarsan; camomile tea would offer greater variety—yet one must take the real cure. Also the spirochetes always remain the same.[12]

As for the accusation that he took no risks, Tucholsky replied that the writers who constantly attacked the Nationalists and the militarists were often beaten and murdered. They seemed to take a risk far greater than those who merely "took a position." Tucholsky believed that Ihering was most unfair when he spoke of the ills of other lands. To say that other countries had failings was not to excuse those of Germany. Even to imply such demonstrated a lack of sympathy for the sufferings of the workers, and the victims of the unjust legal system. Those were the people who remained unsung and unheralded. Tucholsky stated that he would rather write an aesthetically imperfect book dedicated to their silent suffering than remain indolent because of artistic sensitivity.[13]

Perhaps one of the most telling comments on *Deutschland, Deutschland über Alles* was a small Nazi review which Tucholsky found interesting enough to place in his scrapbook of newspaper clippings. Almost all of the Nazis attacked the book, but one particular critic lamented that its author was a Jew, since it provided such good material for the cause of National Socialism: "With this book you have made good prefatory propaganda for us. Heartiest thanks, Monsieur! It was great business for us!"[14]

This perhaps should have been an indication to Tucholsky that Ihering's criticism was more correct than he cared to admit. The spirochetes were not the same; new enemies and problems had arisen. Perhaps Tucholsky had been away too long to recognize the real dangers.

Tucholsky had not spent any length of time in Germany since 1924 with the exception of the brief period of *Weltbühne* editorship. In 1929, he left France and moved to Sweden where he established his residence in Hindas near Göteborg. And it may have been because he lived abroad that Tucholsky's writings began to lack immediacy, to lose touch with the nuances of German life. It is striking how Tucholsky failed to deal with the larger figures and issues during the final years of the Republic. For all of his involvement in political and social development, he curiously did not comment upon the persons and events, which now seem so crucial. The elections of 1930 and 1932 were not discussed in a comprehensive fashion. The economic depression, for all intents and purposes, went unmentioned. Only brief, satirical references were made to Heinrich Brüning. The Nazis were dealt with mainly in satire and song. All in all, his commentary was vague, concerned more with generalization than with specific analysis.

This state of affairs did not go unremarked by Tucholsky's contemporaries, as shown by Ihering's letter in 1929. Two years later, Hans Wesemann in the *Welt am Montag*—in what was more praise than damnation—also upbraided Tucholsky for his seeming lack of touch with German reality:

> … Dear Theobald Tiger. Why do you want to jump over your own shadow? You know German conditions too well to be able really to know them. You are always with events, but you are never in them. The truth is that you are an emigrant. You always write from the outside, from

> beyond the borders. You see our German misery with the endearing hatred of the voluntary expatriate. You move your golden quill against the dusty ghosts of a past which has long hung in the museum with its face to the wall. Your words do not reach the youth! ... Why thus do you always ride against Teutonic windmills that contain nothing? In any event, I say, in confidence, that you sit behind a desk much better than you sit on a horse.[15]

Wesemann believed that in quixotic fashion, Tucholsky continued to fight forces that had long since ceased to be of meaning or importance. He maintained that the old Prussian cant about discipline and militarism had no meaning for a modern youth, brutalized by the war. In other words, Tucholsky seemed, to Wesemann, to be addressing the youth of the Empire, not of the Republic. The problems had become new and different.

Tucholsky's self-imposed exile was not the only reason for the decline in the quality and vitality of his political writings. Although there was no evidence in his publications of his deep personal problems during the last difficult period before 1933, Tucholsky had been for years gripped by intermittent depression and sieges of despair. In 1927, he began a series of restless journeys to Denmark, England, Switzerland and Sweden. The following year his health began to fail and he was forced to take several rest cures:

> I have become very old this year and am in a wicked crisis. If I didn't have my routine it would be noticeable. In truth there is nothing left in me and I want to enter a monastery and have my peace. Hm—.[16]

Although he was writing half in jest, Tucholsky was slowly becoming possessed by a spiritual exhaustion. The complaint that he was devoid of ideas and weary of writing was a constant refrain in 1928. On August 7, he wrote," ... it is very bad because would like to be silent and remain silent." And a month later, "I would like to hold my tongue for years—but who will pay me for that?"[17] The defeatism that eventually would overwhelm him was beginning.

Ironically Tucholsky was ready to give up just as he was reaching his greatest success, for it was in the last years of the Republic that he was most popular with the German public. From 1928 through 1932, Tucholsky became a celebrity in Germany. Three separate editions of selected works appeared and his social satire in the *Vossische Zeitung* brought him fame as a humorist.[18] Most of the major German magazines pursued him for articles. ("So many commissions have come in that no intelligent man would attempt to write them," he wrote.[19]) Yet Tucholsky seems to have lost heart for the battle. In the early twenties, he had attacked the militarists and putschists with zest and vitality. In the early thirties, his polemic was lifeless, almost perfunctory. In 1927 he wrote:

> Since 1913, I have belonged to those who believe the German spirit to be almost unalterably poisoned, to those who have no faith in improvement and who consider this constitutional monarchy to be a facade and a lie.[20]

Tucholsky had, of course, spoken similar words much earlier. The difference was that in 1919 he had criticized the Republic in the hope that it would improve. By 1927 his words of despair were no longer a conscious exaggeration produced for shock effect. They were on the contrary an expression of his deepest convictions. For him, Germany had become a hopeless society.

After 1927 Tucholsky fought a desperate ad hoc battle. He assiduously avoided the larger issues—having given them up as lost. Instead he dealt with the small things as they arose, much as a man fighting a forest fire concentrates on the creeping brush fire, knowing full well that he can do nothing about the crown fire, which threatens the whole forest. In the last years, it was as though Tucholsky continued to fight not out of hope of winning, but out of habit.

A catalogue of Tucholsky's political writings after 1926 demonstrates the spasmodic character, which his crusade assumed—its random thrusting and flailing about. In 1926, an anti-pornography law was passed. Tucholsky attacked it as a disguised censorship.[21] In January 1927, the Reichstag refused to give a press pass to Tucholsky as editor of the *Weltbühne*. One reason for Tucholsky's later personal attack upon Paul Löbe may have been his letter justifying the refusal of the pass:

> In spite of the twenty-three year existence and the significance of your weekly magazine, I regret that in principle I am unable to grant your request for permission to attend Reichstag sessions.[22]

In April 1927, Tucholsky departed from his usual, exclusive concern with German causes. With millions of others, he pleaded with American officials to spare the lives of Sacco and Vanzetti.[23]

In 1929, he began a campaign for better treatment of prisoners. He asked for better food, improved sanitary conditions and for provisions for the sexual satisfaction of prisoners that would be in conformity with standards of human dignity. As they stood, the prisons were ruled by brutality and perversion.

Continuing his Voltaire-like crusade against injustice, Tucholsky in 1929 also attacked the paragraphs of the German Civil Code directed against homosexuals. He defended their right to freedom of sexual expression, calling for a distinction between relations of consenting males and homosexual crimes, just as there was a distinction made between ordinary heterosexual relations and rape.[24]

That same year, Tucholsky defended Erich Maria Remarque, whose All Quiet on the Western Front was attacked by the rightist extremists. When Hollywood made the book into a film, the Nazis raised a storm of protest, which they did not confine to speeches. They employed new strong-arm methods of riots and brawls to such an extent that they forced the government to forbid the showing in early 1931. The Nazis had begun to give an indication of their future ruthlessness and brutality. From 1931 until Hitler came to power, riots, brawls and street fighting between the Nazis and their opponents would be a continual occurrence. Tucholsky, of course, wrote a stinging denunciation of the government's compliance with the Nazi demands. He was beginning to see the real threat that the National Socialists signified.[25]

Organized religion and religious institutions were frequent targets of the intellectual left because religion and state formed a conservative team almost unimaginable in a secular age. State governments undertook to protect the interests of religion with laws against blasphemy. Artists, writers, filmmakers could be prosecuted in the courts if they presented the Christian religion in an unfavorable light. In 1928, the painter George Grosz was again prosecuted for a series of drawings, but the charge this time was for blasphemy. The drawings included the famous crucifixion in which the Christ figure is wearing army boots and a gas mask.[26] Grosz was acquitted, but three years later Walther Victor did not fare as well. As editor of the *Sächsisches Volksblatt*, he was sentenced to four months' imprisonment for an article which purportedly attacked a state-protected religious institution. Tucholsky, in his article on the affair, did not question the right of a religious sect to sue if it believed itself slandered. He questioned the wording of the judgment handed down by the court, for it seemed to have less to do with the particular case than with a general prohibition of freedom of expression. The main justification for finding Victor guilty was that the article had had a *"zersetzende Wirkung"*—a "corrosive effect"—upon the society: "The article, which was available to the broad ranks of the people at large, has a corrosive effect upon the population...."[27]

Here was a clear expression of distrust of dissent, of fear of diversity. "Corrosive effect" was used to describe any opinion or person whom the reactionaries disliked. It was a phrase used almost as much as "cultural

Bolshevism." The right-wing press attacked Tucholsky many times because his writings were *zersetzend*. This would last on until after the war. In 1963, it was proposed before the Wiesbaden City Council that a street be named for Tucholsky. The council refused, saying that Tucholsky was not worthy of a street name. In the course of the report from the council, the word *zersetzend* was used. This created a scandal; a hail of protests against the use of the term came down upon the heads of the councillors. The report of the council does sound like something from the worst days of the Republic:

> To be sure his human fate deserves our sympathy, for the Jew, Tucholsky, was forced to emigrate by the Nazi regime and in the end committed suicide. Yet his writings and opinions are in part today still so corrosive (*zersetzend*) that it would be tactless to name a street after him. If Tucholsky were still alive today, he would be sitting in the DDR (GDR) writing inflammatory articles against the federal government.[28]

The ignorance of the statement in view of Tucholsky's popularity in Germany is striking. Tucholsky was not forced to emigrate by the Nazis; he was already out of the country when they came to power. He was never a Communist and it is highly unlikely that he would have made his home in either the Federal Republic or the GDR. And the use of the term *zersetzend* was inexcusable. One of the best protest articles appeared in *Die Welt*:

> There we have it again: "*Schrifttum*," "*zersetzend*." The old phrases. Except for Mr. Menges, who wishes it were so, no one knows the "Communist," Tucholsky. A consolation that many citizens in Wiesbaden protested against these assertions and that Mr. Menges did not find a majority in the Council. . . .
> That men are in a position to have such sentences quoted, that they play a role in public life, no matter how small, is dangerous indeed. Tucholsky still excites controversy in Germany.[29]

In commenting on the trial against Walther Victor, Tucholsky took particular exception to that portion of the judgment that dealt with Christianity in general. The words of the court ran:

> … Beneath this garment of story, anecdote, satire is concealed the secret intention of spiriting the reader away, unconsciously and indelibly, from a respect for Christianity, and for the moral philosophy taught to the people by Christianity.[30]

Tucholsky believed that the courts might defend a particular religious group against slander, but they had no right to protect Christianity as a religion. In words reminiscent of an eighteenth century philosophe, Tucholsky denounced the idea that Christians had a monopoly upon either truth or morality:

> The Christian religious community is not a refuge of all morality. There is no religious monopoly upon ethics. Millions of upright and moral people do not despise the Church, but they live consciously and completely without its teachings and they are correct in doing so. It is not true that the person who has surmounted the teachings of the Church is a morally inferior individual. Any teaching that violates its own principles in the manner of Christianity during the war, has nothing to tell us of morality. And no punishment will hinder us ... from making use of our legal rights—namely, to say to all our friends and, above all, the women: Leave the church, leave the church, leave the church.[31]

As would be expected, the members of the intellectual left as good rationalists and political liberals were hostile to revealed religion. The most obvious focus for their attacks was the Roman Church. Tucholsky seldom discussed religion in moral and theological terms and he never ridiculed religious believers. He also disapproved of the vulgar attacks upon Roman Catholicism by the left: "I have always emphasized to our like-minded friends that the crude way in which they fight the Catholic Church does not please me. I do not believe that it is proper."[32]

Tucholsky did not mock the Church's religious teachings, but he did criticize its political and social attitudes. He maintained that the spiritual teachings of the Church were a matter best reserved for gentlemanly discussion, but the Church's reactionary interference into politics had to be met with by implacable opposition.[33] Tucholsky had alluded to the malevolent political influence of the Church during the early years of his career, but he did not deal with the subject in any length until 1930. (With the exception of his travelogue about the Pyrenees—Ein Pyrenäenbuch—published in 1927 which described in part life in a monastery and the devotions at Lourdes.)

Tucholsky believed that the Roman Church provided the main support for the censorship of film and radio, and promoted the moralistic laws that interfered with individual privacy. It was the Church, in league with the Nationalists, which upheld the established order to the disadvantage of the workers. The Church's attitude toward marriage, the family and contraception were means whereby the workers were shackled to economic penury.[34]

Of greatest importance to Tucholsky was the political representative of the Church, the Center Party. Although the Center had performed yeoman service for the Republic, Tucholsky attacked it as a confessional party, which would be loyal ultimately only to the interests of Rome. This was a familiar criticism of Catholic parties, but Tucholsky's accusations were not concerned with the old saws about lack of patriotism. He criticized what he believed to be the basic lack of commitment to democracy on the part of a party, which represented a hierarchical organization whose watchword was obedience to authority. He correctly recognized that the good men of the Center would cooperate with the Nazis if it appeared in the interests of the Church to do so. In 1930, he wrote:

> A part of the Center press is suspiciously near to the National Socialists, who do not at all desire this comradeship. But the positions of the Center change. In general, this party always waits to see who maintains the upper hand in a struggle.[35]

Tucholsky contended that the Center would not support the Nazis because it believed in their brutal teachings; it would support them for opportunistic reasons. It was a party without political principle, relying as it did solely upon religious ethics for its direction. Little harm might come as long as the political situation were stable, but in an emergency, the Church would throw its support to any group—no matter how ruthless—which achieved power and would promise protection to the Church. In 1931, Tucholsky was explicit about the weakness of the Church in the face of the Nazis:

> The Church and her political parties will never do anything which does not serve their own interests… and if a few of the braggarts of the Hitler band were not so unspeakably uneducated and foolish, they would cease to annoy the Center by denouncing Rome, proclaiming the somewhat shy cult of Wotan and attacking the Jesuits. Hitler does not need to do that, for I would like to see an instance when they did not bless what provides the greatest reward.[36]

To be sure, when the Center Party members in the Reichstag voted for the Enabling Act on March 21, 1933—the *Ermächtigungsgesetz* that took the power away from the Parliament, the Reichstag, and gave it to the Hitler regime—, they acted under the pressure of extraordinary, and possibly extenuating, circumstances. But the concordat with the Hitler regime, negotiated by the Church the following July, appeared to bear out Tucholsky's worst fears. He was horrified that the Church fell upon its knees so meekly before Hitler, for it was the one supranational force with any persuasive power. On

October 7, 1934, Tucholsky wrote to his friend and frequent collaborator, the playwright Walter Hasenclever:

> According to his faith, a Protestant has to believe in the superiority of the state. But that the Catholics also go along reminds me of the words uttered by our imprisoned friend [Ossietzky] once in the Würzburg Cathedral: "Too bad that for three hundred years, German Catholics have been Protestant!" That the Catholics are cooperating is perverse. God bless this Pope![37]

Tucholsky was surprised that his own worst prophecies concerning the Church had in effect come true. Although he criticized the Church bitterly, he could not comprehend the continuing failure of an organization of such high moral pretension to resist in a forthright manner either the Nazis or the Fascists. By 1935, Tucholsky was so disgusted that he compared Pope Pius XI to Stalin:

> There is only one other fellow who has betrayed his followers as much as Stalin—and that is the Pope. The similarity is astonishing: In both cases, the demand for absolute obedience, in both cases, when the crucial hour strikes, they both in essence make the same gesture: "Unfortunately... we can do nothing else... . Compromise is our best quality." Well not for me. The poor dogs who believed in these knaves.[38]

Tucholsky explicitly expressed his fear of the role the Roman Church would play in the abolition of German democracy. But of far greater importance is his analysis of the principal actors in that dreary drama—the Nazis. Because he was out of the country during the early years of Hitler's rise, Tucholsky had little firsthand contact with the followers of National Socialism. But in late 1929 he returned to Germany to give a lecture and reading tour. It was then that he glimpsed the face of the future. He stopped in the major German cities without incident, but in Wiesbaden he caused a riot. The Nazis held a mass demonstration before the hall in which Tucholsky was to read and they threw stones at his car. The police injured many people and the mob almost martyred one innocent victim, one Dr. Walter Meyer, who looked like Tucholsky and was mistaken for him. Inside the hall, the galleries were so filled with Nazis that the police had to remove them by force before the performance could take place.[39]

The tour and the Wiesbaden riots were sobering experiences for Tucholsky. He entered a political despair from which he would never emerge. He looked at the faces of the rioters and was profoundly shocked by the hatred he saw. As he wrote later in 1935 concerning his tour:

> Such is Germany. The uniform fits them—except that the collar is a bit too high. A little uncomfortable—a little disturbing—so much pathos, so little butter—and what else? As Alfred Polgar says, "The downfall begins when you hear—'Well, you have to let them have at least one thing.' " And they take the one thing, then another thing and finally everything. That is bitter to realize. I've known it since 1929 when I made a reading tour. Then I looked at "our people"—opponents and supporters, one face after the other as they sat before the podium. And then I realized and from then on I grew more and more silent.[40]

Even though Tucholsky saw the Nazis in 1929 and was horrified by them, like many others he did not recognize the true nature of the danger which they posed. In giving any intelligent answer to the question of Tucholsky's estimation of the Nazi threat, it is necessary to return to his views during the early days of the Hitler movement. In the twenties Tucholsky saw Hitler as a Bavarian phenomenon, as but one more reason why tourists should boycott Bavaria.[41] Hitler was just another fanatic leader of a paramilitary organization who preached the gutter doctrines of anti-Semitism and national revival. He was more a pawn in the struggle between Berlin and Munich than anything else. His cheap theatrical attempt at a putsch and "national revolution" was a miserable failure. Although there were other overtones, Hitler's arrest, trial and light sentence appeared to be indications more of a reactionary legal system than of the power of National Socialism.

From May 1924 until September 1930, the DNVP (the conservative *Deutschnationale Volks-Partei*) was the second largest party in the Reichstag. And outside the legislature, the Nationalists in the guise of the Hugenberg press and propaganda apparatus appeared to be the primary bulwark of anti-republicanism.[42] Not until 1929, with the controversy over the Young Plan—a plan to restructure and prolong the German war debt under the auspices of international banks, named after Owen Young, the founder of RCA, the Radio Corporation of America—, did the Nazis again attract national attention. In July 1929, the Nationalists invited Hitler to cooperate with them in combatting the new economic scheme. Hugenberg wanted the Nazis mainly because of their skill as rabble-rousers, for they were to aid in gaining signatures for a petition to introduce in the Reichstag "a Law against the Enslavement of the German People." Although only a little more than four million signatures were found, Hitler and his followers lived up to their demagogic reputations. Throughout the country, they made speeches, circulated literature and started riots. After 1929, the Nazis were able to make a more impressive public appearance because they used the funds flowing from the Nationalists to enlarge and equip the SA and the SS. It was then that the menacing power of the Nazis became apparent.

In 1930, Tucholsky dealt with the Hitler movement in two longish articles. Both were written before Hitler's Reichstag success in September. Both show Tucholsky's conception of the meaning and purpose of National Socialism. The first article, "Der Hellseher" ("The Clairvoyant"), was published in the *Weltbühne* on April 1, 1930. The fact that it was reprinted in the same journal on April 15, 1932, demonstrates how little Tucholsky's view of the Nazis changed in two years.

"Der Hellseher" is in the form of a dialogue between a fortuneteller and a client who has come to hear of the political future. The customer enquires whether the outlook is "white or black."[43] The sage replies that he sees a bloodless putsch and the establishment of fascism. He quickly adds, however, that fascism will be nothing new; it will simply be a front for the Stahlhelm and the Nationalists. There will be no need for bloodshed since the old guard already controls almost everything it wants—the judiciary, the military, the schools. The Nationalists will take control quickly, quietly and simply. "And the Hitler people?" asks the client. The fortuneteller replies that nothing is in store for them except disappointment:

> Not so bad. A frightful amount of screaming and brutality. They will have great fun in organized rowdiness, putting on uniforms, driving trucks and marching in the streets—not so bad. Like a team of horses— as soon as they make the first sudden tug, the drivers will put the brakes on them, the poor chaps. There will be great disappointments.[44]

The client then asks if the President will be deposed and an open dictatorship established. The prophet answers, "Mussolini has his little king; the ones here have their big Hindenburg." According to the seer, everything will be done in a constitutional fashion—the Reichstag, the President, the whole democratic façade will remain. Real power, however, will be in the hands of a committee. As for Hitler, he will be shut out as soon as he has served his purpose. Then the Nationalists will exclude the SPD and pension off untrustworthy members of the bureaucracy. Certain punitive measures will be taken against Jews; the KPD will be made illegal. The new regime will express "platonic love" for Italy and advertise itself as the bulwark against Russia.

In this interesting dialogue, Tucholsky revealed his opinion that Hitler was basically a pawn of the Nationalists. The gentlemen of the right would use

Hitler's following for their own ends and then "put on the brakes." Tucholsky presented Hitler as a simpleton and a poseur who would quickly be put in his place by his more intelligent and powerful masters. Tucholsky believed the Germans would create an imitation fascism resembling Italy only in outward appearance. The real power would continue to be wielded by those who had always had it, i.e., the generals, the Junkers and the industrialists.

Tucholsky and the Nationalists were, of course, united in their conviction of Hitler's basic impotence. The DNVP and the army thought they would be able to control Hitler and rule through him. They were in for a rude surprise. Neither Tucholsky nor the Nationalists recognized Hitler's charismatic appeal, oratorical genius and fanatic will. They also failed to recognize the revolutionary character of his movement.

In the second article, "Die deutsche Pest" ("The German Plague"), published on May 13, 1930, Tucholsky spoke of how un-revolutionary the Nazis were.[45] The phrases "worker party" and "people's party" were employed by the Nazis only for competitive purposes. In actuality, according to Tucholsky, the only power that the Nazis had was given them by the capitalist interests:

> They [the Nazis] have never been revolutionary. The financial supporters of this movement are arch capitalists. The resentment, expressed in the provincial papers of the party and in the unspeakable *Beobachter*, is only of the little people of the party. The success of these papers rests on local gossip and slander. "We ask Herr Alderman Normauke whether he obtained the deliveries to the city through his brother-in-law, who for his part gave the major… " That makes the simple people happy. It shows them that the party accepts their interests; it satisfies their deepest instincts—for the little man has three real passions; beer, gossip and anti-Semitism. The Nazis give all these things in abundance: beer at the meetings, gossip in the papers and noisy anti-Semitism in the swaggering slogans of the party. Now what is revolutionary in this business?[46]

Everything in Tucholsky's analysis of the Nazis was essentially correct, except for his crucial underestimation of the power of their appeal. They were supported by the capitalists. Hitler was cynical in his cant about a worker party. The party did address itself to the little people. What Tucholsky failed to recognize was that the three passions he named would be blended into one of the most powerful mass movements of all time. Tucholsky did not reckon that Hitler's mass following in conjunction with his private army would give him an appearance of overwhelming power before which all the old forces would fall, be they left or right. Given Tucholsky's premise of the old guard's continuing power once Hitler was in office, there was nothing revolutionary about the Nazis. Tucholsky did not see that Hitler would create a change in nation, society and government, which would be different from a Communist triumph, but no less revolutionary. Tucholsky failed to realize that revolutions may come from the right as well as from the left. The main reason for this failure was his basic inability to see beyond the old struggles of the Empire.

For a moment in 1930, Tucholsky had a clearer view of the real power of National Socialism, but he soon returned to the earlier conviction about Nationalist control. The moment came after Hitler's surprising success in the Reichstag election of September 14, 1930. The representation of the Nazis rose from twelve deputies to 107 or from 2.6 percent of the vote to 18.3 percent. One of the most striking parts of the Nazi victory was that it was achieved at the expense of the Nationalists who dropped from seventy-three representatives and 14.2 percent of the vote to forty-one representatives and seven percent of the total votes cast. This gave an indication of the independence of the Nazis from the Nationalists. In October, Tucholsky published a Wendriner story that presented a chillingly accurate description of certain aspects of the later Nazi dictatorship. "Herr Wendriner steht unter der Diktatur" (Herr Wendriner under the Dictatorship") was the last of the series and although it said less about the Nazis than about Jewish attitudes toward them, it is appropriate to mention it here.[47]

In the story, the Nazis have assumed power. Wendriner and his cronies are at the cinema, where in fearful tones they discuss the new dictatorship. Through their conversation, it is learned that Jews must wear yellow markings and live in special, guarded districts. Wendriner contends that "H" knows the German psyche well, that Goebbels is immensely popular with the masses and that the Nazis know how to put on a show as good as anything under the monarchy

The prophetic quality of this story, notwithstanding, Tucholsky remained convinced that the Nationalists would ultimately control the Nazis. He had good reason. Hitler's main financial support came from the old guard and with the fusion of the right wing at Harzburg on October 11, 1931, it appeared that the Nationalists would swallow up the Nazis. The support Hitler gained from the industrialists in Düsseldorf on January 27, 1932, did little to discourage this impression at the time. Tucholsky therefore let "Der Hellseher" be republished in 1932 as being indicative of his views.[48]

That same year he wrote: "Satire has an upper boundary. Buddha is beyond it. Satire also has a lower limit. In Germany it is the governing fascist powers. It doesn't pay—you can't shoot that low."[49] But Tucholsky did "shoot that low" many times, for his main commentary upon the Nazis was restricted to satiric prose and verse. Tucholsky not only considered the Nazis to be puppets of the Nationalists, he also thought them too vulgar and irrational to be worthy of serious analysis. He therefore believed the only recourse was to make them look ridiculous. Many Tucholsky chansons about the Nazis were sung in the Berlin cabarets the winter of 1930–31. There was "Das Dritte Reich" ("The Third Reich") in which Tucholsky mocked the Nazi racist and nationalist theories—"Das Dritte Reich? Bitte sehr! Bitte gleich!"[50] There was also "50 Prozent Bürgerkrieg" ("50 percent Civil War") in which Tucholsky described Hitler as a "Mussolini with beer."[51] The title alone of "Lied der Cowgoys" ("Song of the Cowgoys") could stand as a satiric comment on the Nazis complete in itself.[52] One of the most powerful chansons was "Die Mäuler auf!" ("Mouths Ready!"). The "Tauber of the barricades," Ernst Busch, gave the song its most effective interpretation, hissing out the last lines in a contemptuous sneer—"Kleine Leute, kleine Leute"—"Little people, little people."

Roar of Heil and racist whoopers,
Curt and stiff with Prussian clang.
Staffelführer, little troopers,
Brass bands beat—bang, bang, bang.
Jew baiters, dirty cheaters,
Little leaders, little leaders.

Screaming brutes, dumb and wiser,
A thousand hands in agitation,
Hitler as the holy Kaiser,
Like a cheapened imitation.
Filthy parasitic bleeders,
Little leaders, little leaders.

Sing of race and Germanism,
Grovelling cattle, whipped and lost.
Praise the cheap Romanticism,
Industry will pay the cost.
Also will the Junkers pay,
Working, feverish, night and day—

Always with us—hatred breeders,
Little leaders, little leaders.[53]

Perhaps the only real effect of Tucholsky's jibes and attacks was to get him into legal trouble. The *Weltbühne* was constantly threatened with lawsuits and the verdicts of the courts were an indication of the political and social crisis that was beginning to consume the Republic. In the final days, it was in the courts that Tucholsky saw most clearly that the end had come.

One amusing exception, however, occurred on April 18, 1929, when the *Berliner Volkszeitung* reported that Tucholsky might be prosecuted by the government for a violation of Paragraph 166, the provision protecting religion. The offending publication was a poem, "Gesang der englischen Chorknaben" ("Song of the English Choirboys"), which criticized the attitude of the Anglican Church toward the great coal strike. The case was dropped when Tucholsky's counsel asked the obvious question: "What have we to do with the English Church?"[54]

But there were other suits that were more serious. On October 9, 1928, Tucholsky published in the *Weltbühne* an article entitled "Verhetzte Kinder—Ohnmächtige Republik" ("Children Incited to Hatred—The Republic Remains Unconscious")[55]. The piece was about a geography book for public schools that had been reissued in a new post-war edition by a Professor Wührer.[56] The book was a vast series of lies, which contained statements that the French were lazy while the Germans were industrious and other myths about national character. The general tone of the book was an incitement of German youth to a war of revenge against France. Tucholsky's review did little more than quote from the book, thus letting it damn itself by its own words. Nevertheless, Wührer sued for slander, maintaining that Tucholsky had misrepresented him and the book. Incredibly, the court fined Tucholsky two thousand marks.[57]

The most important legal actions came in 1932. On August 4, 1931, Tucholsky had published an article with a pacifist theme entitled "Der bewachte Kriegsschauplatz" ("The Guarded Theater of War"). In it he stated, "Soldiers are murderers."[58] The Minister of Defense, General Groener, decided to press charges against Tucholsky for defaming the Reichswehr. Carl von Ossietzky, as editor of the *Weltbühne*, was actually the person prosecuted.

When Tucholsky learned of the suit, he had to face the hard choice of whether to go to Germany and give Ossietzky moral support. Although Tucholsky was not mentioned in the charges and thus would not be brought before the court, there was the possibility that the German government would cancel his passport or trump up some other obstructionist action. In addition, if Tucholsky went to Germany, there was the very grave danger of assassination by the Nazis. Yet if he did not go, he would be severely criticized for leaving Ossietzky in the lurch. Tucholsky in the end decided to remain where he was, stating that "noble gestures" were soon forgotten. He was of more worth free and writing than if he were imprisoned and silent.

In a letter to Mary he stated: "Ossietzky is a model of behavior. In any event, for years I have given him the fullest power of censorship over my articles, always with the assertion: I will attend no trials... ."[59]

The trial took place on July 1, 1932, and Ossietzky was acquitted because the word "soldiers" was an abstraction which did not necessarily mean the Reichswehr. But this trial was eclipsed in importance by an earlier one, for Ossietzky was already serving an eighteen-month sentence for "treason." On March 12, 1929, the *Weltbühne* had published an article, "Windiges aus der deutschen Luftfahrt" ("Airy News of German Aviation"), in which Heinz Jaeger reported the existence of a special "Section M." in the *Reichsverkehrsministerium*.[60] The section was responsible for the development of military aviation, which was in violation of the Versailles Treaty. Ossietzky was arrested for revealing military secrets, while at the same time the government announced that the story was without foundation.

The resulting trial was a scandal. The public was excluded and all witnesses had to swear under oath not to reveal anything of the proceedings. Ossietzky was found guilty in November 1931. He began serving his sentence on May 10, 1932. He was released the following December in the Christmas amnesty.

After the amnesty, Ossietzky was urged to flee the country, but he remained in Berlin and continued to edit the *Weltbühne*. He was arrested again on February 27, 1933, the night of the Reichstag fire, and placed in a concentration camp. He was awarded the Nobel Peace Prize in 1936, which caused Hitler to order all Germans to be ineligible for Nobel prizes. Ossietzky died in 1938, as a result of his sufferings. Tucholsky could not understand why Ossietzky refused to take flight since he believed that editors were more valuable out of prison than in. He wrote on March 4, 1933:

> Ossietzky unfathomable. I've been told that they did not give him back his passport after Tegel. Whether that is true, I don't know—he writes no letters. This excellent stylist, this man unsurpassed in civil courage, has a remarkable, lethargic manner which I do not understand and which has alienated many people who admire him. It is too bad for him, for this sacrifice is senseless. My instinct has always told me: martyrs without effectiveness, that is senseless. In no event do I believe they will do anything to him. He is safer under arrest than out. Only an unsuccessful assassination attempt upon Adolf would cause something to happen, for the SA would storm the prisons and would be hindered in nothing by the wardens. Otherwise, I think he'll be out in two or three weeks. (If concentration camps are not created!)[61]

For Tucholsky, Ossietzky's arrest and trial were the last acts in the drama of the Republic. The court conviction convinced him that all was lost and the end was near. Tucholsky wrote perfunctorily, "The weapons are passed on," but the "weapons" had become impotent. The Republic was already dead. The men around the President engineered its burial. With each passing month in 1932, Tucholsky wrote less and less. As he wrote to Hasenclever almost a year later: "We must see things as they are. We have lost. The only thing for an honorable man to do is to withdraw."[62]

At the end of his scrapbook, Tucholsky drew three stair—steps and placed a word under each—*Sprechen, Schreiben, Schweigen*—Speaking, Writing, Silence. After 1932 he did not write another word for publication. The worst that he had predicted and more had come to pass.

NOTES

1   Kurt Tucholsky, *Ausgewählte Briefe*, 1913-1935 (Hamburg, 1962), p. 477. The format of the title page actually said: "Unter Mitarbeit von Kurt Tucholsky, geleitet von Carl von Ossietzky."
2   Quoted by Fritz J. Raddatz, *Tucholsky, Eine Bildbiographie* (Munich, 1961), p. 92.
3   Kurt Tucholsky, *Ausgewählte Briefe*, p. 486.
4   Kurt Tucholsky, "Lottchen beichtet 1 Geliebten," G.W., III, 768-770; P.P., *Vossische Zeitung*, 38 (January 23, 1931). English translation by Cindy Opitz in *Berlin! Berlin" Dispatches From the Weimar Republic* (Berlinica, New York, 2013), pp. 171-172
5   Kurt Tucholsky, "Deutsches Chaos," G.W., III, 901-904; K.H., *Die Weltbühne*, XXVII/31 (August 4, 1931), 179.
6   Kurt Tucholsky, *Deutschland, Deutschland über Alles* (Berlin, 1929), pp. 46-55. (In 1964 Rowohlt Verlag published a facsimile edition of the original book, thus completing the publication of Tucholsky's entire collected writings.). The following quotes are from the original book, pp. 219, 43, 204, 29, 63, 175f, 19, 156-168, 163, 208.
7   Erich Eyck makes this judgment of Löbe: "Löbe, who directed the chamber's affairs from 1920 to 1932, was one of the best presidents the German Reichstag ever had: objective and just, calm, self-assured and polite." Erich Eyck, *A History of the Weimar Republic* (Cambridge, Mass., 1963)' II, p. 291. Löbe was repetedly imprisoned by the Nazis and deported to Gross-Rosen concentration camp in 1944, but he survived the Nazis.
8   Kurt Tucholsky, *Ausgewählte Briefe*, p. 212.
9   Kurt Tucholsky, *Deutschland, Deutschland über Alles*, p. 226.
10   Kurt Tucholsky, *Ausgewählte Briefe*, p. 266.
11   Herbert Ihering, "Polemik," *Das Tagebuch*, XX (Berlin, October 12, 1929), 1693.
12   Kurt Tucholsky, *Ausgewählte Briefe*, p. 133.
13   Ibid., p. 132.
14   Jäcklin Rohrbach, "Das republikanische Bilderbuch," *National-Sozialistische Briefe*, 7 (Berlin, 1929). Contained in Tucholsky, Scrapbook under "Interessanter Tadel," Kurt Tucholsky Archive, Rottach-Egern, Germany. The controversy over the value of the book still continues. See Paul Sethe, "Tucholskys tragische Irrtümer," *Die Zeit*, 14 (April 10, 1964), p. 7, for a severe criticism of Tucholsky's attack upon moderate republicans. For a reply see the issue of *Die Zeit*, April 24, 1964, "Ein Feind der Republik?" a collection of protesting letters from Tucholsky enthusiasts.
15   Hans Wesemann, "Von Rheinsberg bis Schloss Gripsholm oder der sterbende Schwan," *Welt am Montag* (Berlin, June 8, 1931).
16   Kurt Tucholsky, *Ausgewählte Briefe*, p. 486.
17   Ibid., p. 482, 484. (In personal letters to friends, Tucholsky often wrote in an abbreviated, telegraphic style.)
18   The editions of selected works were: *Mit 5PS* (Berlin, 1928); *Das Lächeln der Mona Lisa* (Berlin, 1929); *Lerne lachen ohne zu weinen* (Berlin, 1931).
19   Kurt Tucholsky, *Ausgewählte Briefe*, p. 484.
20   Kurt Tucholsky, "Stahlhelm oder Filzhut?" G.W., II, 790; I.W., *Die Weltbühne*, XXIII/20 (May 17, 1927), 773.
21   Kurt Tucholsky, "Old Bäumerhand, der Schrecken der Demokratie," G.W., II, 558-562; I.W., *Die Weltbühne*, XXII/50 (December 14, 1926), 91. The title is a wordplay on "Old Shatterhand," the fictional hero of Karl May's popular Wild West novels.

22 Quoted by Kurt Tucholsky, G.W., II, 733.
23 Kurt Tucholsky, "An den Botschafter," G.W., II, 770f.; K.T., *Die Weltbühne*, XXIII/16 (March 19, 1927), 638.
24 Kurt Tucholsky, "Paragraph 297 / Unzucht zwischen Männern," G.W., III, 17f.
25 Kurt Tucholsky, "Gegen das Remarque-Filmverbot," G.W., III, 809; K.T., *Die Menschheit* (March 20, 1931).
26 See Tucholsky's comment on the trial, "Die Begründung," G.W., III, 52-56; I.W., *Die Weltbühne*, XXV/12 (March 19, 1929), 435.
27 Quoted by Kurt Tucholsky, "Auch eine Urteilsbegründung," G.W., III, 856; I.W., *Die Weltbühne*, XXVII/19 (May 12, 1931), 680.
28 As quoted in the *Berliner Abendpost*, (Berlin), Feb. 15, 1963
29 *Die Welt* (Berlin), February 21, 1963:
30 Quoted by Kurt Tucholsky, "Auch eine Urteilsbegründung," G.W., III, 856.
31 Ibid, 857
32 Ibid
33 Kurt Tucholsky, "Brief an eine Katholikin," G.W., III, 351; I.W., *Die Weltbühne*, XXVI/6 (February 4, 1930), 198. It is unclear why he suddenly began to attack Catholic social attitudes and political involvement. It does not appear to have been Heinrich Brüning's chancellorship, since "Brief an eine Katholikin" ("Letter to a Catholic Woman") was written before Brüning assumed office. The later articles do not mention the Centrist Chancellor.
34 Kurt Tucholsky, "Von den Kränzen, der Abtreibung und dem Sakrament der Ehe," G.W., Ill, 786; I.W., *Die Weltbühne*, XXVII/7 (February 17, 1931), 237.
35 Kurt Tucholsky, "Brief an eine Katholikin," G.W., III, 349.
36 Kurt Tucholsky, "Von den Kränzen, der Abtreibung und dem Sakrament der Ehe," G.W., III, 785f.
37 Kurt Tucholsky, *Ausgewählte Briefe*, p. 290.
38 Ibid., p. 327.
39 See the letter of sympathy to Meyer in Kurt Tucholsky, *Ausgewählte Briefe*, p. 210. I learned of the Wiesbaden riots from the scrapbook of press clippings, which Tucholsky kept during these years. (It is housed in the Tucholsky Archive in Rottach-Egern.) Tucholsky preserved the more interesting accounts of the disturbance, and the descriptions naturally vary according to the political persuasion of the newspaper. One conservative journal reported that a meeting of the Wiesbaden Literary Society, called to discuss the scandal, was not a total success because Tucholsky was not unqualifiedly denounced. (*Neue Wiesbadener Zeitung* [Wiesbaden, Dec. 3, 1929].) Needless to say, the Literary Society expressed regret that it had invited Tucholsky. For Tucholsky's brief reference to the affair, see *Ausgewählte Briefe*, p. 493. In the light of the dispute about renaming a street after Tucholsky, it is interesting that the only riots occurred in Wiesbaden.
40 Kurt Tucholsky, Ausgewählte Briefe, pp. 336-37.
41 Kurt Tucholsky, "Reisende, meidet Bayern!" G .W. (Hamburg, 1960), I, 1144-48; I.W., *Die Weltbühne*, XX/6 (February 7, 1924), 164.
42 Alfred Hugenberg (1865-1951), press and film magnate, violently nationalistic and dedicated to the overthrow of democracy and the repudiation of the Versailles Treaty. In October 1928, the Nationalists chose Hugenberg to lead their party.
43 Kurt Tucholsky, "Der Hellseher," G.W., III, 398; I.W., *Die Weltbühne*, XXVI/14 (April 1, 1930), 499.

44 Ibid., G.W., III, 398.
45 Kurt Tucholsky, "Die deutsche Pest," G.W., III, 439-443; I.W., *Die Weltbühne*, XXVI/20 (May 13, 1930), 718.
46 Ibid., G.W., III, 439f.
47 Kurt Tucholsky, "Herr Wendriner steht unter der Diktatur," G.W., III , 547-550; K.H., *Die Weltbühne*, XXVI/41 (October 7, 1930), 559. English translation by Harry Zohn in *Germany? Germany! The Kurt Tucholsky Reader* (Berlinica, New York, 2017), p. 54–57
48 Kurt Tucholsky, "Der Hellseher," G.W., III, 397-401; I.W., *Die Weltbühne*, :XXVIII/15 (April15, 1932), 541.
49 Kurt Tucholsky, "Schnipsel," G.W., III, 1029; P.P., *Die Weltbühne*, XXVIII/10 (March 8, 1932), 377.
50 Kurt Tucholsky, "Das dritte Reich," G.W., III, 437; Th.T., *Die Weltbühne*, XXVI/19 (May 6, 1930), 686.
51 Kurt Tucholsky, "50% Bürgerkrieg," G.W., III, 446; Th.T., *Die Weltbühne*, XXVI/21 (May 20, 1930), 754.
52 Kurt Tucholsky, "Lied der Cowgoys," G.W., III, 544; Th.T., *Die Weltbühne*, XXVI/40 (Oct. 1, 1930), 522.
53. Kurt Tucholsky, "Die Mäuler auf!" G.W., III, 502f.; Th.T., *Die Weltbühne*, XXVI/35 (August 26, 1930), 321.
54 Kurt Tucholsky, G.W., II, 1216f. Also reported in *Berliner Volkszeitung* (April 18, 1929).
55 Kurt Tucholsky, "Verhetzte Kinder – Ohnmächtige Republik," G.W., II, 1261-1265; I.W., *Die Weltbühne*, XXIV/41 (September 9, 1928), 553.
56 Michael Geistbeck and Alois Geistbeck, *Geographie für höhere Lehranstalten* (Munich, 1925).
57 Reported in D*eutsche Tageszeitung* (Feb. 12, 1929), contained in the scrapbook.
58 Kurt Tucholsky, "Der bewachte Kriegsschauplatz," G.W., III, 905; I.W., *Die Weltbühne*, XXVII/31 (Aug. 4, 1931), 191.
59 Kurt Tucholsky, *Ausgewählte Briefe*, p. 496.
60 Hein Jäger was a pseudonym for Walter Kreiser, a German aircraft designer.
61 Kurt Tucholsky, *Ausgewählte Briefe*, pp. 247f.
62 Kurt Tucholsky, *Ausgewählte Briefe*, pp. 250-51.

Above: Park Monceau in the heart of Paris, the place where the poet, journalist, and satirist was the happiest during his life.

Below: Berlin now has a Tucholskystraße, as do many German cities.

X.

A MAN WHO WAS ALWAYS HUNTED

By GOOD fortune Tucholsky was in Sweden when Hitler came to power on January 30, 1933. From his rented house in Hindas near Göteborg, he waited and watched as the Nazis consolidated their power and mounted a vicious attack upon him personally. To Tucholsky's grim amusement, Goebbels and his staff began a systematic defamation of his character and writings. In the paranoid Nazi mentality, Tucholsky was the archetype of the corrosive, internationalistic, "stateless" Jew. There were few anti-Semitic pamphlets that did not mention his name. The pseudo-scientific study, *Die Juden in Deutschland*, released by the Institute for the Study of the Jewish Question, devoted twenty-three pages to Tucholsky, more than any other person who was defamed had the honor of receiving.[1] The anonymous author described Tucholsky as a pornographer and destroyer of society who did not have the courage to use his own name. He had desecrated all that was holy to the German people. The article concluded with a typical Nazi description of the Jew as parasite: "... There is nothing of the prophet about him, no indication of a glowing passion—only a gnawing hatred of the national ideal of the people whose bread he eats."[2] Tucholsky, of course, did hate the national ideal, but he was also too much of a prophet for Nazi comfort.

There were other publications devoted to Tucholsky, extending from Wilhelm Stapel's attempt at a scholarly critique[3] down to a scurrilous little picture book entitled *Der Ewige Jude* (*The Eternal Jew*).[4] Tucholsky, however, suffered little real harm from these publications. The greatest inconvenience the Nazis caused him was to deprive him of a livelihood by banning and indeed burning his books on May 10, 1933.

Some three months later, on August 23, Tucholsky's name also stood among those on the first list of Germans to be deprived of their citizenship.[5] Tucholsky's reaction was one of amusement and even relief for the "clarification." When asked if he would undertake legal measures, he replied that such would be pointless. Besides, any action might make it appear that he placed some value on being a German. That, needless to say, was not the case.[6]

But even if Tucholsky placed no value on being a German, citizenship itself had great worth, for it provided something without which it was almost impossible for a European to live—a passport. Without one, travel became difficult and residence in exile uncertain. Bureaucracies did not recognize the rights of the stateless and Tucholsky was unable to obtain citizenship in any other European country. The Swedish government did allow him to remain in Sweden, but only by forcing him to renew his visa from month to month. For three years Tucholsky lived under the constant threat of deportation.

In Sweden, Tucholsky lived a quiet life and saw few people. Only through letters did he have contact with the world at large. Few in fact knew where he really lived, since, in order to elude the Gestapo, he had all mail sent to Switzerland, from where it was forwarded to his Swedish home.[7]

Exile was nothing new for Tucholsky, but before 1933 it had been voluntary. Forced exile was something else, for he began to brood and withdraw into himself. Not only was his livelihood cut off, not only had he lost what he regarded as his battle, but he had also in a sense been rejected by the country which he loved—tempered though that love may have been by hatred. He had been cast out. He believed that no place was left in the world for a person of his sort. On September 14, 1933, he wrote prophetically to his friend and collaborator, the playwright Walter Hasenclever, "We shall see a whole series of suicides."[8] Two years later, Tucholsky became the first of many exiles who chose to end their lives.

There were many possibilities open to Tucholsky. He could have started a new life in America as did his brother and sister, but Tucholsky was too weary in spirit for new beginnings. And he was sick in body. He suffered from a painful nasal infection that required five surgical operations in 1935 alone. His mental depression increased as he lost hope of recovery. This is apparent in his letters to his brother in 1935:

April 15, 1935

Bulletin: Until now, I've had four operations this winter. Now I have to wait. There is a possibility for a fifth. Now I'm getting along; when it hurts, I clear my throat again. I am a great hero.

May 28, 1935

I am not well—this winter I've had 5 (five) operations. I've had eight in all. There is an improvement. I'm beginning to have a sense of smell, something I've not had for four years. The pressure in my head is gone. The doctor, an angel of patience, says that I must wait a very long time until the nerves recover. For the time being, there are still small growths, which are an unending plague. The operations, themselves, no longer bother me.

It's now as though I could say, "Wait just a moment—I'm going to have my nose cut." Just like at the barber. Now I have intestinal catarrh on top of everything, which oppresses me. You can imagine what my condition is.

July 16, 1935

I am not well. The operations are over. I still have the thick catarrh and must wait until it is gone. I notice that four years have gone by in this way—until recently, I've been given the wrong treatment—God bless the doctors. I am very tired.

Tucholsky had always been concerned with words, sentence construction and literary style. Suddenly his talents were useless; he had no audience. (Austria and Switzerland did not interest him.) German was his medium, and it gave him his identity. The greatest harm which the Nazis did to him was to deprive him of his language, a fact second only to his illness in causing his depression. Persons with other professions could learn new languages and employ their talents much as before. Even some other writers could use a different language or be translated. But Tucholsky was a stylist and a satirist, skills that required an intimate knowledge and unique insight into the workings of a society and its language. His literary creations and effects were singularly dependent upon nuance of sound, twists of phrasing, and the particular grammatical construction of German. Not only did he have little to say to any other audience, but his style was more untranslatable than that of most German authors. As Tucholsky said to Hasenclever on November 29, 1935:

> … *You* are easy to translate. You are a poet (*Dichter*) and a proportioned person. I am a writer (*Schriftsteller*) and how I say something is often better than *what* I say. That is lost in translation. In addition, it is true of German and any other language that if a person wants to write it well, he must be in constant touch with the people.… I do not speak German the way it is spoken today and for a—shall we say, humorist—that is a heavy obstacle.

The only answer was to learn another language. For a time, Tucholsky attempted to write in French, but he soon gave up hope of developing a good style. One of the reasons why Tucholsky did not go to the United States was the effort required to learn a new language. In his advice to his brother, Tucholsky repeatedly emphasized that he must learn English if he were to succeed. On April 15, 1935, Tucholsky wrote to Fritz, whom he jokingly called "Kohn":

I don't believe that you will have it easy over there, but, nevertheless I think it is for the best. I say only this: learn English, learn English. If possible, get yourself a German-*American* lexicon. American is a language, not just a variation of English. Both peoples make enormous fun of each other about it. When Whistler, the painter, was asked by Wilde what was new in America, he replied, "Nothing, safe [sic] the language."

And again on May 28, 1935, Tucholsky returned to the same theme:

Learn English! Learn English! Don't let up. Continuously read newspapers, and also an easy novel now and then, but never skip a word, not a single word without looking it up... Not much grammar, but learn the forms, again and again until they flow automatically. And in addition, you will have great difficulty understanding what they say—they speak horribly. But soon it will go much more easily. Language is the A and the O.

When you are in New York, you can look up George Grosz, the painter, and give him my regards. I don't have his address, but the art dealers know it or *The New Yorker* magazine. He is a good man...

yours truuli—is that a language!
bien a vous—that's a language!
K.

In his final letter to Fritz, written on December 8, 1935, Tucholsky again dwelt upon the subject of language and its importance. At the same time, Tucholsky was trying to learn Swedish and there is little doubt that language had become something of a preoccupation with him.

Tucholsky had a distaste for America and sometimes repeated the clichés about its materialism and crassness. Occasionally his advice to his brother assumed a comic note such as when he twice warned him not to be caught without money:

August 19, 1935

Yes, when do you leave? The only thing that pleases me as little as it does you, is that you are going without any money. I would not do that—I'm not writing out of thin air, I've thought carefully about it. In Prague, they won't do anything to you—but over there they are horribly strict about such things.

Don't do it—I believe it is really dangerous. They are capable of locking you up on Long Island until someone saves you. Merciless.

On September 5, Tucholsky again asserted his fear that Fritz would be "locked up" on Long Island. Perhaps it would have been best for Fritz Tucholsky to have followed his brother's advice to remain in Prague a while longer. In that way he might have changed a fatal course of events, for in 1936, shortly after his arrival in America, Fritz Tucholsky was killed in an automobile accident.

After January 1933, Tucholsky claimed that he was finished with Germany, that he was unconcerned. He kept his word in so far as his publication was concerned, but in his private correspondence he was far from indifferent toward his country of origin. In the past, he bad restricted himself to personal matters in his private letters, reserving his political comments for the public. But now that he was deprived of his audience, his letters to friends became intensely political. He wrote scores of such letters to Walter Hasenclever, Arnold Zweig, and to his brother, Fritz—letters, which were concerned mainly with the Nazis and the Jews. He brooded over both the future of Germany and the Jews in the hands of Hitler and his gang.

After January 30, 1933, neither did Tucholsky engage in any kind of deep abstract analysis in his private statements about the Nazis. He did not discuss the nature of Hitler's movement. There was no discussion of totalitarianism. Above all, he never clearly attempted to distinguish between the old conservatives and the Nazis. It would appear that he failed to grasp the revolutionary implications of National Socialism—its nihilism, its new combination of mass support and technological power. In a letter to his brother, Fritz, on August 31, 1933, Tucholsky wrote that the Nazis were justified in taking measures against him such as deprivation of citizenship. Enemies were always treated in such manner after a revolution, but he added:

> Quite another matter are the camps, the repression of the Jews and the disgusting humiliation of people who once held other opinions. What is being done is immoral (*unsittlich*).

"Immoral" seems an almost comically mild word for describing the Nazis. Tucholsky had no illusions about the brutality of the National Socialists, but he was, nevertheless, shocked when that brutality became the ethos of the state. He had believed the Nationalists would be ruthless with their enemies and make matters difficult for the Jews, but he had never thought they would abolish due process of law while institutionalizing cruelty and barbarism. And Tucholsky never basically recognized that the Nazis were creating a new morality ostensibly based upon a racist elitism. In actuality, it was a system in which only the leader himself had the right to individuality or even to a personality.[9]

Tucholsky did not think often about these matters because he was essentially uninterested in them. As a young man, he had repudiated the German past and called for the establishment of new and purer traditions. However, the desire for a revolution in German society proved hopeless, for Tucholsky saw Hitler as a confirmation and consolidation of all that was unsavory in the past. Therefore, Tucholsky rejected the present. He retired to a personal life and preferred to be unconcerned with things German. He had fought and lost; there was nothing more to say. As he wrote to Hasenclever on March 11, 1933:

> I do not need to tell you that our world has ceased to exist in Germany, and therefore: I shall keep my mouth shut.... . We must see the situation as it is: our side has lost.[10]

Tucholsky believed he had fought his battles. He wanted nothing to do with the Nazis. On March 4, he wrote his impressions of Hitler's voice—impressions which are interesting not only in themselves, but also because they showed Tucholsky was unable to understand Hitler's appeal. He concluded that if such a man could gain control of a society, it was beyond salvation:

> Day before yesterday we installed a radio and listened to Adof. [Tucholsky's name for Hitler, "Doof," is German slang for stupid, half-witted, etc.] Dear Max, it was a remarkable thing. First Göring, an evil, old, bloodthirsty woman, who shrieked and incited the people to murder. Very frightening and disgusting. Then Göbbeles with the luminous eyes, who spoke to the people. (*Dann Göbbeles mit den loichtenden Augen, der zum Vollik sprach....* . [a parody of Goebbels's pronunciation.]) Then screaming of Heil and commands and music, gigantic pause—the Führer speaks. After all that went before, he should now be the speaker who—I stepped a few meters away from the apparatus and I confess I listened with my whole body. And then something remarkable happened.
> Then nothing at all. The voice is not as unsympathetic as you would think—it has a little of the odor of dirty underwear or of men—unappetizing, but nothing else. Sometimes he overextends himself with bellowing and sounds like he's throwing up. But other than that—nothing, nothing, nothing. No suspense, no high points, he doesn't hit me. I am too much of an artist myself not to admire the artistic even in such a person as he if it existed. Nothing, no humor, no warmth, no fire, nothing. He said nothing but the most stupid banalities, conclusions that did not follow—nothing.

From force of habit if nothing else, Tucholsky could not cease to take an interest in German events. In his letters to Hasenclever, he wrote down, in a cursory fashion, his thoughts concerning the future of National Socialism and of Europe.

In 1933, Tucholsky formulated a view of the Nazi regime that was essentially the same when he died two years later. He believed that Hitler had managed to establish a permanent power. "There is no use in speaking of collapse." In his view, no opposition movement could be effective. Tucholsky recognized the terroristic methods of Hitler, but he did not believe that they would continue. Tucholsky was convinced that when Hitler had eliminated his enemies, he would have no more need of terror. "The concentration camps will be closed. The game for us is over." In Tucholsky's opinion, Hitler would finally establish a tight, authoritarian government, rigidly bureaucratic and somewhat arbitrary in its administration of justice. Jews, for example, would never know where they stood in relation to the state, but bloodshed would not occur. It would be a society of mediocrity and order.

Again Tucholsky was envisioning a recreation of the Empire or a variation of it, i.e., a minority elite that enforced its will upon the broad majority. Hitler's power was different, for it was based on mass support and mass hysteria. To maintain both, Hitler had to have enemies with which he could both frighten and consolidate the masses. In addition, the terror would never cease, for it not only helped maintain Nazi power, it was also an end in itself. Hitler's revolution was destructive and nihilistic, not conservative and concerned with order, as Tucholsky suggested.

On June 11, 1933, Tucholsky implied more clearly that he believed the Hitler regime was still basically controlled by the old conservative elements in the army and the bureaucracy. He maintained that the only possible alternative to Hitler would be a military dictatorship with a monarchical head. Unfortunately the Crown Prince was too stupid to command a following, but Tucholsky contended that if the Hohenzollerns could have provided a dynamic leader, they would have been able to establish the most successful dictatorship. Tucholsky was convinced that the middle class by and large disapproved of the form of Hitler's power, but not of its content. They would prefer the monarchical form for their military dictatorship rather than the fascist shell. However, Tucholsky believed that Hitler would remain in power. On May 17, 1933, he wrote, "If Hitler survives the winter, we shall be buried with him." Even though Tucholsky did not recognize the revolutionary qualities of National Socialism, he did not entertain any false hopes that its rule was temporary.

Tucholsky was extremely pessimistic concerning the future of Europe. In July 1933, he maintained that war would come with Poland, but unlike 1925, he did not believe it would lead to a world conflict. It would be a local affair and Hitler would win it. Tucholsky predicted it would be four years before

Hitler was ready and then he would slowly establish hegemony over all of Eastern Europe.

Tucholsky did not live to see Hitler's great successes, but he predicted that the timidity of the European powers would make them possible. On December 12, 1934, he wrote to Hasenclever:

> ... How these dead democracies accept the atrocities, happening all around them... Certainly Germany will create a good foreign policy... They [Nazis] beat on the table with their fists. The table is not paid for, but they are correct in saying: "This is the language which the world understands!" In the great conferences, which the British will arrange in Geneva or somewhere else, the Germans will hold all the trumps. My deepest disappointment is France.
>
> ... The question is not whether people are beaten to death in concentration camps; it's been a long time since I was that optimistic. The question for France is whether Germany can be a serious partner, which she can trust. She [Germany] can't be trusted. Now the poor French are floundering about for allies and they deceive themselves about the English. England feels a closer affinity to Germany than to France. And the French fail to perceive that they are sliding down to the rank of a second-rate power.

Tucholsky thus predicted that England would attempt to move closer to Germany, while leaving France alone to fend for herself. He correctly perceived that relations with Germany would be determined not by whether people were starving and dying in concentration camps, but by the advantages that Germany might be able to offer.

The trends that Tucholsky perceived in 1934 were to become apparent to all in the years 1936-38 when England all but supported Nazi foreign policy, discouraged a Franco-Russian alliance, drove Italy into the arms of Germany and failed to draw up a firm alliance with France. The leading power of Western Europe, England, was unable or unwilling to recognize that the character of National Socialism was expansion and war. As early as August 17, 1933, Tucholsky recognized the lethargy that would overwhelm Europe. Its civilization would stand idly by watching the preparation of its own destruction:

> I do not believe that Hitler will topple. Why should he? As though she were crippled, Europe looks on while a new war is being prepared—the war industries grow, M. Daladier is tactful, the Foreign office ice cold. And so that one will have the three years that he needs in order to cut

loose. My conviction continually grows that he will win this war. Perhaps we should find out the conditions in Bali—for a Europe in which the Germans run around as proud conquerors—not for me.

According to Tucholsky, Poland would be Hitler's key to Eastern Europe, for the French would lose interest in the Polish. "How would they get there anyway," he asked in 1934, "through Germany?" Tucholsky believed the French might send money to Poland, but they would never send people and tanks. The English would do little more. Tucholsky despaired that the English would ever become cognizant of their own true interests again. He stated that the Conservatives were plagued by weakness and the Labourites could see no evil. " … Labour is the last straw … I don't like them—they are the ruin of Europe," Tucholsky wrote on January 5, 1934.

It appeared to Tucholsky that every power fell helplessly before the Nazis. To expect resistance from within Germany was useless. He came to believe that all vestiges of his world had been wiped out; there was left no remnant to speak for the "other Germany" of Goethe and the Enlightenment. Geist had been overwhelmed by Macht. There was nothing to be gained by protest. Tucholsky concluded in 1934—"Hitler is Germany."

One of the most curious and even tragic aspects of Tucholsky's exile was that his bitterness was extended not only to the Nazis but to their victims as well. He had always had an ambivalence toward his Jewish origin, but in 1935 it erupted into the invective which could only be the product of a wounded and defenseless spirit. At the end of his life he wrote, "In 1911, I 'seceded from Jewry.' I know one can't do anything of the sort, but that was the legal formula."[11]

Although Tucholsky had long ceased consciously to identify himself as a Jew, he was aware that others, especially his enemies, regarded him as one. No matter how neutral Tucholsky might be toward things Jewish, his origin remained an inescapable nuance and overtone throughout his life and career. At this point it is essential to investigate more closely Tucholsky's early relation to Judaism if we are to attempt to understand those harsh words at the end of his life that gained for him the epithet of anti-Semite.

Tucholsky was born into an upper-class Jewish family, but he received little formal religious training. His background and education were almost identical to those of any wealthy middle-class non-Jew. The milieu, however, was Jewish in that Tucholsky's parents called themselves Jews, were regarded as Jews by others and probably had only Jews as close friends. It was not a question of their being despised or disliked as Jews, it was simply an almost indefinable awareness that they were Jews. Tucholsky tried to explain it with a quotation from Alfred Kerr:

> Even people of sensitive nature did not find it so rough when on the Day of Atonement a boor would call a gentleman with a prayer book "damned Jewish dung!" Or if a Major of the "Eleventh" would publicly declare on the streetcar, "There are so many pregnant Jewish women—makes you want to vomit!" Those things made no wounds. But when enlightened friends, well-meaning, and considerate, said, "The Jewish gentlemen"—that hurt.[12]

It was not the vulgar anti-Semitism of ruffians that wounded. Rather, Tucholsky was saying, it was the vague or subtle distinctions made by non-Jewish friends, which made a Jewish background seem to be a kind of stigma impossible to eradicate.

On the other hand, there was the pride that Jews took in their own separate traditions. No child could be raised in a Jewish home, no matter how religiously lax, without being made aware of past Jewish history. The two parts of the Judeo-Christian tradition had more to distinguish them than the question of the divinity of Jesus. Exclusion, persecution, separation became a part of the Jewish tradition and after emancipation, the hostility of gentile society was recalled and kept alive in the memories of those who might never have experienced it directly. Thus in Germany in the nineteenth and twentieth centuries, the idea of apartness was kept alive during a time of assimilation.

Certainly this simultaneous rejection and acceptance of German society by Jews as a group played a part in Tucholsky's development. And in turn the attitudes of the society toward Jews were no less important. This is a delicate matter to analyze since Tucholsky said almost nothing about it explicitly. Only the bitterness toward Jews expressed by him shortly before his death gave a sure indication of the importance of Tucholsky's Jewish background. In his famous letter to Arnold Zweig of December 15, 1935, Tucholsky revealed why he left Judaism. "I did it because in my earliest youth, I developed an ineradicable abhorrence of those unctuous Rabbis—because I sensed more than knew the cowardice of this society."[13]

Although these words were written in the disillusionment of 1935, they nevertheless demonstrated that Tucholsky had assumed something of the prejudice of the society around him. He was also ashamed of the way Jews let themselves be treated. As a youth he expressed his protest by officially repudiating the Jewish religion.[14] It would be extreme to call this what the Nazis liked to term "Jewish self-hatred," but by his action Tucholsky expressed uncertain feelings about his background. Above all, in his comment and satire on Jews, Tucholsky betrayed an ambivalence toward his origins.[15] He seemed to expect more of Jews, somehow, and was disappointed when they acted as ordinary people. On the one hand he criticized Jews for remaining separate, for being "clannish." On the other hand, he upbraided them for not showing group solidarity in the face of anti-Semitism. He wanted Jews simultaneously to be a part of and separate from German society. And, of course, in his *Hassliebe* toward Germany, that was precisely the position he himself occupied—simultaneous alienation and involvement.

Tucholsky's reaction was not so great that he became indifferent to Jews. Just as he was interested in almost all social and political matters, so was he concerned with the Jews as a group within a larger society. Just as he defended any group or individual who was the object of injustice, so naturally he defended the Jews against anti-Semitism and against isolation by the rest of society.

Shortly after the war, Tucholsky became aware of a growing anti-Semitism in Germany. In 1920, he published a chilling letter by a liberal army officer describing conditions in the rural areas and small towns. The officer stated that the provinces were seething with hatred for the Jews and that sophisticated city dwellers should not be deceived concerning the gravity of the problem. Furthermore, he reported that anti-Semitic nationalists were preaching race hate to the gullible youth in the villages and army. In fact, the situation had become so bad that the officer added, "It is no longer discussed *if* the Jews should be killed, but *how* they should be killed."[16]

It was in Tucholsky's attack upon anti-Semitism that his conflict with himself as Jew-German was illustrated. Tucholsky was an assimilationist, for he repudiated Judaism and contracted a marriage with a non-Jew. By his actions, he indicated that Jews should merge with the society at large. But when he attacked anti-Semitism, he also upbraided the Jews for not showing greater unity in the face of their enemies. He accused them of wanting to become German so badly that they had begun to view their Jewishness as a kind of shameful sickness. In 1921, he wrote:

> Their behavior is not blameless. There are a great number of persons among the German Jews (especially in Berlin) who seem to be ashamed of their Jewishness as though it were a sickness. When in a restaurant, they stop the children from mentioning the word "Synagogue" with a fearful "*Stike!*" [quiet!]. These good merchants and poor musicians were happy to give their sons to the Kaiser—but they are not happy to give their taxes to this regime, which has to pay for the adventures of imperial Germany. And they are ready to support any group, which promises order because of their senseless fear of Bolshevism, which they have always feared and never advocated. If the German Nationalists were not so stupid as to be anti-Semitic, the greatest part of conservative Jewry would flock to them. I know of cases where Jews have lost any sense of honor to the extent of voting for the German Nationalists.[17]

Here, Tucholsky was expressing his hatred for German society and his horror that Jews could become subject to its shortcomings. Tucholsky said many times that there was no danger of the Germans assuming the faults of the Jews; it was rather the Jews who were being Germanized.

The assassination of the (Jewish) foreign minister Walther Rathenau on June 24, 1922, appeared to be the climax of anti-Semitic and anti-republican terrorism. Shocked by the murder, Tucholsky was inspired again to express his contempt for the Jews who merged with a society that hated them. He stated his feelings through the invention of the fictional character, Herr Wendriner.

As a businessman who was also Jewish, Wendriner had assumed what Tucholsky believed were the worst German character traits. Wendriner was subservient before authority, arrogant to inferiors, and narrow in his wide view of the world. Always on the side of "order," Wendriner expressed an unenlightened self-interest and political timidity that Tucholsky believed would insure the triumph of reaction and be the ruin of the Jews.

In the first Wendriner sketch published on July 6, 1922, entitled "Ten Minutes" (later changed to "Herr Wendriner Telephones"), Tucholsky presented his idea of a Germanized Jew. The sketch opens with Herr Wendriner, the Jew. After a brief vacillation it closes with Herr Wendriner, the Jew turned conservative Prussian. The brilliance of the story was that Tucholsky managed to limit it to a paragraph of less than fifty lines.

The piece is a soliloquy by Herr Wendriner as he attempts to make a business telephone call and finds the lines closed in mourning for Walther Rathenau. (On the day of Rathenau's burial, all communications in Germany were suspended for ten minutes in his honor.) At first, Wendriner is pleased—"absolutely proper. The man was a princely merchant and our greatest statesman. That is uncontested. Scandalous that they shot him!" While waiting for the ten minutes to elapse, Wendriner continues to reminisce how impressive were the mourning ceremonies in the Reichstag and how excellent was the lead article in the newspaper. He tries to call again and is surprised the ten minutes are not yet up. He speculates about the murderers, makes an automatic mental association with officers and thinks how proud he was when his son received his commission.

As he waits, his impatience begins to grow—"The ten minutes are a bit long"—until he questions the whole idea of paying tribute to the dead in such manner: it certainly would not bring Rathenau back. Wendriner asserts that it would have been better to honor the former Foreign Minister by creating a fairer taxation system. Wendriner wonders who will suspend the telephone system when he dies. Suddenly he realizes with disgust that the person he is trying to reach has probably left his office. Wendriner concludes with the inevitable reflection that things were better under the monarchy: murder is one thing, but interference with business?—In the end, it is even bad for the Jews:

> What is this? In broad daylight, they cut off the telephone right in my face! Many things happened under the Emperor, but I've never experienced anything like this! Unheard of! This is an imposition on the public. They can shoot each other or not—but they must not interfere with business. And besides: a Jew shouldn't make such a spectacle of himself! That incites anti-Semitism. There's been no order in this country since the ninth of November. Is it necessary to cut off the telephone? Who will pay my damages if I don't reach Skalitzer? Operator! Oh listen to that—they're demonstrating again—look at that—with red flags—I don't like that! What are they singing? They will do that until they make another revolution. Operator! As far as I'm concerned they can take their republic and… Operator! Finally! Operator, Königstadt… .[18]

The Wendriner stories were extremely popular in Germany, but a few persons found them harmful. Some saw the portrayal of Wendriner as a Jew to be a contribution to an already raging anti-Semitism. In 1966, at the World Jewish Congress in Brussels, the Israeli scholar, Gershom Scholem, had harsh words for Tucholsky as the author of the Wendriner sketches:

> It is, after all, to a German Jew who left Judaism—though, as he said, he "of course, knew that this was impossible"—that we owe what a critic once called "the most naked exposures" of the Berlin Jewish bourgeoisie which exist anywhere and which will endure as a sinister document of the German-Jewish reality; l am referring to the monologues of Herr Wendriner written by Kurt Tucholsky. The anti-Semites took pains to make the Jews look as bad as possible, but their writings are curiously overstrained and hollow. The hatred is there, but there is no knowledge of the subject and no feeling for atmosphere. Small wonder, then, that it remained for one of the most gifted, most convinced and most offensive Jewish anti-Semites to accomplish on a definitive level what the anti-Semites themselves were unable to bring about.[19]

It must have been painful for men such as Scholem to read the Wendriner monologues, seeing in them another thrust from the anti-Semitic dagger. Perhaps Tucholsky should have recognized that the time was too serious for any kind of satire at the expense of Jews—that the enemies of the Jews were too powerful for anyone to run the risk of contributing to their strength. However that may be, it is grossly unfair to accuse Tucholsky of being anti-

Semitic. Tucholsky neither loved nor hated anyone because of religion or race. He hated Wendriner not because he was Jewish, but because he was selfish, narrow and crass. Tucholsky disliked the bourgeoisie as a class and he believed that the Gentile and Jewish varieties of that class were separated by different, particular prejudices and modes of expression. But they were united in the fact of their prejudice, in the fact of their pettiness. Perhaps Tucholsky should have selected a Gentile bourgeois for his caricature, but it was the Jewish milieu which he knew best.

The Wendriner stories also show that somehow Tucholsky expected more of Jews. Wendriner was an expression of a kind of reverse prejudice on the part of Tucholsky. There were thousands of Wendriners in Germany—all products of a capitalist society but the fact that there were also Jewish Wendriners was a disappointment for Tucholsky. He exposed Wendriner, not because he hated Jews, but because he wanted there to be no Wendriners among the Jews—because he wanted the Jews to be an exemplary people within the society. Yet this sentiment was complicated by the fact that Tucholsky also wanted the Jews to be assimilated within the society at large, to "disappear."

The "Wendriner mentality" was, of course, in the end fatal to the Jews and Tucholsky recognized that it could be. Again we have the dilemma of alienation and involvement. Wendriner was a businessman first and a Jew second. He was so involved in making money in the German economy and in praising the traditional values of German culture that he could not recognize when the same culture excluded and harmed him. Tucholsky despised the Wendriners because they were both German and "Jewish." By "German" Tucholsky meant that they were Germanized—they were authoritarian and "Prussian." By "Jewish" he meant that they took pride in being Jews only when it was of some material value to them to do so. Tucholsky believed that if a crisis came they would be unable to associate themselves with the persecuted group either to lead it or to defend themselves. This is illustrated in "Herr Wendriner steht unter der Diktatur" ("Herr Wendriner under the Dictatorship"), a story mentioned earlier in another context. Tucholsky's main concern in this Wendriner sketch was the anti-Semitism of well-to-do Jews and what he believed would be their toleration of the Nazis.

In this last of the Wendriner stories, the Nazis have assumed power. Herr Wendriner and his friends are in a theater that is filled with SA men. Wendriner constantly admonishes his cronies to speak more softly:

> ... Those are Jewish matters. We—not so loud! Speak quietly! Don't make me any unpleasantness—the times are too grave for that. All in all the people [the Nazis] are absolutely correct when they demand that we show restraint in public. They are absolutely justified.[20]

Here Tucholsky was effectively portraying the destructive self-hatred of the anti-Semitic Jew. Wendriner goes on to say that the SA man who guards his street is a regular fellow as long as he receives his cigarette bribe. And Wendriner boasts that his "connections" got him his yellow badge sooner than anyone else.

Tucholsky was thinking of the Wendriners when he said, "It is not true that the Germans have become Jewish. The German Jews are Germanized (*verbocht*)."[21] The Jewish dilemma was that exclusiveness, in a sense, fostered anti-Semitism; while a lack of solidarity rendered them impotent against it. In their eagerness to be Germans, the German Jews could not recognize their own best interests when the "Germans" rejected them. They did and yet did not feel themselves to be a separate group. Some were so much a part of the society that they even despised themselves as Jews, thus leading to Wendriner's lunacy when he said, "They [the Nazis] are absolutely correct."

On the other band, Jews were so much apart of German society that they could feel no solidarity as a group when placed in that category by the Nazis. In other words, the Nazis placed Jews into a separate group that the Jews did not really believe existed. They were thus all the more vulnerable.

After the advent of Hitler, Tucholsky watched with horror and disgust what he believed to be the weak Submission of the Jews to their fate. He expressed his bitterness on many occasions, but the climax came four days before his suicide. On December 15, 1935, he wrote the letter to Arnold Zweig, which unmercifully criticized the Jews of Germany. It was a harsh and biting statement, which the Nazis used for anti-Semitic purposes by claiming that it was an example of Jewish self-hatred and recognition that Judaism was lost.[22] But Tucholsky spoke out of a sense of disillusion and disappointment, not out of hatred. "I speak not because of resentment. Also I do not belong to the notorious Jewish anti-Semites."[23] The letter, nevertheless, was a denunciation of the Jews through the ages—their alleged docility, complicity with authority and lack of resistance to attack. In Tucholsky's opinion, the Jews' obsequiousness had led them to the predicament of the twentieth century.

> Jewry has suffered defeat, a defeat, which it deserves—and it is not true that it has fought for thousands of years. It does not fight.

Tucholsky further contended that the Jews had never been responsible for their own fate. The emancipation had not been the work of Jews. The French Revolution had freed the Jews and not they themselves. And the Jews had always, in Tucholsky's opinion, accepted their own fate. They were not brave, they were not proud and thus they were downtrodden. "The ghetto is not a consequence—the ghetto is fate. A master race would have crumbled—this one 'must live.' No, one must not live that way, not that way."

Tucholsky was saying that it was better to die than suffer humiliation. He despised the lack of resistance on the part of the Jews in Germany. He could not understand how they could allow themselves to be treated as they were by the Nazis. In his thinking, it was because German Jews accepted the idea of the ghetto. They were cowardly; they had no idea of heroism. "The Jew is a coward. He is happy when he doesn't get a kick in the pants." To add to the shame was the lack of leadership:

> But the great moment found a weak generation... Was there one Rabbi who was the leader of his people? Just one man? Not a single one.

Tucholsky asked how could it be that Julius Streicher thrived in Nuremburg, a city with one of the richest and most influential Jewish communities? How could the Jews of Frankfurt have gone quietly into their houses when forced off their own streets? Why did they all refuse to heed the warnings? Tucholsky contended that in March 1933 nine out of ten Jews should have left the country instead of one in ten. There should have been a mass exodus, but when urged to leave, the cry was, "But my business... ":

> "I can't leave! ... Think of my losses! What do you mean—think of my business!" And now they crawl out, sad, beaten, up to their ears in shit, broke, robbed of their money—and without honor. (But thinking themselves better.) Heroism would have been the better business here. Why did they not choose that way? Because they are not able to be heroic; because they have no idea what that is.

In his letter, Tucholsky revealed more about his own feelings than he said about the behavior of Jews. He was correct in implying that merely to be victimized is not to be noble, but he had no sympathy for their plight as victims. What Tucholsky expressed most was a deep disappointment in the Jews and, as Arnold Zweig said in his "Answer," a sense of insult as a Jew:

> Your letter made an assumption something like this: Above all, this Zweig moves in circles concerned with Jewish questions, and one has to talk about these problems with him. The way in which you did it was moving and brave, but it was something more. A deeply wounded soul made its appearance, wounded not as a leftist, not as an intellectual, not as a Cassandra-like prophet, but as a Jew.[24]

Tucholsky's vehement denunciation betrayed a love, and a wound. Like Shakespeare's lady, be protested too much and revealed his underlying expectations. As before, Tucholsky expected Jews to be better, nobler, more heroic than ordinary people. He demanded superhuman efforts such as mass emigration and a sense of separate identity after a century of assimilation. When the Jews failed to meet these impossible expectations, in his disappointment, Tucholsky made their quite ordinary behavior as victims, the result of a unique cultural deficiency. Tucholsky committed out of love the same error the Nazis committed out of hate—he made the Jews different, separate and berated them when they did not act so.

Tucholsky said the Jews were *verbocht*. And so they were. They were Germans; they were not separate until they were separated. In his sense of hurt, Tucholsky failed to recognize that German Jews in 1933 had as little relation to medieval Ghetto Jews as Junkers to Teutonic knights.

Tucholsky's letter to Arnold Zweig was one of the last acts in his long drama of despair. Yet the question arises of why Tucholsky lost so completely his old combative spirit, why he gave in so totally to his feelings of impotence and depression. The answer lies in part in the fact that he became absolutely convinced that he had been defeated, that his cause had been swept away, his message had become passé. He believed that he had outlived his time and there was nothing left for him but silence. "*Schweigen, schweigen, schweigen,*" he counseled his brother.[25] "Ich bin ein aufgehörter Schriftsteller" ("I am a writer who has ceased to write")."

Tucholsky contended that the future was measured by the interests of youth and youth was ignoring the antifascist cause. He saw no young persons rushing to join the *emigré* leftist writers. As he wrote on April 11, 1933, "For the time being. I have no plans. If there were somewhere a group of *young* men who were antifascist, I would cooperate." And in another letter to Hasenclever the following year on September 26, be said, "The boys, the girls, many young people in spite of all criticism, disappointment and many ifs and buts, are completely lost to us. In their minds, we are *ci-devants*. As for myself, I certainly have nothing more to do with it."

Tucholsky believed that he and the other leftist writers had become anachronisms. Therefore, he had nothing to do with the literature in exile that developed. In his opinion, the only purpose such efforts served was to enable the writers to eke out a small living. Otherwise, their activities were hopeless. As early as March 4, 1933, he wrote to Hasenclever:

> Under no circumstances should one take part in the emigration literature now in its beginnings. Dear Max, first, there will not be a large emigration because, unlike the Russian Revolution of 1917, Europe is not prepared to accept such people. They will starve. Secondly, like every emigration, the Germans will also break up into 676 little groups, who

will fight each other much more than Adof (we'll take the L away since we need it for Eckner, Hei Adof!). Thirdly, you shouldn't do it because it ruins character. You'll get wrinkles around your mouth and become, with all due respect, a rather comic figure.

For Tucholsky, the defeat had been too overwhelming to expect anything to result from a few journals in exile. "You can't tackle an ocean," he said in 1933. How, he asked, could the emigrant writers expect to accomplish from the outside what they found it impossible to effect from the inside? Tucholsky saw a pathetic quality about the *emigrés* with their naive hope that their articles—read only by other exiles—would be effective. He foresaw an increasingly narrow audience for them as Hitler's giant propaganda apparatus shouted down their feeble voices. As he wrote in April 1933: "Sometimes the exiled gentlemen are like little boys playing Indians.... Our people are naive—!"

Tucholsky recognized the impotence of the *emigrés* and in his deep mental depression, he was repelled by the optimism implicit in their activities. To him, they seemed to behave as though nothing had changed; their words were all so familiar. He wrote Arnold Zweig in 1935:

> Here is what so annoys me about the German emigration: everything continues as though nothing has happened. On and on—they write the same books, give the same speeches and make the same gestures. None of that was of any use when there were still possibilities and we had some power—how can anything be done now from the outside! Look at Lenin in emigration: steel and greatest clarity of thought. And these here—? Pure muck, *Doitsche Kultur* [sic]. The conscience of the world—good night.

Tucholsky wanted nothing to do with the emigrant groups because he had lost all concern for Germany. The Germans had rejected him and he rejected them. On April 20, 1933, he remarked that the Nazis seemed to be attacking him often on the radio and in the papers, but he admitted he could not care less—"I can scarcely even make up jokes about the Nazis, I am so unendingly indifferent to all that." At the same time, he resolved not to buy any German goods, read any German newspapers or speak with any Germans who were not absolutely free of Nazi taint.[26]" —Am unfortunately unable to understand any German while traveling."[27]

Again and again, Tucholsky wrote Hasenclever of the fact that he read no German, spoke as little of the language as possible and had no interest in what was happening. It was in this constant repetition of his rejection of Germany that he unconsciously revealed how deeply he had been wounded. In all of the letters, written immediately before his death, to Walter Hasenclever, Fritz Tucholsky, and Arnold Zweig, he repeatedly emphasized his indifference to things German. It was in the letter to Zweig that he expressed his hurt most violently:

> My life is too valuable to sit under an apple tree and beg it to produce pears. No more for me. I have nothing more to do with this land whose language I speak as little as possible. May it perish—may Russia conquer it—am finished with it.

Beginning in November 1935, Tucholsky's letters told the story of a man in decline. Constantly he spoke of feeling ill and tired. He lost all sense of purpose and began to brood about the Jews and the meaninglessness of his past career. He wrote his brother on December 5, "It is not your duty to fight for Germany. You will only waste your life as I have done. (For what purpose was all that?) ." He saw no hope for the future in any form and confessed that even if the Nazis were to fall from power, the society that he and his friends had envisioned would not be created. It was too late for that.[28]

He believed his world was dead and he finally chose not to live in the world that had replaced it. Toward the middle of December, Tucholsky calmly decided to end his life. But there was one unfinished matter to attend to—a final, parting letter to his former wife, Mary Gerold Tucholsky (referring to her as "Mala" and "Him," and to himself as "Nungo," as he used to during their marriage). A letter of love, it was also the anguished cry of a man broken by the arduous time in which he lived. Tucholsky wrote the letter on December 19, 1935. On the outside of the envelope he wrote:

> [Hindas]   [December 19, 1935]
> If He is married or seriously attached, I beg Him to destroy this letter unread. I do not desire to intrude upon unknown happiness—I want nothing. I have nothing to conceal, nothing to say which He does not know better than me. I only want to ask for His forgiveness. If the above is true, promise to burn this—nothing should be stirred up again.
>   Wish Him all the happiness
>   N.

Inside the envelope was the following:

> Dear Mala.
> Want to take His hand for the last time and ask Him for forgiveness for what has once done to Him. Had a lump of gold and fished for pennies; did not understand and did stupid things—did not betray, but deceived and did not understand.

I know that He is not vengeful. What He has endured on the return trip to Berlin; what took place later: I have richly atoned for it. In the end, it was clear to me—as clear as the reflection in a polished mirror. Now, everything comes back, images, words... and how I let Him go—now that it's all is over, I know: I bear the whole, complete guilt.

... And now it is almost seven years to the day since gone away, no—since let go away. And now the memories are splashing down, all of them together. I know what I complain to Him and about Him—our unlived life.

If the times were normal (and if I were also), we would have a child of, say, twelve years—and what's more, we would have the unity of our memories.

Did not dare to call Him anymore. Hopes that He has followed my plea on the envelope—the alternative would not be good. I may assume that when He reads this, I'm not disrupting a happiness I myself was not able to earn.

No, not dared to call Him anymore. For reasons easy to understand, I have never made any kind of "inquiries": If He were married, I would have heard—but not anything else. And above all did not dare because had no right to tear Him a second time from work and everything—: am sick and can defend me no longer—much less someone else. I lack nothing important or grave—it is a series of small disturbances that make it impossible for me to work. I could not call Him into sure misery—quite aside from the fact that I never hoped He would come.

Still. Knew.

If He had come, He would not have found another person, but a transformed, matured one. I never published a line about what happens in Germany now—in spite of all requests to do so. It is no longer my concern. It is not cowardice—what's the big deal to write for the exile press! But I'm *au dessus de la mêlée*, it is no longer my concern. I'm done with it. And now so much has been freed, now—now I know—but now it's of no use. Was stupid in the beginning—the usual *coup de foudre* for 2.50 francs, half important things and I had good friendships. But I still see myself after His departure, sitting in Parc Monceau where I began my Paris. I was "free"—and I was sad and empty and not at all happy. And that's how it remained.

His loving patience to participate in this madness—the unrest, the patience to live next to a man who was as if always hunted; who always had fear—no, anxiety. The anxiety that has no basis and could not name one reason—today, it would no longer be necessary. Today, I know. If love is what turns you upside down, which maddens every fiber of your be-

ing—then such can be felt anytime and anywhere. But when it comes to real love, which lasts, which returns over and over again:—then I loved only once in my life.
Him.
… Had imagined a ridiculous "freedom" on the other side—whereas such a thing truly does not exist. Lived more and more quietly—and now washed up on the shore—the vehicle is stuck—can't keep going.
I only want to ask Him for forgiveness.
I was once a writer and I learned from S.J. the joy of quotation. If He wants to know how it sounds in the classics, He should read the parting letter by Heinrich von Kleist to his sister in Wannsee, 1811. And perhaps also look through a few pages of *Peer Gynt*; I don't know if we saw the play together, it is not really performable. Toward the end, the hero rushes around the forest and happens upon a hut in which this chocolate image, Solveig, sits and sings something syrupy. But then the lines: "He arose—deadly pale." Then he speaks four more lines. These are the ones I mean.
"Oh, Angst," … not because of the end. I don't care about that, like everything which happens around me and to which I no longer have a connection. The reason to struggle, the bridge, the inner force, the *raison d' etre* is gone. I did not understand.
Wish Him everything—everything good—
and please forgive.

Nungo[29]

Shortly after completion of the letter, Tucholsky swallowed the poison which be had long carried on his person. He left a note written in French asking to be allowed to die in peace. He was discovered and rushed to a hospital in Göteborg where he died on December 21, 1935.

NOTES

1   Institut zum Studium der Judenfrage, *Die Juden in Deutschland* (Munich, 1935), pp. 223-246.
2   Ibid., p. 224, 234.
3   Wilhelm Stapel, "Kurt Tucholsky," *Forschungen zur Judenfrage, Sitzungsberichte der zweiten Arbeitstagung der Forschungsabteilung Judenfrage des Reichsinstituts für Geschichte des neuen Deutschlands vom 12 bis 14 Mai 1937, II* (Hamburg, 1937), 182-216.
4   Hans Diebow, *Der ewige Jude. 265 Bilddokumente* (Munich, 1938).
5   Twenty-three people composed the first group to be treated in this manner. In addition to Tucholsky's name, the list contained artists, writers, and luminaries such as Lion Feuchtwanger, Alfred Kerr, Heinrich Mann, Philipp Scheidemann, Leopold Schwarzschild, Friedrich Stampfer, Ernst Toller, and Otto Wels.
6   Kurt Tucholsky, Letter to Walter Hasenclever of August 1933, *Ausgewählte Briefe, 1913-1935* (Hamburg, 1962), p. 271.
7   When Tucholsky's brother, Fritz, passed through Switzerland on his way to America, he was somewhat baffled as to why Tucholsky was unable to meet him. Not until Fritz had reached the United States did Tucholsky dare tell him that be had been in Sweden an along. See *Ausgewählte Briefe*, pp. 310-330.
8   These and the following quotes are from Kurt Tucholsky: *Ausgewählte Briefe*, pp. 273. 319-322, 307, 318, 320f., 323, 315. Hasenclever himself also committed suicide in the prison camp of *Camp des Milles* in the south-east of France on 22 June 1940, as not to fall into the hands of the Nazis.
9   See Bruno Bettelheim, *The Informed Heart, Autonomy in a Mass Age* (Glencoe, Ill., 1960), pp. 267-300 and passim.
10   This and the following quotes are from: Kurt Tucholsky, *Ausgewählte Briefe*, pp. 251, 247., 258, 253, 250f, 260, 258, 265, 293f, 269, 275, 280, 275.
11   Kurt Tucholsky: *Ausgewählte Briefe*, p. 333. Translated by Ralph Mannheim in *Politics*, V/3 (New York, Summer, 1948), 173.
12   Alfred Kerr, quoted by Kurt Tucholsky, *Ausgewählte Briefe*, p. 337.
13   Ibid., p. 333.
14   Under the Empire, a Jew could register his renunciation of faith before a local law court (*Amtsgericht*). In 1918, Tucholsky officially became a Protestant for reasons of expediency. As he said, "... It was bearable to be a Jew under the Empire, but not to be an atheist" (Ibid.).
15   Ibid., p. 462.
16   Kurt Tucholsky, "Das leere Schloss," G.W. (Hamburg, 1960), I, 601; I.W., *Die Weltbühne*, XVI/8 (Feb. 19, 1920), 240.
17   Kurt Tucholsky, "Hepp hepp hurral" G.W., I, 790; I.W., *Die Welt am Montag* (Feb. 14, 1921).
18   Kurt Tucholsky, "Herr Wendriner telefoniert," G.W., I, 990f.; K.H., *Die Weltbühne*, XVIII/27 (July 6, 1922), 19. English translation by Cindy Opitz in *Berlin! Berlin! Dispatches From the Weimar Republic* (Berlinica, New York, 2013), pp. 96f.
19   Gershom Scholem, "Jews and Germans," *Commentary*, XLII/5 (November, 1966), 36.
20   Kurt Tucholsky, "Herr Wendriner steht unter der Diktatur," G.W., III, 547-550; K.H., *Die Weltbühne*, XXVI/41 (Oct. 7, 1930), 559. English translation by Harry Zohn in: *Germany? Germany! The Kurt Tucholsky Reader* (Berlinica, New York, 2017), pp. 54–57.

21 Kurt Tucholsky, *Ausgewählte Briefe*, p. 334.

22 The letter was printed in abridged form—unflattering references to Stalin and the Communists carefully excised—in the Communist-controlled *Die neue Weltbühne* in January 1936 (the paper, now forbidden in Germany, was published in exile in Prague). Thereby the Nazis found it and reprinted it with their own excisions and commentary.

23 This and the following quotes are from: Kurt Tucholsky, *Ausgewählte Briefe*, pp. 333, 334, 335.

24 Arnold Zweig, "Antwort," *Die neue Weltbühne*, XXXII/3 (January 16, 1936), 165-170.

25 This and the following quotes are from: Kurt Tucholsky, *Ausgewählte Briefe*, pp. 293, 329, 339, 251, 290, 246, 251, 256, 338, 254.

26 He wrote to Hasenclever on April 20, 1933 (*Ausgewählte Briefe*, p. 255): With exactly the same ruthlessness, with exactly the same power and force with which the Germans drill, imprison and humiliate our friends—making them sing the Horst Wessel growl, starving and tormenting them—with exactly the same quiet ruthlessness, I refuse to sit at the table with any German who is not absolutely pure. I don't care what he may be called. You know me and have seen me in many situations. It is not my shortcoming to give political editorials in the salon or forcefully to "convert" other people. But here it ends. I have made a rule for myself. I will buy no German newspapers, no German products and will associate with no German unless I have had exact previous knowledge about his position on the subject... .

27 This and the following quotes are from: Kurt Tucholsky, *Ausgewählte Briefe*, pp. 280, 337, 327.

28 Ibid., p. 290. Tucholsky expressed this sentiment explicitly on September 7, 1934, in a letter to Hasenclever, but it is implicit in his letters of the last months of his life.

29 Ibid., pp. 500-502.

PUBLISHER'S AFTERWORD

BY EVA C. SCHWEITZER

WHEN HAROLD L. Poor published his book about Tucholsky in 1967, the author had already made a comeback in Germany. "In 1935, Tucholsky died thinking he would be a forgotten man," Poor wrote in the afterword of the original book, *Kurt Tucholsky and the Ordeal of Germany 1914-1935* (published by Scribner, New York). "But ironically his fame has risen in double measure in both of the post-war Germanies. Because of Mary Tucholsky's efforts, Tucholsky was republished almost immediately after the war and may indeed be said to have become Germany's most popular writer."

As of 1967, Tucholsky had sold some four million books since 1945 (in 1980, it was more than six million books, and today most likely more than ten million). Up to 1967, his works had appeared in over thirty German editions and have been translated into almost every European language, let alone the additional large secondary literature. Over forty phonograph recordings had been made of his songs and stories. Tucholsky "evenings" were regular events in the post-war theaters of Germany and many radio programs had been devoted to discussions of his works and impact. A film has been made of his novels *Schloss Gripsholm* and *Rheinsberg*. The latter, starring Cornelia Froboess and Christian Wolff, premiered in 1967. (His screenplay *Christoph Kolumbus oder Die Entdeckung Amerikas* became a TV movie in 1969, and *Schloss Gripsholm* was turned again into a movie in 2000, starring Ulrich Noethen, Heike Makatsch, and Jasmin Tabatabai, with Pippi-Longstocking-actress Inger Nielson in a supporting role.) "Tucholsky may be said to have triumphed over those who attempted to silence him," Poor wrote.

The late 1960s—when Poor began teaching at Rutgers—was the decade when German students protested against the heritage of Nazism, the police state and the oppressive jurisdicial structure Tucholsky had written so much about, but also against U.S. foreign policy culminating in Iran, Latin America, and Vietnam. And Tucholsky was still controversial. German reactionaries, as Poor observed, "continued to attack Tucholsky's writings as though he were still active and living." Many students, however, bought Tucholsky's books to use them in their struggle against the conservative establishment.

"In West Germany, he remains the great republican wit, the greatest critic of statist ideology, the most insistent satirist of the shibboleths of German middle-class culture," Poor wrote. In 1960s East Germany, most of his writings had evaded the censor and appealed to a population starved for criticism of government and politics. That did change eventually; the GDR cracked down on Tucholsky as well.

Nowadays, the Iron Curtain has fallen and Europe is united—struggles non-withstanding—at least politically. However, in the last few years right-wing and populist parties have made a comeback, mostly in Eastern Europe, but also in Germany. In the United States, Donald Trump is in the White House; the man who represents a dangerous, illiberal current in American society and who encourages violent partisan fighting, hateful language, a militarized society, and disdain for the press. The highly partisan situation in America today even reminds some historians of Weimar Germany.

"Kurt Tucholsky was one of the most brilliant writers of republican Germany... More than any other person, he foresaw what was coming.... What his readers had enjoyed as the capricious fantasies of a clever satirist has now been enacted in bitter reality, even to a satirical forecast of his own mode of death," wrote *The New York Times* in its 1936 Obituary. Yet Tucholsky, who would have had so many answers to today's quarrels, was virtually unknown in the United States when World War II ended.

That changed only when Harry Zohn, a Jewish refugee from Vienna who became a professor at Brandeis University, translated numerous Tucholsky-works in the 1950s and 1960s. In more recent times, Berlinica Publishing, our New-York-based company has commissioned, as of now, four English-language Tucholsky-books, starting with *Berlin! Berlin! Dispatches From the Weimar Republic* in 2013, followed by *Rheinsberg. A Storybook for Lovers*. Both were translated by Cindy Opitz, as well as *Hereafter. We Were Sitting On a Cloud, Dangling Our Legs*, which came out in 2019. And Peter Appelbaum and James Scott have translated Tucholsky's poems and stories from World War I, titled *Prayer After the Slaughter*. Berlinica has also picked up the now out-of-print Zohn translation; the book is available under the title *Germany? Germany! Satirical Writings: The Kurt Tucholsky Reader*.

In addition to Berlinica, *The New York Review of Books* will reprint the English edition of *Schloss Gripsholm*, originally published by Overlook Press, in a new translation by Michael Hofmann. And also *The New York Times* has re-discovered Tucholsky; the paper called him in a recent story "the most brilliant, prolific and witty cultural journalist of his time". "The pith and the punch of his cabaret work translated brilliantly to his anti-Nazi satires," writes William Grimes in *The Times*. "Too brilliantly, in the end".

Kurt Tucholsky

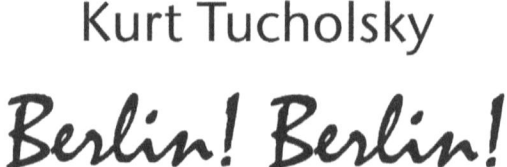

Dispatches from the Weimar Republic

Foreword by Anne Nelson
Introduction by Ian King

Kurt Tucholsky:

**Berlin! Berlin!
Dispatches
From the
Weimar Republic**

Translated by
Cindy Opitz

Foreword by
Anne Nelson/
Introduction by
Ian King

Softcover:
5.5" x 8.5"
202 pp.

ISBN
978-1 935902-20-1
978-3-96026-027-1

Sugg. Retail:
$14.95 /
ebook $7.99

BERLIN! BERLIN! is a selection from the "man with the acid pen and the perfect pitch for hypocrisy," as New York author Peter Wortsman puts it. This book is a collection of Tucholsky's news stories, features, satirical pieces, and poems about his hometown. It depicts its cabarets, its policies, its follies, and its celebrities, from Bert Brecht to Claire Waldoff to Friedrich Hollaender. The book contains some of Tucholsky's most famous pieces, among them the Berliner on the phone, on vacation, or doing "bizness", the holes in the cheese, the lion who escaped the zoo, and more than one satirical biography of the author himself. Herr Wendriner, the chatty Berlin businessman makes an appearance, as well as Tucholsky's friends Karlchen and Jakopp, and Lottchen, the flapper, modeled after one of Tucholsky's real-life girlfriends.

Kurt Tucholsky:

Germany? Germany! Satirical Writings: The Kurt Tucholsky Reader

Translated by
Harry Zohn

Foreword by
Ralph Blumenthal

Softcover:
5.5" x 8.5"
208 pp.

ISBN
978-3-96026-025-7
978-3-96026-086-8

Sugg. Retail:
$14.95 /
ebook $7.99

Kurt Tucholsky made his name as one of the Weimar era's most acid, incisive satirists; but to read his writings in GERMANY? GERMANY!, this panoramic selection of essays, monologues, dialogues and aphorisms, is to be reminded that he was also a brilliant literary shape-shifter, able to take on the persona of an embryo, a squirrel, a suite of pulp novels, or a prophet of post-apocalyptic hope with equal felicity, writes George Prochnik, the author of *Stranger in a Strange Land*. "Tucholsky's words sound alarmingly poignant today." Harry Zohn, who fled the Nazis from Vienna to America where he became a professor and also a prolific editor and translator, presented Tucholsky to an American audience for the first time. His iconic translation is now finally reprinted.

Kurt Tucholsky:

**Rheinsberg
A Storybook
For Lovers**

Featuring: Among
City Wizard / Love
Poems for Claire

Translated by
Cindy Opitz

Afterword by
Peter Boethig

Hardcover
5" x 8"
96 pp.

ISBN
978-1-935902-25-6

Sugg. Retail:
$12.95 /
ebook $7.99

One summer before World War I, a young couple escapes on a romantic weekend getaway to the small German town of Rheinsberg, north of Berlin, in the midst of a rural landscape filled with country houses and castles, cobble-stone streets, lush forests, and dreamy lakes. RHEINSBERG, the story of Wolfie and Claire, told with a fresh, new style of ironic humor, became Kurt Tucholsky's first huge literary success and the blueprint for love for an entire generation. Binnie Kirshenbaum calls it "at once a delightful and a deeply disquieting story.," and Victoria Zackheim writes: "In *Rheinsberg*, Tucholsky delivers the newness and intensity of young love, sweet, sometimes strident, with repartee juxtaposed against the sylvan landscape of rural Germany. Poignant, biting, tender: a reminder of what love promises…and can be."

Kurt Tucholsky:

**Hereafter
We Were Sitting
On a Cloud,
Dangling Our Legs**

Translated by
Cindy Opitz

Foreword by
William Grimes

Also availabe
in German

Hardcover
5" x 8"
96 pp.

ISBN
978-1-935902-89-8

Sugg. Retail:
$12.95 /
ebook $7.99

What happens after you die? Where will you go? Will you have a harp, and featheriy wings? Will you still have your sharp wit? Does it do you any good? Were you happy with your life? Did your family love you? Or, at least, your mistress? And do you want a second chance to return to earth and start anew? In HEREAFTER. Kurt Tucholsky, the iconic German Jewish author and poet of the Weimar era, explores the afterlife between golden clouds and far-away stars, with floating spirits, masquerade balls on lunar satellites, quivering astral lights, time travel through the night, meteor showers, a planet where the water is cured, a mountain of laughter, and, of course, God himself. With its whimsical tone and its sepia colored pictures of Berlin's little angels, this is a book that warms the heart.

Kurt Tucholsky:

Prayer After The Slaughter Stories and Poems From World War I

Translated by Peter Appelbaum and James Scott

Preface by Noah Eisenberg

Softcover 5" x 8", 112 pp.

ISBN 978-3-96026-096-7 978-3-96026-020-2

Sugg. Retail: $11.95 / ebook $4.99

No one before or after Kurt Tucholsky has captured the horrors of the "Great War," as World War I was known, in this book, PRAYER BEFORE THE SLAUGHTER. The famed Weimar writer, who would become one of Germany's best-known satirist and journalists, describes surviving in the trenches and fighting a losing battle, the arrogance of the officers and the desperation of the loved ones back home. His writing is similar to that of Heinrich Heine, his role model, in that it appears superficially simple but is replete with hidden meanings. His works are touching, stirring, and precisely to the point. He brings alive the war that still looms even into our own 21st century. This is the first bilingual anthology in German and in English of his works on World War I.

Coming Soon!

Kurt Tucholsky/
Walter Hasenclever

Christopher Columbus or: The Discovery of America

Translated by
Max Spalter
and George E.
Wellwarth

Softcover
5" x 8",
ca 160 pp.

ISBN:
978-1-935902-09-6
978-3-96026-065-3

Sugg. Retail:
$14.95 /
ebook $8.99

CHRISTOPHER COLUMBUS, a comedy? This is what you get when Kurt Tucholsky and the playwright Walter Hasenclever set out to tell the story of the discovery of the new world anew. The#e Spanish conqueror is depicted as a tool of Royal imperialism, courageous, but naive. And the play is astonishingly forward looking: After the conquerors meet their first Native Americans, the landscape morphs into Times Square — and back to a Spanish pub where the seafarers are telling tall tales after their return. Written in 1932 shortly before the Nazis came to power, this is the only collaboration between Tucholsky and his best friend Hasenclever. The play was only successful long after World War II. Now the iconic translation by Max Spalter and George E. Wellwarth is available for an American audience again.

Important Dates in Tucholsky's Life

January 9, 1890:	Born the son of Alex and Doris Tucholsky in Berlin.
1899-1903:	Student in French Gymnasium in Berlin.
1903-1907:	Student in Royal Wilhelms-Gymnasium in Berlin.
November 22, 1907:	First publication: "Märchen" in *Ulk*.
1909-1912:	Legal studies at the University of Berlin.
1910:	Summer semester at University of Geneva.
1912:	Publication of his first novella *Rheinsberg*
1913-1915:	Active in editorial offices of *Die Schaubühne*.
January 9. 1913	His first story is printed in the *Schaubühne*, soon to be renamed *Die Weltbühne*. He will be writing under five different names.
November 19, 1914:	Receives the degree, "Doctor of Jurisprudence."
1915-1918:	Soldier on Eastern front in WWI.
1917:	At a military flying school in Latvia, then in the occupation of Romania. Becomes acquainted with Mary Gerold in Latvia.
1918-1920:	Editor-in-chief of *Ulk*.
May 3, 1920:	Marries Else Weil, the "Claire" in *Rheinsberg*.
1923:	Employed in a bank, Bett, Sirnon & Co.
August 30, 1924:	Marries Mary Gerold, after divorcing his first wife.
1924:	Becomes Paris correspondent of Die *Weltbühne* and the *Vossische Zeitung*.
December 7, 1926:	Siegfried Jacobsohn dies. For ten months, Tucholsky becomes editor of *Die Weltbühne*.
1927	The *Pyrenäenbuch*, a travel story book about the Pyrenees comes out.
1928:	Mit *5 PS* and *Das Lächeln der Mona Lisa* come out. Both are story collections mainly from *Die Weltbühne*.
1929:	Together with John Heartfield, he publishes *Deutschland, Deutschland über Alles*.
1929:	Tucholsky moves to Sweden where he lives until his death. (In Hindas near Göteborg.)
1931:	His novel *Schloss Gripsholm* appears, based on his girlfriend Lisa Matthias. It takes place in Sweden.
August 23, 1933:	Tucholsky's citizenship is revoked by the Nazis; his books have already been burned.
December 21, 1935:	Tucholsky commits suicide. He is buried in the Mariefried cemetery near the Gripsholm Castle.

SOURCES

I

Kurt Tucholsky Archive, Rottach-Egern, Germany. Letters, notebooks, scrapbooks and other personal papers. The director of the Archive, Frau Mary Tucholsky, has collected a formidable number of recordings of radio broadcasts dealing with Tucholsky's life and career. In addition, the Archive contains a complete library of secondary works on the Weimar era. [Today, as of 2019, the Archive is within the Deutschen Literaturarchiv Marbach, in Marbach, Germany.]. www.dla-marbach.de/archiv/

II

Journals and Periodicals in which the Majority of Tucholsky's Writings Appeared. (Tucholsky was published in over eighty publications, but only seven are mentioned here in descending order of importance. The vast majority of his works may be found in the first two.)

Die Weltbühne (until 1918: *Die Schaubühne*, Berlin). Weekly. 1905-1933.

Vossische Zeitung (originally: *Berlinische privilegierte Zeitung*, Berlin). Daily. 1704-1934.

Berliner Volkszeitung (Berlin). Daily. 1853-1939.

8 Uhr Abendblatt (formerly: *Nationalzeitung*, Berlin). Daily. 1910-

Die Welt am Montag (Berlin). Weekly. 1895-1933.

Die Menschenrechte (Berlin). Monthly. 1926-1933. (Organ of the Liga für Menschenrechte.)

Die Menschheit (Bern; later Wiesbaden). 1914-1931. (Changed in 1930 to *Chronik der Menschheit*.)

III

BOOKS PUBLISHED BY TUCHOLSKY DURING HIS LIFETIME

Tucholsky, Kurt. *Rheinsberg. Ein Bilderbuch für Verliebte*. Charlottenburg: Axel Juncker, 1912.

KT. *Der Zeitsparer. Grotesken von Ignaz Wrobel*. Berlin: Reuss & Pollack, 1914.

KT. *Fromme Gesänge. Von Theobald Tiger mit einer Vorrede von Ignaz Wrobel*. Charlottenburg: Fritz Lehmann, 1919.

KT. *Träumereien an preussischen Kaminen*. Von Peter Panter. Charlottenburg: Fritz Lehmann, 1920.

KT. *Ein Pyrenäenbuch*. Berlin: Die Schmiede, 1927; Rowohlt, 1930.

KT. *Mit 5 PS*. Berlin: Rowohlt, 1928.

KT. *Das Lächeln der Mona Lisa*. Berlin: Rowohlt, 1929.

KT. *Deutschland, Deutschland über Alles*. Berlin: Neuer deutscher Verlag, 1929.

KT. *Schloss Gripsholm*. Berlin: Rowohlt, 1931.

KT. *Lerne lachen ohne zu weinen*. Berlin: Rowohlt, 1931.

KT. and Walter Hasenclever. *Christoph Kolumbus oder Die Entdeckung Amerikas. Komödie in einem Vorspiel und sechs Bildern*. Bühnenmanuskript, 1932.

IV:
POSTHUMOUS COMPILATIONS OF TUCHOLSKY'S WRITINGS

Two compilations of Tucholsky's works have appeared in English: Kurt Tucholsky, *What If--? Satirical Writings of Kurt Tucholsky* (trans. Harry Zohn and Karl F. Ross); and *The World Is a Comedy. A Tucholsky Anthology* (ed. and trans. Harry Zohn). As of 2018, they are both lout of print; however, the former has been reprinted as a paperback under the title *Germany? Germany! The Kurt Tucholsky Reader* (Berlinica, 2017)

Tucholsky, Kurt. *Gesammelte Werke*. Eds. Mary Gerold Tucholsky and Fritz J. Raddatz. 3 vols. Hamburg: Rowohlt, 1960-61.

KT. *Ausgewählte Briefe, 1913-1935*. Eds. Mary Gerold Tucholsky and Fritz J. Raddatz. Hamburg: Rowohlt, 1962.

KT. *Gruss nach vorn. Eine Auswahl*. Ed. Erich Kästner. Stuttgart: Rowohlt, 1946.

KT. *Na und-? Eine neue Auswahl*. Ed. Mary Gerold Tucholsky. Hamburg: Rowohlt, 1950.

KT. *Und überhaupt. Eine neue Auswahl*. Ed. Mary Gerold Tucholsky. Hamburg: Rowohlt, 1953.

KT. *Kurt Tucholsky hasst — liebt in Prosastücken, Gedichten und Briefen*. Ed. Mary Gerold Tucholsky. Hamburg: Rowohlt, 1957.

KT. *Ausgewählte Werke*. Selected and edited by Fritz J. Raddatz. 6 vols. Berlin: Volk und Welt, 1956–1963. 1) *Rheinsberg und anderes*, 1956. 2) *Schloss Gripsholm und anderswo*, 1956. 3) *Panter, Tiger und andere*, 1957. 4) *Deutschland, Deutschland unter anderen*, 1957. 5) *Kurt Tucholsky, ganz anders*, 1961. 6) *Unter anderem in den Pyrenäen*, 1963 (Roland Links, ed.).

KT. *Zwischen Gestern und Morgen. Eine Auswahl aus seinen Schriften und Gedichten*. Ed. Mary Gerold Tucholsky. Hamburg: Rowohlt, 1952.

KT. *Panter, Tiger und Co. Eine neue Auswahl aus seinen Schriften und Gedichten*. Ed. Mary Gerold Tucholsky. Hamburg: Rowohlt, 1954.

KT. Tucholsky. *Ein Lesebuch für unsere Zeit*. Ed. Walther Victor. Weimar: Volksverlag, 1952.

KT. *Ausgewählte Lyrik und Prosa*. Berlin: Bibliothek fortschrittlicher deutscher Schriftsteller, 1952.

KT. *'n Augenblick mal!* Eine Auswahl. Hamburg: Deutsche Hausbücherei, 1955.

KT. *Nachher*. With drawings by Herbert Mende. Darmstadt: Georg Büchner Verlag, 1956.

KT. *Das Wirtshaus in Spessart*. Drawings by Lieselotte Mende-Neupert. Darmstadt: Georg Büchner Verlag, 1956.

KT. *Vier Szenen fürs Kabarett*. Leipzig: Hofmeister, 1956.

KT. *Man sollte mal—* Eine Auswahl. Ed. Hermann Kesten. Frankfurt a.M.: Büchergilde Gutenberg, 1957.

KT. *'n Augenblick mal—!* Freiburg: Hyperion Verlag, 1958.

KT. *Drei Minuten Gehör. Prosa, Gedichte, Briefe*. Leipzig: Reclam, 1961.

KT. *So siehst du aus! Eine Auswahl*. Ed. Willy Haas. Gütersloh: Bertelsmann Lesering, 1962.

KT. *Kurt Tucholsky, zeitkritische Gedichte und Aufsätze*. Stuttgart: Special publication of the upper technical school for graphic art of Stuttgart, produced in 320 copies, 1963.

KT. *Morgen wieder—?* Ed. with an Afterword by Fritz J. Raddatz. Frankfurt a.M.: Büchergilde Gutenberg, 1964.

KT. *Ausgewählte Werke*. Selected and edited by Fritz J. Raddatz. 2 vols. Reinbek: Rowohlt, 1965.

KT. *Ksiega pieciu szydercow.* Edited and translated by Antoni Marianowicz. Warsaw: Czytelnik, 1955.

KT. *Fristil om mennesket og andre betragtninger.* Edited and translated by Brita Vogel Rasmussen. Copenhagen: Hasselbalch, 1956.

KT. *The World ls a Comedy. A Tucholsky Anthology. Edited and translated with a critical introduction by Harry Zohn.* Cambridge, Mass.: Sei-Art Publishers, 1957.

KT. *Különös lopokot elünk.* Budapest: Europa Könyvkiad6, 1959.

KT. *Alligator a Szinpadon* (Panter, Tiger es Tarsaik). Budapest: Magvetö Könyvkiad 6, 1959.

KT. Kurt Tucholsky, *Panoptikum.* Prague: Mlada fronta, 1963.

KT. Kurt Tucholsky: *Eine Auswahl.* Ed. Egon Schwarz. New York: Norton & Co., 1963.

KT. *Schloss Gripsholm und anderswo.* 3 vols. in Braille. Leipzig, 1958.

KT. *Kurt Tucholsky, What If --? Satirical Writings of Kurt Tucholsky.* Translated by Harry Zohn and Karl F. Ross. New York: Funk & Wagnalls, Company, Inc., 1968.

V.

ANALYSIS AND CRITICISM OF TUCHOLSKY'S WRITINGS

Brandl, Bruno. "Kurt Tucholsky. Ein Satiriker der Weimarer Republik." *Der Bibliothekar,* VI (1952), 569-575.

Csokor, Franz Theodor. "Der deutsche Jeremias." *Der Monat,* IV (1952), 651-653.

Drescher, Hans. "Die geistige Entwicklung Kurt Tucholskys." Unpublished. *Examensarbeit,* University of Leipzig, 1956.

Drews, Richard. "Der, den wir schmerzlich vermissen." *Die Weltbühne,* II (1947), 16-18.

"Ein schmähender Brief von 8 namentlichen Studenten gegen Tucholsky und einer Antwort von Karl Ludwig Schneider," *Hamburger Akademische Rundschau,* I (1946-1947), 236-259.

Filion, Guy. *Tucholsky als Satiriker.* Diplôme d'Études Supérieures d'Allemand. (Sorbonne.) Paris, 1963

France, Ade. "Kurt Tucholsky. Politiek satirious tijdens de Weimar Republik." Unpublished essay, University of Ghent, 1955/1956.

Gallasch, Walter. "Es darf laut geproben worden. Das Kurt Tucholsky-Archiv in Rottach," *Geist und Zeit,* 4 (1958), 135-138.

Gallasch, Walter. "Kurt Tucholsky, Gewissen seiner Zeit," *Die Andere Zeitung* (Dec. 22, 1955).

Haas, Willy. "Kurt Tucholsky, zu seinem 60. Geburtstag," *Die Welt am Sonntag,* VIII, 1 (1950).

Halperin, Josef. "Abschied von Kurt Tucholsky," *Die neue Weltbühne,* XXXII, 1 (1936), 5-9.

Herrmann-Neisse, Max. "Ein lächelnder Rebell. Kurt Tucholsky," *Die neue Bücherschau,* VII (1929), 131-135.

Herzog, Wilhelm. "Ein Emigrant weniger," *Arbeiterzeitung* (Basel, January, 1936).

Heyn, Wolfgang. "Ich bin das Schwert, ich bin die Flamme. In memoriam Kurt Tucholsky," *Geist und Tat,* VIII, 2 (1953), 50-53.

Hoche, Klaus. "Der Humor und die Bitterkeit. Gedanken über Kurt Tucholsky," *Deutsche Rundschau,* LXXVIII (1952), 1254-1260.

Holitscher, Arthur. "Der Mann mit den 5 PS!" *Die neue Bücherschau*, VI (1928), 170-173.

Ilberg, Werner. "Tucholsky unter uns," *Neue deutsche Literatur*, V (1957), 110-118.

Institut zum Studium der Judenfrage. *Die Juden in Deutschland*. Munich: 1935, 223-246.

Jänicke, Helga. "Kurt Tucholsky als Gegner des Krieges und des Militarismus." Unpublished *Examensarbeit*, Humboldt University, Berlin, 1951.

Jens, Walter. "Was wir von Tucholsky lernen können," *Die Zeit* (November 3, 1961), 11.

Karsch, Walther. "Ein Mann und fünf Namen," Tagesspiegel, XIII, 2 (1946).

Kästner, Erich. "Kurt Tucholsky, Carl von Ossietzky, 'Weltbühne'," *Die Weltbühne*, I (1946), 21-23.

Kesten, Hermann. "Kurt Tucholsky," *Der Monat*, X, 113 (1958), 70-76.

Kleinschmidt, Karl. *Kurt Tucholsky. Sein Leben in Bildern*. Leipzig: VEB Verlag, 1961.

Kuby, Erich. "Ganz ohne Tucholsky," *Alles im Eimer, siegt Hitler bei Bonn—ein politischer Monolog, 1944-1960*. Stuttgart: Henry Goverts Verlag, 1960.

Ludwig, Emil. "An die Herren Polgar und Tucho," *Vossische Zeitung* (December 20, 1927).

Mehring, Walter. "Kurt Tucholsky. Ein freundschaftliches Bekenntnis," *Der Monat*, V (1953), 556-558.

Prescher, Hans. "Dr. Kurt Tucholskys publizistischer Kampf in den Jahren 1919-1932." Unpublished Ph.D. Dissertation, University of Munich, 1956

Prescher, Hans. *Kurt Tucholsky*. Berlin: Colloquium Verlag, 1959.

Raddatz, Fritz J. *Kurt Tucholsky. Eine Bildbiographie*. Munich: Kindler Verlag, 1961.

Röhl, Claus Rainer. "Kurt Tucholsky und der Kalte Krieg," *Konkret*, 23-24 (December 10, 1960), 15-16.

Sahl, Hans. "Kurt Tucholsky," *Politics* (Summer, 1948), 171-176.

Schelker, Markus. "Kurt Tucholsky — ein Gewissen, das niemals schlief," *Basler Arbeiterzeitung* (March 17, 1962).

Schröder, Heinrich. "Polemik und Satire im Kampf um eine Weltanschauung." Unpublished Ph.D. Dissertation, University of Vienna, 1958.

Schulz, Klaus-Peter. *Kurt Tucholsky in Selbstzeugnissen und Bilddokumenten*. Hamburg: Rowohlt Verlag, 1959.

Schümann, Kurt. *Im Bannkreis von Gesicht und Wirken. Max Brod. Else Lasker-Schüler. Kurt Tucholsky. Alfred Polgar*. Munich: 1959.

Seidel, Gerhard. "Kurt Tucholsky als Literaturkritiker," *Sinn und Form*, XIV, 5-6 (1962), 937-946.

Stapel, Wilhelm. "Kurt Tucholsky," *Forschungen zur Judenfrage* (Hamburg, 1937), 182-215.

Victor, Walther. "Einige Bemerkungen zum Gesamtwerk Kurt Tucholskys," *Die Weltbühne*, LVII (August 9, 1961), 1007-1013.

Walberer, Ulrich. "Wenn Tucholsky wiederkäme," *Die Presse* (Vienna, June 23, 1962).

Welse, Horst G. "Kurt Tucholsky als Literaturkritiker." Unpublished Ph.D. Dissertation, Harvard University, 1962.

Zweig, Amold. "Antwort an Kurt Tucholsky," *Die neue Weltbühne*, XXXII (1936), 165-170.

VI
OTHER SOURCES FOR THE WEIMAR ERA

Angress, Werner T. *Stillborn Revolution, the Communist Bid for Power in Germany, 1921-1923*. Princeton, N.J.: Princeton University Press, 1963.

Apfel, Alfred. *Behind the Scenes of German Justice, 1882-1933*. London: John Lane, 1935.

Barkeley, Richard. *Die deutsche Friedensbewegung, 1870-1933*. Hamburg: Hammerich und Lesser, 1948.

Bell, Daniel. *The End of Ideology*. Glencoe, Ill.: The Free Press, 1960.

Bergsträsser, Ludwig. *Geschichte der politischen Parteien in Deutschland*. Munich: Günter Olzog Verlag, 1960.

Berlau, A. Joseph. *The German Social Democratic Party, 1914-1921*. New York: Columbia University Press, 1949.

Blume, Bernhardt. "Professor Tucholsky's Facts," *New Statesman and Nation*. (November 26, 1961.)

Borkenau, Franz. *European Communism*. London: Faber and Faber, 1953.

Bracher, Karl D. *Die Auflösung der Weimarer Republik*. Villingen/Schwarzwald: Ring Verlag, 1960.

Bracher, Karl D. *Die Entstehung der Weimarer Verfassung*. Hannover: Niedersächsische Landeszentrale für Politische Bildung, 1963.

Bracher, Karl D. "Die Weimarer Republik im Spiegel der Memoiren-Literatur," *Politische Literatur*, II, 1 (January 1953), 339-350.

Braun, Otto. *Von Weimar zu Hitler*. New York: Europa Verlag, 1940.

Brecht, Arnold and Glaser, Comstock. *The Art and Technique of Administration in German Ministries*. Cambridge, Mass.: Harvard University Press, 1940.

Brecht, Arnold. *Federalism and Regionalism in Germany, The Division of Prussia*. New York: Oxford, 1944.

Brecht, Arnold. *Prelude to Silence*. New York: Oxford, 1944.

Brod, Max. *Streitbares Leben, Autobiographie*. Munich: Kindler, 1960.

Bullock, Alan. *Hitler, A Study in Tyranny*. London: Odhams Press, 1952.

Carsten, F. L. *The Reichswehr and Politics, 1918 to 1933*. New York: Oxford University Press, 1966.

Chalmers, Douglas A. *The Social Democratic Party from Working-Class Movement to Modern Political Party*. New Haven: Yale University Press, 1964.

Craig, Gordon A. *From Bismarck to Adenauer, Aspects of German Statecraft*. Baltimore: The Johns Hopkins Press, 1958.

Craig, Gordon A. *The Politics of the Prussian Army, 1640-1945*. Oxford: Clarendon Press, 1955.

Deak, Istvan. "The World of Carl von Ossietzky: Germany's Homeless Left in the Weimar Republic." Unpublished Ph.D. Dissertation, Columbia University, 1964.

Dovifat, Emil. "Die Presse," *Zehn Jahre Deutsche Geschichte, 1918-1928*. Berlin: 1928, pp. 501-512.

Drews, Richard, and Alfred Kantorowicz. *Verboten und Verbrannt: Deutsche Literatur 12 Jahre unterdrückt*. Berlin: H. Ullstein; Munich: H. Kindler Verlag, 1947.

Dyck, Harvey Leonard. *Weimar Germany and Soviet Russia, 1926-1933*. New York: Columbia University Press, 1966.

Ebermeyer, Erich. *Denn heute gehört uns Deutschland... Persönliches und politisches Tagebuch von der Machtergreifung bis zum 31 Dez. 1935*. Hamburg: Paul Zsolnay, 1959.

Enseling, Alf. *Die Weltbühne.* Münster: Verlag J. C. Fahle, 1962.

Epstein, Klaus. *Matthias Erzherger and the Dilemma of German Democracy.* Princeton, N.J.: Princeton University Press, 1959.

Erdmann, Karl D. "Die Geschichte der Weimarer Republik als Problem der Wissenschaft," *Vierteljahreshefte für Zeitgeschichte,* 111, 1 (January 1955), 1-19.

Eschenburg, Theodor; E. Fraenkel; K. Sontheimer; et al. *Der Weg in die Diktatur, 1918 bis 1933.* Munich: Piper, 1962.

Eschenburg, Theodor. *Die improvisierte Demokratie, Gesammelte Aufsätze zur Weimarer Republik.* Munich: Piper, 1963.

Fischer, Ruth. *Stalin and German Communism. A Study in the Origin of the State Party.* Cambridge, Mass.: Harvard University Press, 1948.

Flechtheim, Ossip K. *Die Kommunistische Partei Deutschlands in der Weimarer Republik.* Offenbach/a.M.: Bollwerk-Verlag, Karl Drott, 1948.

Fliess, Peter J. *Freedom of the Press in the German Republic, 1918-1933.* Baton Rouge, La.: Louisiana State University Press, 1955.

Forsthoff, Ernst (ed.). *Deutsche Geschichte von 1918 bis 1938 in Dokumenten.* Stuttgart: A Kröner Verlag, 1943.

Frank, Leonhard. *Der Mensch ist gut.* Zürich: Max Rascher Verlag, 1917.

Frank, Leonhard. *Heart on the Left.* Transl. Cyrus Brooks. London: Artbur Barker, 1954.

Gay, Peter. *The Dilemma of Democratic Socialism, Eduard Bernstein's Challenge to Marx.* New York: Columbia University Press, 1952.

Gerlach, Hellmut von. *Von Rechts nach Links.* Zürich: Europa Verlag, 1937.

Gessler, Otto. *Reichswehrpolitik in der Weimarer Zeit.* Stuttgart: Deutsche Verlags-Anstalt, 1956.

Grossmann, Kurt R. *Ossietzky, ein deutscher Patriot.* Munich: Kindler, 1963.

Grosz, George. *A Little Yes and a Big No.* New York: The Dial Press, 1946.

Gumbel, Emil J. *"Verräter verfallen der Feme": Opfer, Mörder, Richter, 1919-1929.* Berlin: Malik Verlag, 1929.

Gumbel, Emil J. *Vier Jahre politischer Mord.* Berlin: Malik Verlag, 1922.

Gumbel, Emil J. *Vom Fememord zur Reichskanzlei.* Heidelberg: L. Schneider, 1962.

Haas, Willy. *Die literarische Welt. Erinnerungen.* Munich: Paul List, 1957.

Hafkesbrink, Hanna. *Unknown Germany. An Inner Chronicle of the First World War Based on Diaries and Letters.* New Haven: Yale University Press, 1948.

Handbuch der deutschen Tagespresse ("Deutscher Institut für Zeitungskunde.") Berlin: Carl Duncker Verlag, 1932.

Heidegger, Hermann. *Die deutsche Sozialdemokratie und der nationale Staat, 1870-1920.* Göttingen: Musterschmidt-Verlag, 1956.

Heller, Erich. *The Disinherited Mind.* New York: The World Publishing Company, 1959.

Herzog, Wilhelm. *Menschen, denen ich begegnete.* Bern: Francke Verlag, 1959.

Hiller, Kurt. "Aufstieg, Glanz und Verfall der Weltbühne," *Konkret* (Hamburg), 3-7 (March-July 1962).

Hiller, Kurt. *Köpfe und Tröpfe.* Hamburg: Rowohlt, 1950.

Hunt, Richard N. *German Social Democracy, 1918-1933.* New Haven: Yale University Press, 1964.

Hüttig, Helmut. *Die politischen Zeitschriften der Nachkriegszeit in Deutschland. Leipzig: 1928* (printed Ph.D. Dissertation).

Jacob, Herbert. *German Administration Since Bismarck.* New Haven: Yale University Press, 1963.

Jasper, Gotthard. *Der Schutz der Republik Studien zur staatlichen Sicherung der Demokratie in der Weimarer Republik. 1922-1930*. Tübingen: J.C.B. Mohr (Paul Siebeck), 1963.

Kantorowicz, Alfred. *Deutsches Tagebuch*. 2 vols. Munich: Kindler, 1959.

Kantorowicz, Alfred. *Porträts: Deutsche Schicksale*. Berlin: Chronos Verlag, 1947.

Kaufmann, Walter H. *Monarchism in the Weimar Republic*. New York: Bookman Associates, 1953

Kempf, Rosa. "Der Deutschen Pazifismus in seiner Presse," *Süddeutsche Monatshefte*, XXI, 6 (June 1924), 186-194.

Kessler, Harry Graf. *Tagebücher, 1918-1937*. Ed. Wolfgang Pfeiffer-Belli. Frankfurt a.M.: Insel Verlag, 1.961.

Kesten, Hermann. *Meine Freunde, die Poeten*. Vienna: Donau Verlag, 1953.

Klemperer, Klemens von. *Germany's New Conservatism*. Princeton, N.J.: Princeton University Press, 1957.

Kohn, Hans. *The Mind of Germany*. New York: Charles Scribner's Sons, 1955.

Koplin, Raimond. *Carl von Ossietzky als politischer Publizist*. Berlin: Verlag Annedore Leber, 1964.

Koszyk, Kurt. *Zwischen Kaiserreich und Diktatur: Die sozialdemokratische Presse von 1914 bis 1933*. Heidelberg: Quelle und Meyer, 1958.

Krieger, Leonard. *The German Idea of Freedom*. Boston: Beacon Press, 1957.

Laqueur, Walter Z. *Young Germany: a History of the German Youth Movement*. New York: Basic Books, 1962.

Lehmann-Russbüldt, Otto. *Der Kampf der Deutschen Liga für Menschenrechte, 1914-1927*. Berlin: Hensel und Co., 1927.

Lewinsohn, Richard (Morus). *Das Geld in der Politik*. Berlin: S. Fischer Verlag, 1930.

Mann, Erika and Klaus. *Escape to Life*. Boston: Houghton Mifflin Company, 1939.

Mann, Erika and Klaus. *The Other Germany*. New York: Modern Age Books, 1940.

Mann, Golo. *Deutsche Geschichte des neunzehnten und zwanzigsten Jahrhundert*, Frankfurt/M. Fischer Verlag, 1961.

Mann, Golo. "The Intellectuals," *Encounter*, IV, 6 (June 1955), 42-49.

Mann, Heinrich. *Sieben Jahre: Chronik der Gedanken und Vorgänge, 1921-1928*. Vienna: Zsolnay Verlag, 1929.

Mann, Thomas. *Betrachtungen eines Unpolitischen*. Berlin: S. Fischer Verlag, 1920.

Marcuse, Ludwig. *Mein zwanzigstes Jahrhundert: auf dem Wege zu einer Autobiographie*. Munich: Paul List Verlag, 1960.

Matthias, Erich and Rudolf Morsey (eds.). *Das Ende der Parteien, 1933*. Düsseldorf: Droste Verlag, 1960.

Meinecke, Friedrich. *The German Catastrophe: Reflections and Recollections*. Transl. Sidney B. Fay. Boston: Beacon Press, 1963.

Mendelssohn, Peter de. *Zeitungsstadt Berlin*. Berlin: Ullstein, 1959.

Mertens, Carl. *Verschwörer und Fememörder*. Berlin-Charlottenburg: Verlag der Weltbühne, 1926.

Morsey, Rudolf. *Die deutsche Zentrums-Partei, 1917-1923*. Düsseldorf: Droste Verlag, 1966.

Mosse, George. *The Culture of Western Europe*. Chicago: Rand McNally and Co., 1961.

Neumann, Franz. *Behemoth, the Structure and Practice of National Socialism*. New York: Oxford University Press, 1942.

Neurohr, Jean F. *Der Mythos vom Dritten Reich, zur Geistesgeschichte des Nationalsozialismus*. Stuttgart: J.G. Cotta'sche Buchhandlung, 1957.

Noske, Gustav. *Erlebtes aus Aufstieg und Niedergang einer Demokratie*. Offenbach a.M.: Bollwerk-Verlag, 1147.

Noske, Gustav. Von Kiel bis Kapp. *Zur Geschichte der deutschen Revolution*. Berlin: Verlag für Politik und Wirtschaft, 1920.

Osborn, Max (ed.). *50 Jahre Ullstein, 1877-1927*. Berlin: Ullstein, 1927.

Pfeiler, William K. *War and the German Mind*. New York: Columbia University Press, 1941.

Pross, Harry (ed.). *Die Zerstörung der deutschen Politik: Dokumente, 1871-1933*. Frankfurt a.M.: Fischer Bücherei, 1959.

Pross, Harry. *Literatur und Politik: Geschichte und Programme der politisch-literarischen Zeitschriften im deutschen Sprachgebiet seit 1870*. Olten: Walter Verlag, 1963.

Reinisch, Leonhard (ed.). *Die Zeit ohne Eigenschaften. Eine Bilanz der zwanziger Jahre*. Stuttgart: W. Kohlhammer Verlag, 1961.

Roch, Herbert. *Deutsche Schriftsteller als Richter ihrer Zeit*. Berlin: Horizont Verlag, 1947.

Rühle, Jürgen. *Literatur und Revolution: die Schriftsteller und der Kommunismus*. Köln: Kiepenheuer und Witsch, 1960.

Schlawe, Fritz. *Literarische Zeitschriften, 1910-1933*. Stuttgart: J. B. Metzler, 1962.

Schorske, Carl E. *German Social Democracy, 1905-1917*. Cambridge, Mass.: Harvard University Press, 1955.

Schüddekopf, Otto-Ernst. *Das Heer und die Republik: Quellen zur Politik der Reichswehrführung, 1918 bis 1933*. Hannover: Norddeutsche Verlagsanstalt 0. Goedel, 1955.

Schüddekopf, Otto-Ernst. *Linke Leute von Rechts: die national-revolutionären Minderheiten und der Kommunismus in der Weimarer Republik*. Stuttgart: W. Kohlhammer Verlag, 1960.

Schultz, Edmund (ed.). *Das Gesicht der Demokratie, ein Bilderwerk zur Geschichte der deutschen Nachkriegszeit*. Leipzig: Verlag von Breitkopf & Härte!, 1931.

Schwarzschild, Leopold. *Von Krieg zu Krieg*. Amsterdam: Querido Verlag, 1947.

Schwarz, Albert. *Die Weimarer Republik*. Constance: Akademische Verlagsgesellschaft Athenaion, 1958.

Seeckt, Hans v. *Aus seinem Leben, 1918-1936*. Ed. Friedrich von Rabenau. Leipzig. von Hase und Koehler Verlag, 1940.

Seil, Friedrich C. *Die Tragödie des deutschen Liberalismus*. Stuttgart: Deutsche Verlags-Anstalt, 1953.

Sokel, Walter H. *The Writer in Extremis: Expressionism in Twentieth-Century German Literature*. Stanford, Calif.: Stanford University Press, 1959.

Sontheimer, Kurt. *Antidemokratisches Denken in der Weimarer Republik*. Munich: Nymphenburger Verlagsbuchhandlung, 1962.

Stampfer, Friedrich. *Die ersten 14 Jahre der deutschen Republik*. 2d ed. Offenbach a.M.: Bollwerk Verlag, 1947.

Stern, Fritz. "The Political Consequences of the Unpolitical German," *History*, 3 (September 1960), 104-134.

Stern, Fritz. *The Politics of Cultural Despair, A Study in the Germanic Ideology*. Berkeley: The University of California Press, 1961.

Stürmer, Dietrich. *Maximilian Harden: der "geheimnisvolle Gewaltige."* Leipzig: Kurt Vieweg Verlag, 1920.

Sutton, Eric (ed. and trans.). *Gustav Stresemann, his Diaries, Letters and Papers.* 2 vols. London: Macmillan, 1937.

Tjaden, K. H. *Struktur und Funktion der "KPD-opposition" (KPO).* Meisenheim am Glan: Verlag Anton Hain, 1964.

Toller, Ernst. *I Was a German: an Autobiography.* Trans. Edward Crankshaw. London: John Lane, 1934.

Toller, Ernst. *Prosa, Briefe, Dramen, Gedichte.* Introduction by Kurt Hiller. Hamburg: Rowohlt, 1962.

Treue, Wolfgang. *Deutsche Parteiprogramme 1861-1956.* Vol. III. Göttingen: Musterschmidt Verlag, 1956.

Turner, Henry A., Jr. *Stresemann and the Politics of the Weimar Republic.* Princeton, N. J.: Princeton University Press, 1963.

Ullstein, Heinz. *Spielplatz meines Lebens: Erinnerungen.* Munich: Kindler Verlag, 1961.

Ullstein, Hermann. *The Rise and Fall of the House of Ullstein.* New York: Simon and Schuster, 1943.

Victor, Walther. *Es kommt aber darauf an, sie zu verändern.* Publizistik, Polemik, Porträts. Weimar: Volksverlag, 1962.

Victor, Walther. *Kehre wieder über die Berge: eine Autobiographie.* New York: Willard Publishing Co., 1945.

Waite, Robert G. L., *Vanguard of Nazism, The Free Corps Movement in Postwar Germany, 1918-1923.* Cambridge, Mass.: Harvard University Press, 1952.

Waldman, Eric. *The Spartacist Uprising of 1919 and the Crisis of the German Socialist Movement: a Study of the Relation of Political Theory and Party Practice.* Milwaukee: The Marquette University Press, 1958.

Wemer, Bruno E. *Die Zwanziger Jahre. Von Morgens bis Mitternachts.* Munich: Bruckmann, 1962.

Wheeler-Bennett, John W. *The Nemesis of Power, The German Army in Politics, 1918-1945.* New York: St. Martin's Press, 1954.

Witkop, Philipp (ed). *Kriegsbriefe gefallener Studenten.* Munich: Georg Müller, 1928.

Young, Harry P. *Maximilian Harden: Censor Germaniae.* The Hague: Nijhoff, 1959.

INDEX

Aktion, Die (periodical), 73
Alienation, social criticism and, 88-90
Ankermann, Lt., 123-26
Anti-Pornography law (1926), 189
Anti-Semitism, see Jews
Arco-Valley, Count von, 103
Army, see German Army
Article 48 of the Weimar Constitution, 160
"Asphaltliteratur," 75
"Auf dem Nachttisch" ("On the Night Stand"), 154
Austria
  Tucholsky's prediction of Anschluss with, 170
  Barmat Committee, 126
  Barres, Maurice, 37
  Bauer, Gustav, 110
  Bäumer, Gertrud, 73
Bavaria, 110, 117-18, 195
  reactionary governments in, 116
  republic proclaimed in, 56
  Bavarian People's Party, 158
  Bell, Daniel, on social criticism, 88-89
Berlin
  birth of Tucholsky in, 15
  defeat and revolution in, 53-67
  French Gymnasium in, 15, 23
  Paris compared to, 152-54
Berlin, University of, 15
Berliner Illustrirte (periodical), 74-75
Berliner Tageblatt (periodical), 24
Berliner Volkszeitung (periodical), 130-31, 200
  Bertens, Rosa, Tucholsky's critique of, 22
  Bett, Sirnon and Company, 15
  "Bewachte Kriegsschauplatz, Der" ("The Guarded Theater of War"), 200-1
  Binding, Rudolf, 39
  Blaich, Hans Erich, see Owlglass
  "Blick in ferne Zukunft" ("Glance into the Distant Future"), 145-46
  Book burning, 17, 207

Bourgeoisie, see Middle class
Braun, Otto, 158
Brecht, Bertolt, 17
Breuer, Robert ("Germanicus"), 73
Brod, Max, 25, 154
Brüning, Heinrich, 181, 187
Bullock, Alan, 142
Bureaucracy, 114-16
Busch, Ernst, 59, 199
Cabaret theater, Tucholsky's chansons for, 10-11, 33, 58-71, 199
Center Party, Tucholsky on, 193-94
Chaplin, Charles, 150
Christianity, Tucholsky on, 82, 191-92
Communism, international, 143-46
Communist Party (German), 55, 135-39, 141-145
  cooperation with Nazis, 146
  with Moscow, 139-40, 142
  in 1925 presidential elections, 159-61
  ousted in Saxony and Thuringia, 18, 127, 149
  in Reichstag, 157
  Spartacists and, 137
  Tucholsky's attitude to, 90, 135-46, 159-60, 161
Conrad, Hans, 141
Courland, Tucholsky in, 42, 44-50, 64
"Cultural Bolshevism," 92-95
Cultural criticism, 71-104
  by nationalists, 78-79, 85
  by Nietzsche, 81-82, 84-86
  role of alienation in, 88
  by Tucholsky, 71-104
  "barracks mentality," 84-89, 98
  German spirit as poisoned, 75, 82, 98, 189
Czechoslovakia, Tucholsky's predictions on, 170
Da Da trial, 122
Daladier, Edouard, 214
Danehl, Erich, nickname of, 29
"Dank an Frankreich" ("Thanks to France"), 153-54

"Das will kein Mensch mehr wissen" ("Nobody Wants Hear That Anymore"), 149
Dawes Plan, ISS, 156-57, 167, 181
"Deutsche Pest; Die" ("The German Plague"), 197
"Deutsches Chaos" ("German Chaos"), 181-86
Deutschland, Deutschland über Alles (Tucholsky's book), 15, 81, 135-36, 183-87
DNVP, see German Nationalist Party
"Dritte Reich, Das" ("The Third Reich"), 199
DVP, see German People's Party
East Prussia, 80, 118
Ebert, Friedrich, 54-57, 109-112
  accused of treason, 125-26
  agreement with Army by, 54-57, 129, 239
  Barmat and, 126, death of, 125-26
  Tucholsky on, 126-30, 157-58
"Ebert Legende, Die" ("The Ebert Myth"), 126-30
Eggebrecht, Axel, 72
Eichhorn, Emil, 56
Einstein, Albert, 19
Eisner, Kurt, 103
Elections
  1924 (Reichstag), 157
  1925 (presidential), 157-60
  1930 (Reichstag), 198
Emigration, Tucholsky on, 223-25
Enchanted Princess, The, 41
Erzberger, Matthias, 19, 119
"Face of a German," 83-84
Fackel, Die (periodical), 64
Feuchtwanger, Lion, 241
"SOS Bürgerkrieg" ("SOS Civil War"), 198
Flake, Otto, 73
"Flecke, Die" ("The Spots"), 62
Foreign relations, Tucholsky on, 153-56, 161-67, 170-173, 211-13
Forum (periodical), 73
France
  foreign policy of, 155-56, 161, 166-67, 172-74, 214-16

Tucholsky in, 15, 149-61, 178-79, 187
Frankfurter, Kitty, 25
Free Corps
  Baltic campaigns of, 131
  Noske and, 102, 109
  recruiting in high schools for, 116
  used against Spartacists, 56, 109-10
Freiheit (periodical), 71
French Gymnasium (Berlin), 15, 23-34
Freud, Sigmund, 17, 86
Pritsche, Hans, nickname of, 29
Front, Die (periodical), 140-41
"Führer?" ("Leaders?"), 137-38
Geneva, University of, 24
Georg, Manfred, 105
Gerlach, Hellmut von, 72
German Army
  antipathy to Republic of, 114
  Grosz case brought by, 122
  Kaiser's birthday celebrated by, 111
  in Kapp Putsch, 110-111
  rearmament
  Ossietzky's 1929 article on, 74, 200-01
  Stresemann and, 169-71
  Social Democratic cooperation with, 18, 55-57, 59, 109-12
  Soviet Union and, 171-73
  Tucholsky article prosecuted by, 200-01
  Tucholsky's proposals for reform of, 110-15
  See also Militarism
German Nationalist Party (DNVP
  Jews and, 197
  Nazis and, 197-98
German People's Party (DVP), 168
Germanic Religion, 77-78, 85
"Germanicus" (Robert Breuer), 73
Gerold, Mary, see Tucholsky, Mary Gerold
"Gesang der englischen Chorknaben" ("Song of the English Choirboys"), 200
Gessler, Otto, 112
Gide, Andre, 154
Goebbels, Joseph, 198, 207, 212
Goldschmidt, Alfons, 72, 143
Moskau 1920, 143
Göring, Hermann, 212

Graetz, Paul, 59, 180
Great Britain, Tucholsky on, 214
Grenz, Albert Wilhelm, 123-24
Groener, Gen. Wilhelm, 55-56, 200
  Ebert's agreement with, 55-56
Grosz, George, 83, 152, 210
  blasphemy trial of, 190
  defamation trial of, 122-23
Harden, Maximilian, 73, 122-25, 151, 155
Harzburg Front, 198
Hasenclever, Walter
  nickname of, 29
  Tucholsky's letters to, 88, 144, 194, 202, 208-09, 211-14, 223-24
    Hauser, Kaspar (pseudonym), 32-33, 155
Heartfield, John, 15, 183, 185
Heidelberg Program, 130
Heine, Heinrich, 76, 145, 186, 236
Held, Heinrich, 158
Hellpach, Willy, 158
"Hellseher, Der" ("The Clairvoyant"), 196-98
Herr Wendriner
  "Herr Wendriner" sketches, 33, 95-98, 155, 179, 198, 218-21
  "Herr Wendriner erzählt eine Geschichte" ("Herr Wendriner Tells a Story"), 95-98
  "Herr Wendriner steht unter der Diktatur" ("Herr Wendriner under the dictatorship), 198
  Holl, Gussy, 59
  Holländer, Friedrich, 59, 232
Hugenberg, Alfred, 172, 195
Ihering, Herbert, on Deutschland, Deutschland über Alles, 186-88
Independent Socialists, see Socialists, Independent
  Inflation, 66, 136, 149, 153, 157,
  "Interview mit sich selbst" (Interview with Myself'), 30-32
"Ja, früher . . . !" (Yes, formerly ... !), 150
Jacobsohn, Siegfried, 15, 18, 73-74, 140, 151
  author-editor relationship between Tucholsky and, 27-28, 178
  death of, 15, 177

Jaeger, Heinz (Walter Krelser), 201
Jarres, Karl, 158
Jena, University of, 27
Jews
  attitude toward Nazis of, 146, 187, 196, 198-99, 207, 216, 220
  as "enemy" in World War I, 101
  in Harden trial, 122-25
  Nazi attacks on, 200, 207-9, 224
  Tucholsky and, 21, 23, 29-30, 33-34, 87, 94-95, 211-25,
  on Weltbühne, 75
Joyce, James, 154
Justice in Weimar Republic, 19, 91, 104, 113, 119-30, 186, 190
Kafka, Franz
  death of, 154
  on Tucholsky, 25-27, 30, 40
Kahr, Gustav von, 18
Kapp Putsch, 110-13
Kästner, Erich, 10, 34
Kerr, Alfred, 27, 215-216
Kiel, mutiny at (1918), 54
Kleist, Heinrich von, 227
"Köpfe" ("Heads"), 184
Koralle (periodical), 74
Kraus, Karl, 73, 119
Krelser, Walter ("Heinz Jaeger"), 201
"Krieg dem Kriege" ("War against War"), 60-61
Kühl, Kate, 59
Lagarde, Paul Anton de, 78
Langbehn, Julius, cultural criticism of, 77-78
Lawrence, D. H., 154
League of Nations, 165, 167-68, 172
Lenin, Vladimir I., 139, 143
"Lerne Lachen ohne zu Weinen" (Learn to Laugh Without Crying), 34
Lewis, Sinclair, 33, 154
Liberalism
  Nietzsche's criticism of, 81-86
  right-wing criticism of, 78-80
Liebknecht, Karl, 55-58, 118-19, 137
"Lied der Cowgoys" ("Song of the Cow-goys"), 199
Löbe, Paul, 185, 189
Locarno agreements, 161, 165-74

"Lottchen beichtet 1 Geliebten" ("Lottchen Confesses One Lover"), 179-81
Ludendorff, General Erich, 19, 60, 118, 158
  Tucholsky's song dedicated to, 60-62
Luxemburg, Rosa, 56-57, 119, 137
Manchester Guardian (periodical), 171, 174
Mann, Golo, 87
Mann, Heinrich, 17
Mann, Thomas, 40, 48
  cultural criticism of, 86, 89-90
  Tucholsky on, 84
"Märchen" ("Fairytale"), 15, 24
Marx, Wilhelm, 158-159
Marxism, Tucholsky on, 135, 141, 144-45
Matthias, Lisa, 15, 179
"Mäuler auf!, Die" ("Mouths Ready!"), 199
Maurras, Charles, 37
Max von Baden (Maximilian, Prince of Baden), 54
Mehring, Walter, 72
Meinecke, Friedrich, 40
Menschheit, Die (periodical), 158
"Menschliche Paris, Das" ("Humane Paris"), 153
Meyer, Dr. Walter, 194
Middle class
  conservative attitude to, 92
  Tucholsky's attitude to, 33, 92-98, 128-30, 136-38, 213
  Militaria series, 99-100
  Militarism, Tucholsky's opposition to, 58, 60-64, 86, 98-104, 110-16
  Milne, Gen. Sir George, 171
Murder, political, 19, 119-27, 218
Music, German, Nietzsche on, 82
" 'N Augenblick mal!" ("One Moment Please"), 33
"Nachgemachten, Die" ("Imitations"), 149
"Nachher" ("Afterward"), 155
Nauman (editor), 73
Nazis
  anti-Semitism of, 195-97, 216-18, 221

Nazis (cont.)
  Church and, 194-97
  come to power, 142, 190, 193, 196, 207
  Communist cooperation with, 142
  1923 putsch of, 110-14, 149-150, 195-96
  in 1925 presidential elections, 157-160
  in Reichstag, 142, 157, 193, 195-98
  Tucholsky and, 90-91, 145-46, 181-83, 188-89, 191-202
  books burned, 12, 15, 17, 207
  "Herr Wendriner" sketch, 33, 95-98, 155, 179, 198, 218-21
  1929 Wiesbaden riot, 194
  1930 articles, 192-98
Nazis, Tucholsky and review of *Deutschland, Deutschland über Alles*, 15, 81, 135-36, 183-87
  Tucholsky's last views, 211-24
Nelson, Rudolf, 56-60
Nelson Theater (Berlin), 59, 66
"Neuer Militarismus" ("New Militarism"), 102
Neumann, Franz, on German bureaucracy, 115
Nietzsche, Friedrich, cultural criticism by, 81-82, 84-86
Noske, Gustav, 59, 102, 109-12, 126
"Offizier und Mann" ("Officer and Man"), 99, 121
Olden, Rudolf, 72
Ossietzky, Carl von, 18, 72, 74, 140, 178, 194, 200-02
  as editor of Weltbühne, 140, 178
  tried for defaming Army, 200-2
  tried for revealing "military secrets," 72, 201-2
  on Weimar Republic, 18
Owlglass, Dr. (Hans Erich Blaich), 25, 43,
  Stresemann and Poland, 173-74
  Tucholsky's predictions on, 169-70, 213-15
Polgar, Alfred, 195
Politics
  rejection of, 85-90
  See also Tucholsky, Kurt, political and social views of

Prager Tageblatt (periodical), 151
Prague, Tucholsky in, 25-26, 211
Preuss, Hugo, 117
"Preussenhimmel, Der" ("The Prussian Heaven"), 102-4
Professors, as true "intellectuals," 66
Prussia, in German federal system, 114
Pyrenäenbuch, Ein (A Book of the Pyrenees), 191
Querschnitt (periodical), 74
Quidde, Ludwig, 72
Rapallo Treaty, 161, 168, 174
Rathenau, Walter, 40,
  assassination of, 19, 119, 122-23, 218-19
Rearmament
  Ossietzky's 1929 article on, 74, 201
  Stresemann and, 171-72
Religion, Tucholsky's attitude to, 49, 184, 190-92, 200
Remarque, Erich Maria, 190
Rembrandt, Langbehn on, 78
Revolution of 1848, 38, 79
Revolution of 1918, 17, 53-58, 126-29
Rheinsberg, 15, 25-27
Rhineland Pact, 172
"Richter und Henker" vs. "Dichter und Denker," 119
Röhm, Ernst, Tucholsky's defense of, 91
Roman Catholic Church, Nazis and 194-97
Rote Fahne, Die (periodical), 73, 137, 142, 151
"Rote Melodie" ("Red Melody"), 60-62
"Rue Mouffetard, Die," 153
Ruhr occupation, 155-57
Romania, Tucholsky in, 15, 47-50, 64
Sacco and Vanzetti, 189
Sächsisches Volksblatt (periodical), 190
Saxony, Communist government in, 18, 149
"Schall und Rauch" ("Noise and Smoke") (Berlin cabaret), 59
Schaubühne, Die (periodical), 15, 27-28, 42, 73
  See also *Weltbühne, Die*

Scheidemann, Philipp, 127-28, 171
  proclaims republic, 54
Scheler, Max, 39
Schloss Gripsholm (*Gripsholm Castle*), 15, 26
Scholem, Gershom, on "Herr Wendriner" sketches, 219
School system in Weimar Republic, 116
Schützinger, Hermann, 130
Seeckt, Gen. Hans von, 114, 160, 167-68, 171, 174
Simplicissimus (periodical), 25, 43
Social Democratic Party (SPD) (Majority Socialists)
  cooperation with Army by, 18, 55, 59, 109-14, 128
  Heidelberg Program of, 130
  left intellectuals' criticism of, 128-29
  in 1925 presidential elections, 157-60
  in Reichstag, 157
  Tucholsky's attitude to, 87, 90-92, 102-4, 109-10, 125-31
  Verbürgerlichung of, 129
Stael, Madame de, 119
Stalin, Josef, 139, 143-145, 194
Stapel, Wilhelm, 207
Sternberg, Fritz, 72
Stettin, Tucholsky in, 22
Streicher, Julius, 222
Stresemann, Gustav, 156, 158
  foreign policy of, 165-74
Ströbel, Heinrich, 72
Sturm, Der (periodical), 73
Sweden, Tucholsky in, 15, 26, 187-89, 207-10
Szafranski, Kurt, 24-27, 43
Tagebuch, Das (periodical), 178, 186,
Teutschtum, 23,
Thälmann, Ernst, 158-59
Theater, Tucholsky's chansons for, 28, 33, 58-59, 83, 199
Thuringia, Communist government in, 18, 127, 149
"Tiger, Theobald" (pseudonym), 32, 41, 58, 155, 187
Tirpitz, Adm. Alfred von, 158, 160
Toller, Ernst, 17-18, 72

Treitschke, Heinrich von, 78
Troeltsch, Ernst, 40
Trotsky, Leon, 139, 143
True German, The (story-poem), 22-23
Tucholsky, Alex (father), 15, 21-23
  death of, 23
Tucholsky, Doris (mother), 15, 21-22
Tucholsky, Ellen (sister), 8, 32 nickname of, 17
Tucholsky, Else Weil (first wife), 25-26
  Tucholsky's marriage to, 64-65, 58
Tucholsky, Fritz (brother), 209-11, 225
  nickname of, 29
Tucholsky, Kurt
  attitude toward Germany of, 38, 50, 75-77, 79-84, 86, 92-93, 119, 135, 142-43, 166, 170, 191-96, 189, 195, 207-8, 210-217, 224-25
  birth of, 15
  "book bar" of, 27
  childhood of, 21-24
  cultural criticism of, 71-104
  "barracks mentality," 84, 98
  German spirit as poisoned, 75, 82, 98, 189
  deprived of citizenship, 207-8, 211
  education of, 15, 23-24, 27, 29
  employment in bank, 15, 149
  as a Jew, 21, 23, 29-30, 33-34, 87, 94-95, 211-25
  as a "left intellectual," 18, 71
  legal actions against, 200-201
  Nazis and, 23, 84, 146, 188-89, 193-99
  books burned, 12, 15, 17, 207
  "Herr Wendriner" sketch, 33, 95-98, 155, 179, 198, 218-21
  1929 Wiesbaden riot, 194
  1930 articles, 196-99
  review of *Deutschland, Deutschland über Alles,* 15, 81, 135-36, 183-87
  Tucholsky's last views, 207-8, 210-217, 224-25
  personal characteristics of despair and depression, 26, 29, 66, 177, 188, 208-9, 223-24,
  hatred of barking dogs, 26
  opposition to provincial autonomy, 117-19

Kurt Tucholsky, political and social views of (Cont.)
  pacifism, 49-50, 153-154
  prediction of balkanization of Europe, 50
  support of democracy and pluralism, 79-80, 92-93, 110-112, 114-116
  pseudonyms of, 28-33, 41, 79
  rationalism of, 79-81
  suicide of, 225-26
  Weimar Republic and, 72, 90, 109-112
  women and, 25-26, 32, 179-81
  See also Tucholsky, Else Weil; Tucholsky, Mary Gerold
  writings of at age of seven, 22
  chansons, 28, 33, 58-59, 83, 199
  epitaph, 34
  poems, 28, 41, 47, 56-60, 152-54, 184, 200
  satire, 28, 33, 41, 72, 102-103, 150-51, 181-88, 191, 198, 216-219
  Tucholsky ceases to write for publication, 29, 202, 211, 223
  use of dialect, 25, 82-83, 102-103
  See also specific writings
Tucholsky, Mary Gerold (second wife)
  in World War I, 44-50
  divorce of, 179
  estrangement of (1920), 63-66
  final estrangement of, 178-79
  marriage of Tucholsky to, 154-55
  nickname of, 29
  Tucholsky's correspondence with, 26, 47-50, 53-55, 62-63, 151-52, 201, 225 28
  Tucholsky's meeting with, 44-50
Uhu (periodical), 74, 154
Ulk (humor supplement), 24
Ullstein publishing house, 71, 74, 154
United States, Tucholsky and, 209-10
"Unterwegs 1915" ("Underway 1915"), 42
USPD, see Socialists, Independent
Valetti, Rosa, 59, 60
Verdun, Tucholsky's pilgrimage to, 153
"Verhetzte Kinder – Ohnmächtige Republik" ("Children Incited to Hatred—The Republic Remains Unconscious"), 200

"Verpflegung" ("Food Supply"), 100-103
Versailles Treaty, 80, 101, 156
  Stresemann and, 167, 169-73
  Tucholsky on, 101-104, 111
Victor, Walther, trial of, 190-191
Vienna, at outbreak of World War I, 40
"Volk, Das," 136
Volk, mystic union of, 85
"Vormerkung aus 1179 BGB und ihre Wirkungen, Die" ("The Memorandum from Paragraph 1179 of the German Civil Code and its Effects"), 27
Vorwärts (periodical), 27, 56, 71, 73, 151
Vossisehe Zeitung (periodical), 71
  Tucholsky's writing for, 151, 188
  Waiden, Herwarth, 73
  Waldoff, Claire, 59
  Walpurgisnacht, 41
"Was nun-?" ("What Now-?"), 159
Weimar Republic
  Tucholsky's criticism of, 72, 90, 109-112
  See also specific topics
  Welt, Die (periodical), 191
  Welt am Montag (periodical), 178, 187
Weltbühne, Die (periodical), 15, 28-29, 72-75, 99, 101, 111, 119, 126, 154, 160, 165, 196
  Communists and, 140-141
  criticism of, 130
  described, 72-75
  Ossietzky as editor of, 18, 140, 174
  trials of, 199-201
  Tucholsky's defense of, 74-75
  Tucholsky as editor of, 71, 177, 187, 189,
  Tucholsky as Paris correspondent of, 151
"Wendriner, Herr," see "Herr Wendriner" sketches
  Wesemann, Hans, on Tucholsky's self-imposed exile, 187-188
  Wiesbaden, Nazi riot against Tucholsky in, 191, 194
"Wilde Bühne" ("Wild Stage") (Berlin cabaret), 59

William II (Wilhelm II, German Kaiser) abdication of, 54
  SPD and, 129
  Tucholsky's satire on, 24, 166
  William, Crown Prince, 172-211
  Wilson, Woodrow, caricature of, 101
"Wir alle Fünf" ("All Five of Us"), 79-80
"Wir Negativen" ("We Negativists"), 75-77, 91
"Wo kommen die Löcher im Käse her?" ("Where Do the Holes in the Cheese Come From?"), 33
  Working class, Tucholsky on, 135-140
World War I, 37-50
  cultural propaganda during, 80, 98
  Tucholsky in, 39-50
  Tucholsky's series on Officer Corps in, 114, 121
World War II, predicted by Tucholsky, 165-68, 172-73, 212-13
  Writers, popular suspicion of, 75-78
"Wrobel, Ignaz" (pseudonym), 32-33, 110, 155, 157
Wührer, Professor, 200
Young Plan, 181, 195
Youth Movement, 37-38
  Nietzsche and, 85
  Tucholsky and, 78
Zukunft (periodical), 73
Zweig, Arnold, 211, 216, 221-25
Zweig, Stefan, on outbreak of World War I, 39-40
"Zwischen zwei Kriegen" ("Between Two Wars"), 165-69

Berlinica Presents:

Books and More 2010-24

Softcover, bw, 80 pics; $22.95
Dimensions: 240 pp; 6 x 9"
ISBN: 978-1-935902-54-6
  978-3-96026-067-7

Softcover, color, 44 pics; $18.00
Dimensions: 170 pp; 5.5 x 8.5"
ISBN: 978-3-96026-073-8
  HC: 978-1-935902-73-7

Softcover, bw, 2 pics; $13.95
Dimensions: 144 pp; 5 x 8"
ISBN: 978-3-96026-071-4
  978-1-935902-49-2

Softcover, bw, 177 pics; $24.95
Dimensions: 218 pp; 8.5 x 11.0"
ISBN: 978-3-96026-014-1
       978-3-96026-002-8

Softcover, s/w, 51 pics; $12.99
Dimensions: 90 pp; 7' x 10"
ISBN: 978-3-96026-006-6
       978-3-96026-090-5

Softcover, color, 165 pics; $25.00
Dimensions: 224 pp; 7 x 10"
ISBN: 978-1-935902-59-1
       978-3-96026-081-3

Softcover/French flaps, full color
140 pics and maps; $14.00
Dimensions: 176 pp; 5 x 8"
ISBN: 978-1-935902-44-7

Softcover, bw, 67 pics; $14.00
Dimensions: 176 pp; 5.5 x 8.5"
ISBN: 978-3-96026-069-1
Hardcover is forthcoming

Softcover, bw, 12 pics; $16.00
Dimensions: 176 pp; 5.5 x 8.5"
ISBN: 978-3-96026-066-0
  978-3-96026-064-6

Hardcover, bw, 12 pics; $20.00
Dimensions: 208 pp; 6 x 9"
ISBN: 978-1935902-65-2
  978-3-96026-016-5

Softcover, color, 117 pics; $16.95
Dimensions: 102 pp; 8.5 x 8.5"
ISBN: 978-1-935902-10-2
  978-3-96026-079-0

Softcover, color, 123 pics; $20.00
Dimensions: 100 pp; 7.5" x 9.25"
ISBN: 978-3-96026-092-9
   HC: 978-1-935902-14-0

Music CD, $15.95
Run time 48 minutes
CD available in English
and in German on Amazon

Softcover, full color, 66 pics; $18.00
Dimensions: 100 pp; 6x 9"
ISBN: 978-3-96026-080-6
   978-3-96026-089-9

Softcover, bw; $12.00
Dimensions: 110 pp; 5 x 8"
ISBN: 978-1-935902-40-9
   978-3-96026-091-2

Berlinica Presents:

Upcoming Books 2024-25

Softcover, bw, 41 pics; $25.00
Dimensions: 320 pp; 6 x 9"
ISBN: 978-1-935902-00-3
      978-3-96026-040-0

Softcover, bw, 2 pics; $14.95
Dimensions: ca 160 pp; 5 x 8"
ISBN: 978-1-935902-09-6
      978-3-96026-065-3

Softcover, bw, 4 pics; $13.95
Dimensions: 136 pp; 5.5 x 8.5"
ISBN: 978-3-96026-056-1
      978-1-935902-01-0